FIXING
TRADITION

D1479308

For John L. Spicher and Virginia Peachey Spicher

Let us now praise famous men, and our fathers that begat us. . . . Such as found out musical tunes, and recited verses in writing: Rich men furnished with ability, living peaceably in their habitations: All these were honored in their generations, and were the glory of their times. There be of them, that have left a name behind them, that their praises might be reported. And some there be, which have no memorial; who are perished, as though they had never been; and are become as though they had never been born; and their children after them. But these were merciful men, whose righteousness had not been forgotten.
—Ecclesiasticus 44: 1, 5-10

The C. Henry Smith Series

The C. Henry Smith series is edited by J. Denny Weaver. As is expected to be true of many future books in the CHS series, Volumes 1 through 4 are being published by Pandora Press U.S. and copublished by Herald Press in cooperation with Bluffton College and also Mennonite Historical Society. Bluffton College, in consultation with the publishers, is primarily responsible for the content of the studies.

FIXING TRADITION

Joseph W. Yoder, Amish American

Foreword by Marlene Epp

 Pandora Press U.S.
Telford, Pennsylvania

copublished with **Herald Press**
Scottdale, Pennsylvania

Pandora Press U.S. orders, information, reprint permissions:
pandoraus@netreach.net
1-215-723-9125
126 Klingerman Road, Telford, PA 18969
www.PandoraPressUS.com

Copublished with Herald Press, Scottdale, PA
Library of Congress Catalog Number: 2002030714
ISBN: 1-931038-06-6
Printed in the United States by Mennonite Press, Inc.
Book design by Pandora Press U.S.
Cover design by Jim L. Friesen and Denise Siemens

The paper used in this publication is recycled and meets the
minimum requirements of American National Standard for Information
Sciences—Permanence of Paper for Printed Library Materials,
ANSI Z39.48-1984.

Unless otherewise noted, all Bible quotations are from *The King James Version*.
Special thanks are offered to Jan Gleysteen for preparing the map
shown on pages 270-271.

Library of Congress Cataloguing-in-Publication Data
Kasdorf, Julia, 1962-
    Fixing tradition : Joseph W. Yoder, Amish American
    p. c.m. (C. Henry Smith series ; v. 4)
    Includes bibliographical references and index.
    ISBN 1-931038-06-6 (trade paper : alk. paper)
    1. Yoder, Joseph W. (Joseph Warren), 1872-1956. 2. Amish--United
States--Biography. 3. Amish--United States--Ethnic identity. 4. Amish--
United Sstates--Social life and customs. 5. Musicians--United States--Biogra-
phy. 6. Authors, American--Biography. 7. Mifflin County (Pa.)--Biography.
8. Huntingdon County (Pa.)--Biography. 9. United States--Ethnic relations--
Case studies. 10. Religious minorities--United States--Case Studies. I. Title.
II. Series.

E184-M45 Y655 2003
974.8'041'092--dc21
[B]

                                                                2002030714

    10 09 08 07 06 05 04 03 02   10 9 8 7 6 5 4 3 2 1

CONTENTS

FOREWORD

Mennonites and Amish, with their dual-kingdom theological traditions and church/world separatist models, have oft labeled individuals according to insider/outsider status. One is either "in" the church and its ethnic lineage, or one is "out" of the church and community, holding neither membership nor ancestral ties. Sometimes persons move from one status to another; usually the movement is from inclusion to marginality. As a pure dichotomy, the insider/outsider framework is a simplistic and false way of portraying the unsettled way in which individuals position themselves and are positioned in relation to the group. Nor does it address the dynamic aspect of self-definition, whereby individuals zigzag across psychological and sociological boundaries.

In her exploration of the life of Joseph W. Yoder, author Julia Kasdorf well recognizes the mistake of fixing people either inside or outside of the group with which they are associated, as the subtitle of *Fixing Tradition* reveals. Joseph Yoder is not Amish *or* American, he is Amish American. He was simultaneously in and out and his life filled with "lines of departure and return."

Yoder, best-known as author of *Rosanna of the Amish* (1940), was a complex individual with multiple identities that shifted according to the changing contexts of his life and the influences bearing upon him. While Yoder himself attempted to "fix" the tradition of the Amish, to try to fix any one label to Yoder is folly and Kasdorf excels at demonstrating the ways in which Yoder continually reinvented himself—as Amish, as Irish, as a man, as a teacher, as a writer, as a musician, as an ideologue.

A person with distinct idiosyncracies and unique responses, Yoder was nevertheless also a product of a particular social era. Kasdorf models an approach to writing ethno-religious history that situates individuals and events within diverse circles of influence, ranging in Yoder's case from his cloistered Amish family and community to the organizational and ideological spheres that shaped the progressive era in early twentieth century America. She demonstrates how Yoder was inspired by the highly gendered reform movement called "muscular Christianity" that promoted physical health and athleticism alongside a militaristic evangelicalism. Unmarried for most of his life, Yoder was representative of a larger societal culture of autonomous, gentlemanly bachelors. Later in life, Yoder's modernist sensibilities were vehemently directed at specific issues, like the Amish-Mennonite woman's head covering and the inscription of Amish hymn tunes. His ongoing interest in creative educational models also connected him to broader reform movements.

Fixing Tradition is biography and social history written with the literary sensitivity of a poet. The text is a rich mixture of the "fact" offered up by archival research and the creative imagination a biographer must bring to her subject to bring him to life. Readers may not be drawn to like Yoder; he seems arrogant, opinionated, self-centered—actually situating himself at the center of every group photograph—yet a certain identification with his life struggles is unavoidable.

Indeed, upon reading the book's thoughtful epilogue, one understands why Kasdorf was drawn to explore Yoder's life. Growing up in the same geographical and cultural environment as Yoder, and sharing his artistic proclivities, Kasdorf has felt both the pull of embrace and disdain for the conformist, undemonstrative "plain" people. As someone whose profession includes teaching and writing about Mennonites, I could relate to Yoder's occasional zeal to correct misplaced perceptions and stereotypes and "get the story right," fully realizing that I, like Yoder, bring my own interpretive biases to the task. With equal intensity I could identify with his desire to distance himself from that story and envy the "other" (regrettably I don't have an Irish ancestor).

Yoder's famous book about the Amish was described as a "hybrid of biography, history, and autobiography." Kasdorf's reflection on the process of writing this book might lead one to use the same terms to describe *Fixing Tradition*. As such, it offers wonderful insight into Kasdorf, Yoder, and a unique era of Amish-Mennonite American history.

—*Marlene Epp*
Conrad Grebel University College, Waterloo, Ontario

SERIES EDITOR'S PREFACE

The first three volumes of the C. Henry Smith Series dealt with postmodern theory, theology, and rhetorical philosophy. Volume 4 now ventures into new areas, with *Fixing Tradition: Joseph W. Yoder, Amish American*, Julia Kasdorf's literary biography of the author of the well-known (among Anabaptist-Mennonite or Amish readers) *Rosanna of the Amish*. Even though something like 425,000 volumes of *Rosanna* are in print, outside of his own family and circle of acquaintances Joseph W. Yoder has been virtually an unknown. Kasdorf's interesting book fills that void.

This story fits well the intent of the C. Henry Smith series to publish interdisciplinary and multi-disciplinary scholarship for the service of the church. Kasdorf uses two kinds of data to recreate the life of Yoder: living memories and archival materials. She treats him as one of what James Loewen has called the "living dead"—those who "still live in the memories of the living"—as well as one of the "dead," namely an individual no longer known personally by any living person.[1] The distinction is important because people who lived an experience can bring a kind of critique to an author's work that cold archival materials cannot. Readers will appreciate Kasdorf's sensitivity to the still-living witnesses and her skill in weaving together their memories and anecdotes about Yoder with very extensive data from archival sources.

Joseph W. Yoder was a "character," someone out of the norm, and Kasdorf does not present him as a model for emulation. However, her analysis of the tension in his life between identity with the Amish and with American society is thought-provoking for any experiencing the tension of being Christian in but not of the world. Kasdorf's scholarship is a model for studying such tension. And it does what good biography should do—opens windows to wider worlds and experiences through the life of one person. Readers will, for example, not only experience Amish worlds but also catch fascinating glimpses of the now-expired bachelor society and world of manly men of the early twentieth century.

In terms of issues discussed in earlier volumes of the C. Henry Smith series, this is a postmodern book. Without celebrating relativism and pluralism, which we do not espouse in any case, it makes us aware again that there is no ultimately normative cultural mainstream and that each of us must reflect upon the multiple ways that the church chooses to give expression to the truth that is Jesus Christ. In particular, Yoder's response to World War I raises questions are raised about willingness or ability to maintain a peace church's commitment to nonviolence in the face of a desire to fit into the dominant culture.

Yoder wrote *Rosanna*, the work for which he is best known, when in retirement at age sixty-eight. Intending to correct blatantly false and stereotypical images of the Amish in some contemporary novels, he wrote to fix—as in preserve—the image of the Amish as he knew them. A lack of positive response to his efforts from the Amish provoked subsequent literary efforts, in which Yoder attempted to fix—as in correct or reform—the Amish themselves. Kasdorf's captivating account develops the entire life of the man known beyond his immediate circle of acquaintances only for what he did in supposed retirement. After reading *Fixing Tradition*, those who have not yet encountered *Rosanna* will certainly be inspired to meet Rosanna and her boys, and those who have already read it will want to read it again, as a very different book.

Working with Julia on this volume has been a pleasure. I appreciate her willingness and thoroughness in responding to requests from the editor. It was a delight to share her enthusiasm at the discoveries and new interpretations that emerged in turning her dissertation into this book and in viewing the book's illustrations with her for the first time. Readers will catch that enthusiasm as well. I am also grateful to Zachary J. Walton for his invaluable editorial assistance on this manuscript.

—*J. Denny Weaver, Editor*
The C. Henry Smith Series

AUTHOR'S PREFACE

I came to the life of Joseph W. Yoder (1872-1956) as neither a historian nor a biographer but as a poet and writer. Initially, I believed he could show me how a person can become an author and also remain part of the Mennonite community. I believed he might exemplify how anyone from an ethnic or traditional background can become an artist without breaking ties with his place and people of origin. During the course of my research, however, the question shifted. As I began to see how fraught his relationships were, I became more interested in understanding how this particular Amish-born individual became an American, engaged in public life and discourse, even as he maintained conversations with individuals from his community of birth.

The story and methods of my research are described more fully in the Epilogue, but here I wish to recognize the voices, thought, work, and generosity of many people who made this book possible. This project began as a New York University doctoral dissertation, and I appreciate the selflessness of scholars who supported my efforts on a topic they knew little about themselves: director Gordon Pradl and readers Judith Weissman, Denice Martone, John Mayher, and Berenice Fisher. Fellow graduate students Marylou Graham and Jennifer McCormick were my sharpest and most loyal critics in those years.

Historians of Anabaptist groups Steven Reschly and Leonard Gross provided helpful commentary on the text; John and Beulah Stauffer Hostetler and John Ruth were guiding lights along the way; and Peter Powers offered useful critique of an earlier draft. Among those who provided valuable assistance and access to archival materials are Donald Durnbaugh and Nancy Seigel at Juniata College; John Sharp, Dennis

Stoez and Joe Springer at Goshen College; Joel Alderfer at the Mennonite Heritage Center in Harleysville, Pennsylvania; Caroline Wenger and Lloyd Zeager at the Mennonite Historical Society in Lancaster, Pennsylvania; David Luthy at the Heritage Historical Society in Aylmer, Ontario; Janet Olson at the Northwestern University Archives; Paul Schrock at Herald Press; and Rosalie A. Long at the Ross Library in Lock Haven, Pennsylvania.

I am especially thankful to those individuals who reflected on personal memories of Yoder in conversations that were critical to this project: Maude Brenneman, Abner Beiler, Sadie Byler, Elam Glick, Daniel King, Twila Peachey, Kore N. Peachey, John and Salina Renno, Jesse and Annie Spicher, Dorothy Yoder, Katie B. Yoder, John D. Yoder, Mary Yoder, Naomi Yoder, Percy Yoder, Yost and Amelia Zook, and Martha Zook. Jane Crosby, Tom and Sharon Spicher, Sara and Raymond Hartzler, Miriam and Elsie Peachey, and Lois Yoder provided help and hospitality during my field work in Mifflin County, and John D. Remple offered a guest room in New York City as often as it was needed.

Valuable in the work of revision and expansion of the dissertation was the research assistance of Christopher Weinmann at the Pennsylvania State University and the extraordinary efforts of S. Duane Kauffman, both in the public archives and the local Ivyland/Richboro, Pennsylvania, community. I am grateful to J. Denny Weaver and advisors of the C. Henry Smith Series for their critique, faith, and patience with this manuscript, to Jan Gleysteen for his map-making, and to publisher Michael A. King. Financial assistance from the Pennsylvania State University, the Historical Committee of the Mennonite Church, and the Pennsylvania Council on the Arts made publication of this book possible. Finally, I am indebted to my family, especially my father, whose reflections on a childhood in the Spicher (Zook) Church have influenced my thinking in many ways. And I thank David, who has lived patiently with J. W. for the past six years.

—*Julia Kasdorf*
  Bellefonte, Pennsylvania

INTRODUCTION

J. W. Yoder's best known work, the nostalgic memoir *Rosanna of the Amish*, recently released in a new paperback edition, remains a popular source of information about Amish life. Yet aside from some book reviews and a flurry of eulogistic sketches from the mid-1950s, little has been written about Yoder's life. Whereas he is a controversial figure in the memory of those who knew him in Mifflin County, Pennsylvania, the painful and complicated relationships Yoder maintained with Amish and Mennonite people there have been almost entirely veiled in silence. This may be because most people found him to be a troublesome and contradictory figure. When my father told his father that he wanted to go to college, Grandpa Spicher responded "What? And get as *grosshensich* [big headed] as J. W. Yoder?"

With the exception of S. Duane Kauffman and John A. Hostetler, Mennonite historians have not noted the essential paradox of Yoder's existence as a writer and musician within their community, nor have they considered his life in any depth.[1] To do so, one must simultaneously accept his artistic accomplishments on behalf of the subculture while acknowledging that his loud and flamboyant personality constantly called the community's values into question. Although he came from and contributed much to local culture, he refused to conform to its norms and often flagrantly challenged them. Neither a churchman nor an institution builder, he could not refrain from commenting on matters of doctrine and religious practice.

This study explores Yoder's marginal position in relation to Amish and Mennonite society and describes some ways that he used that position as a source of insight and as a means of articulation. At the same time, it traces the events of his life and education during a period when notions of masculinity and national identity were being formed in American popular culture.

Featuring himself as a character in *Rosanna of the Amish* and in its sequel, *Rosanna's Boys*, J. W. Yoder provided many details related to his family, childhood, education, and early career. Written in old age, these memoirs contain only the events that Yoder could recall or chose to reveal, and his thoughts on Amish culture are influenced by insights and desires formed later in life. Nonetheless, he claimed to write these books with great care to be accurate, conscious of a conservative reading community that would recall the events he described and that holds authors to a standard of literal truthfulness. Although there is now reason to doubt many of the details about his mother's and maternal grandparents' background as described in *Rosanna* and its sequel, these two books nonetheless provide some of the data for the first chapter, which offers some family history and follows Yoder from his birth in 1872 through initial study at Brethren Normal School (Juniata College), until he left central Pennsylvania to teach at the Elkhart Institute in 1897.

At Elkhart and then at Northwestern University, Yoder embraced a strain of Christianity inflected by Midwestern progressivism and the muscular ideals of the YMCA. The second chapter, largely informed by institutional archives, chronicles these events as well as his subsequent return to Juniata College, where he served as Athletic Director and an advocate of Theodore Roosevelt's "strenuous life." Chapter three covers the transient period of Yoder's life that began with his graduation from Juniata College in 1904 and lasted for nearly thirty years. He deliberately obscured details of this period in his published narratives and surviving personal files, so data from this era was gleaned from newspaper accounts and some interviews. During this time, he worked as a traveling college recruiter and an itinerant teacher, soloist, and singing master in various settings. For about two decades during this period, he made his base in the home of a companion from his youth, John Hooley, along with Hooley's wife and children. This long period ended in 1932 when, at the age of sixty, he married Emily Lane and bought a home in Huntingdon, Pennsylvania.

The final three chapters, based on Yoder's personal correspondence and extensive interviews in Mifflin and Huntingdon Counties, deal with his work as a writer and public figure. The lines of his relationships with Amish and Mennonite communities are traced through stories of his engagements with several individuals from those groups. (The sources of these stories are named only when the identity of the inform- ant seems important or essential to understanding the episode; other- wise, I have respected the privacy of my informants, some of whom are no longer living, and all of whom are named in the appendix.)

In 1940, at the age of sixty-eight, Yoder published his first and most successful book, *Rosanna of the Amish*, and in 1942 *Amiche Leider*, the first compilation of Amish sacred music, which previously had been pre- served only through oral tradition. Chapter four deals with these proj- ects. Both were motivated by a desire to protect and preserve Amish cul- ture, and they identified Yoder with that community and drew him closer to its people. Subsequent books, *Rosanna's Boys* (1948) and espe- cially *Amish Traditions* (1950), were motivated by a desire to challenge and reform traditional beliefs and practice, and are treated in chapter five.

Chapter six considers Yoder's final booklet, *The Prayer Veil Analyzed* (1954), published two years before his death at age eighty-four. It fo- cuses on the woman's head covering or prayer veil, a particular point of doctrine and practice among plain people that became for Yoder an em- blem of religious literalism, dogma, and injustice. His final days were di- vided between making cases for "healthful living" and a kind of "liberty" that had both spiritual and political implications.

Yoder's story has meaning not only for individuals from traditional backgrounds who wish to become artists, but for anyone interested in considering the complex relationships between individual authority, sectarian community, and liberal society. As Carl F. Bowman said of M. G. Brumbaugh, the early twentieth-century educator, author, minister, and Pennsylvania governor who was also J. W. Yoder's mentor, "He tried to bridge two worlds, felt pressure from both, and satisfied neither."[2] This assessment describes Yoder as well, and perhaps even speaks to the predicament of some conservative religious groups in contemporary America.

FIXING TRADITION

ONE CHAPTER

TWO-LANGUAGE CHILD

It seems that our home in the spirit of Patrick McGonegal mellowed the Amish austerity somewhat and allowed us a faint gleam of the liberty that Paul speaks of in the book of Galatians. Patrick, you will recall, was my maternal grandfather, and came from the land of the shamrock and the shelalie [sic], where wit and merriment temper religious ardor, and the song of the milkmaid quickens the heart beat of the "homeward plodding plowman." —Joseph W. Yoder, *Rosanna's Boys*

Joseph W. Yoder began his story in *Rosanna of the Amish* with the figures of his grandparents: a couple of Irish-Catholic immigrants and a pair of Amish Americans whose forebears had crossed the Atlantic before the Revolution. Children of potato farmers laboring under British rule, the Irish couple boldly emigrated to escape crushing political and economic conditions. The Amish were descendants of the Swiss Radical Reformation, offspring of those drawn to William Penn's promise of a "Peaceable Kingdom" where they could maintain a distinct way of life unmolested by civil and religious authorities. No historical evidence of the Irish immigrants has been found, but the duality expressed in this celebrated story remained an important theme for Yoder, whose restless nature was constantly plagued by conflicting desires for liberty and change as well as for the preservation of tradition.[1]

As he tells it, Yoder's maternal grandparents grew up on neighboring farms in Ireland, but the brothers of Bridget O'Connor opposed her romance with Patrick McGonegal. Early in the nineteenth century, Bridget's older brothers William and John migrated to northeastern Pennsylvania following the promise that "a man can be whativer [*sic*] he has a mind to."[2] In Scranton, center of the growing anthracite coal region that later provided much of the fuel for the nation, one brother became a store keeper and another opened a hotel, later sending for their sister to manage it. When Bridget's suitor, Patrick McGonegal, appeared one day at the hotel, her brother was so transformed by his taste of self-determination and freedom that he said, "In the auld country I was against ye, but as I see you and hear you now here in free America with all its opportunities, I believe that since you have shown gumption enough to cross the ocean for Bridget, that you will have gumption enough to be a good husband for her, and that is all I am interested in."[3]

Having previously worked in the iron-ore mines of Cornwall, Patrick struck off for the newly developed ore fields near Bellefonte in Center County. Years later, Yoder imagined interactions between two of the groups then living in the ore region of Half Moon Valley: "The Amish farmers supplying the Catholic iron ore miners with food; the Catholic iron ore miners providing the Amish with a market for what they produced. Each complementing the other. Different? Yes, but much alike in one thing, each faithful to the rules of his own church."[4]

In Half Moon Valley, in a small Amish settlement between Stormstown and Warriors Mark, Patrick found lodging with Elizabeth Yoder, a single Amish woman, according to Yoder's account. After the wedding of Patrick and Bridget in Scranton, Patrick took his bride to live with Elizabeth Yoder for a few months before the newlyweds could rent a home of their own, and Bridget and Elizabeth became close friends. Bridget died in December 1837, several days after giving birth to their fourth child. Shortly thereafter, Patrick took the older children to Philadelphia, where friends could help to care for them, but the newborn Rosanna—who became the mother of Joseph Yoder—he left behind with Elizabeth. For a few years, Elizabeth cared for Rosanna alone until she married Christian Kauffman, another member of the Half Moon Valley Amish community.

Never larger than twelve families, the settlement in Half Moon Valley was comprised mostly of relatives of the brothers Hannes Yoder (Yotter Hannes) and Yost Yoder (Red Yost) who had moved there in the early nineteenth century from a larger settlement near Belleville in Mifflin

County. (In many Amish communities, the similarity of first names and family names derived from common ancestral lines often necessitates the adoption of nicknames that are bestowed on an individual by others in the community and that often express a distinctive trait or allude to an event in that person's life.) By 1840, limited marriage prospects, poor soil, and conflicts over land titles with their Quaker neighbors caused members of the Amish community to move on to Ohio or back over the mountain to larger settlements in Juniata and Mifflin Counties.[5] At this time, Rosanna, Elizabeth and Christian Kauffman, moved to the Lost Creek Valley in Juniata County.

Meanwhile, just over the mountains in the Kishacoquillas Valley of Mifflin County, Joseph Yoder's paternal grandparents, Lame Yost and Catherine (Zook) Yoder, had been living on a farm near the town of Belleville. Their large limestone mansion was part of the original 700 acres Joseph (Yost) Yoder bought when he migrated north and west from Lancaster County, Pennsylvania, in 1796. The acreage was part of a parcel granted to Colonel John Armstrong for his service in the French and Indian War, and the house was the finest in the new Amish settlement.[6]

The eldest son of Lame Yost and Catherine Yoder was Christian Z. Yoder, called "Little Crist." He was among the young Amish men who filed conscientious objector depositions during the Civil War, and instead of serving, he probably paid a $300 commutation fee.[7] Little Crist fell in love with Rosanna McGonegal, the orphaned child of Patrick and Bridgit, who in the 1850s moved to a nearby farm with her foster parents, Elizabeth Yoder and Elizabeth's second husband, Bishop Shem

1.1 Joseph W. Yoder's childhood home in Belleville, Pennsylvania.

Yoder. Rosanna and Crist were married and moved into a new home built on land divided from the original Armstrong homestead and within sight of both of their parents' farms.

On September 22, 1872, Little Crist and Rosanna's fourth son, Joseph Warren, was born. He was so small that he was not expected to survive and so frail that he had to be carried on a pillow. Rosanna, in her mid-thirties by then, had already lost a baby daughter to cholera in 1860. Afraid that this child might die too, she asked a neighbor skilled in *Brauche* to "powwow" over him for the "take-off." This traditional form of sympathy healing, common among German immigrants in colonial America, is a secret art involving charms, physical manipulations, rhymes that refer to Bible verses, and formulations, some of which have been traced to German texts from at least the eleventh century.

Despite, or perhaps because of, his early struggle for life, Yoder grew into a large, robust man who never shrank from conflict, and often seemed to be in its center—if not its source. Moreover, he was born in the aftermath of the Civil War and during a period of tension in the Amish community as it sought to respond faithfully to cultural, economic, and theological changes within the church and in the nation.

Community Context

In his first book, Yoder described the pain of a congregational schism that divided his family shortly before his birth. Probably following his parents' view of events, Yoder placed blame on his mother's foster father, Bishop Shem Yoder, whom he described as a man grown conservative with age. Friction erupted between Shem, who favored strict observance of the old rules and order, and Christian K. Peachey, a young, change-minded preacher. According to Yoder, the innovations favored by Peachey were: using colored fabric for work shirts rather than the traditional white muslin, covering carriages with yellow oil-cloth rather than muslin, buying straw hats rather than requiring women to make them, and allowing the young girls to set their caps back to reveal their hair or to use broader cap strings to make larger bows. Yoder wrote, "All these encroachments on worldliness and manifestations of pride were very objectionable."[8]

Other accounts of this era suggest that the sources of the dispute were older and more complex.[9] In any event, tensions mounted until a portion of the congregation refused to participate in a communion service, signaling a rupture in the community's accord. The more progressive group, Yoder's parents among them, withdrew in 1864 and appointed Peachey to be their leader. Yoder described this schism with pathos: "That was the beginning of the Peachey church, and it divided many families."[10] Both pairs of Yoder's grandparents and one aunt, Shem's daughter, remained with Bishop Shem in the *die Alt Gmay* (the old church), later known as the Beiler Church, and today distinguished by their yellow-topped buggies. Yoder's parents, an uncle, Bishop Shem's son, as well as two other uncles and an aunt on his father's side, joined the progressive Peachey group, later known as the Renno Church, which now uses black buggies.

This division was symptomatic of rifts that spread throughout the North American Amish community and which finally solidified the distinction between the Old Order Amish and more progressive Amish Mennonites. Between 1862 and 1878, through a series of annual meetings, leaders from more traditional colonial communities along with those from more recent Amish immigrant settlements, located in communities scattered from Ontario to Maryland and Pennsylvania to South Dakota, met to negotiate a consensus in their religious practice and formulate common responses to cultural change.[11]

Theron Schlabach has described this period as a time of "sorting out" between those American groups who held to the "old order" and its distinctive signs of a separate and visible church in the world—the descendants of whom we recognize and call Amish today—and a change-minded majority. Many of the latter became Amish-Mennonites and then Mennonites in the twentieth century.

Sandra Cronk offers a key to understanding this period by contrasting the Amish subculture with the American mainstream. She delineates a distinction between the "redemptive rites" of American culture during this era—technology and industrialization, a political ideology of democracy, and Evangelical Protestantism—and the traditional Amish processes of *Gelassenheit*. This attitude of powerlessness, yieldedness, and sacrifice is a theme that Cronk finds in all that the Amish value, from stories about Anabaptist martyrdom and pacifism, to the election of their leaders by lot, to their work ethic and resistance to technology. For the Amish, Jesus is regarded primarily as a "suffering servant," not the heroic savior portrayed by American Evangelical Protestants, and believers follow him by living a quiet life of nonresistance and selfless service to family and community, and by abstaining from secular and self-promoting involvements.[12]

Whereas J. W. Yoder blamed seemingly trivial details for the painful congregational division in his community, Cronk's interpretation shows that those small moves toward cultural assimilation may have been deeply at odds with traditional Amish values. Colored shirts, "store-bought" or manufactured hats, wide cap strings, and rain-resistant buggy covers were expressions of individual status and wealth that became available with greater prosperity and the arrival of industrialization and transportation to rural areas.

Rather than getting old and cranky, as Yoder suggests, Bishop Shem may have sensed in these small changes a threat to accustomed communal patterns of human relationship and spirituality. In the words of Cronk, "one could not be lowly, selfless and simple if one wore clothes because they were stylish . . . or bought expensive horse drawn transportation because it was more comfortable."[13] In other words, one could not faithfully follow a suffering, selfless Savior and pursue such pleasures. Many of Yoder's frustrations with the Amish community, whether they pertained to self-expression, aesthetics, fashion, education, sport, or technology, were deeply lodged in this dilemma, and his life was marked by the tensions of this era.

Consequently, he described his own Amish upbringing mostly in terms of obedience, learning to comply with family rules and the *Ordnung,* or church conduct code. If a person complied, he earned the right to exist within the bounds of the community and family; if he did not, he was excluded: "The training of Amish children begins very early in life. The first general lesson is obedience," Yoder wrote.[14] To obedience he added the related ethic of hard work, so that submission of the will or spirit accompanies submission of the body. With revealing precision and detail, Yoder described a young, genderless "it" learning these lessons:

> Probably the very first training in obedience and endurance comes as the child is taken along to preaching and is required to sit with its mother and keep reasonably quiet for almost three hours. It may sleep if it wishes, but it must not disturb the services. If, however, it cries too much, it is taken out and quieted and taken into the service again, and if it repeats the crying stunt too often, it is taken out of the house out of hearing distance and

punished. In that way the child is impressed that to be taken out of the preaching services is no lark, and it learns to endure the long services without much complaint.[15]

Thus, Yoder's experience lends another perspective to *Gelassenheit* that may get overlooked if one focuses only on Cronk's abstract and totalizing concept. Historian Paton Yoder, who has studied and chronicled this schismatic era, points out that although the word *Gelassenheit* was used by early Anabaptists, the Amish of the nineteenth century preferred the simpler words *Gehorsamkeit* (obedience) and *Demut* (humility). In fact, he finds that the concrete terms *Gehorsamkeit* and *gehorsam* (obedience and obedient) and their opposites were the words most often used in Amish sermons of the last century.[16]

Although he may be served a snack, kick the straw on the barn floor, sleep, or play with the fingers and feet of nearby family members, a child learns early to hold his body still and remain quiet during three-hour church services. Today observers find that Amish parents feel a responsibility to instill within their children a yielded and humble spirit, and they resort to physical discipline only when children refuse to submit their wills to family rule. Children thus learn to obey their parents and to work hard in preparation for a life of cooperation and submission to the authority of the community and its leaders.[17] The authority of parents over their children is critical because father and mother exercise the primary control over the child's behavior until the child joins the church and vows to follow its *Ordnung*, often near the age of marriage. Thereafter, individuals are subject to the rule of the church, and Amish adults submit their desires to the needs and authority of the community.

As a child, Yoder witnessed a powerful example of submission to authority in his father's struggle to obey the church. In 1879 or 1880, Little Crist was among candidates nominated from within the congregation to be put in the lot to become a preacher.[18] Following custom, selection by lot took place during a religious service designed for this purpose. Each candidate stood before the congregation and selected a book, with only one book containing a hidden slip of paper on which was written the Bible verse referring to the appointment of Matthias, the apostle chosen to replace Judas (Acts 1:26). Little Crist received the Bible with the hidden paper, so the lot "fell on him" and he was ordained.

In Yoder's view, it was clear that his father had not wished to receive the book that would call him to preach. To satisfy his "aesthetical inclinations," and as a result of knowledge gained from studying a secret "horse doctor book," Crist had established a profitable horse trading business in which he took great pleasure, and the family was occupied with working the fields at the nearby Maclay farm in addition to their own. Crop records indicate that in 1878 Crist was the Valley's leading producer of wheat and oats, harvesting 1,364 bushels from sixty-one acres; in the year of his ordination, twenty-seven acres also yielded a record bounty of 2,650 bushels of corn.[19]

Because Amish preachers must deliver lengthy sermons constructed largely from verbatim recitation of Scripture, the unpaid job required time-consuming study and memorization of the Bible in High German in addition to leadership and pastoral responsibilities. Little Crist's selection put "a tremendous weight on his shoulders and an aching void in his heart," and the children sensed this heavy burden on their parents:

> When Crist and Rosanna returned from Communion that day, it was already almost dark. The weight of responsibility so crushed both of them that they were as those having met with great sorrow. Even the younger boys noticed their mother's tear-stained eyes, and when they inquired the cause, she simply said, "Pap was made preacher today. He is very much broken up; let us all be considerate of him." Even the smaller boys, John and little Joseph, only five, understood the solemn gravity of the situation and sharing the apparent burden and gloom with father and mother, kept very quiet all evening thinking thus to show their sympathy. They knew that to preach the gospel in the German language and to be God's direct representative is considered a very weighty and serious duty.[20]

Because selection by lot is considered to be a divine and communal call to serve the community, preachers generally obey and manage to rise to the occasion. Moreover, the lot enables a community to discern the talents of its members and to enlist and occupy the energies of the most gifted for the greater good. In this case, Crist's outstanding accomplishments as a horse trader and grain farmer were checked by his ordination, and his wealth and status brought closer to the levels of his neighbors. To help their father in preparation for his new vocation, the Yoder boys assumed greater responsibility for the livestock and field work; even little Joseph handled a plow and team of horses. Crist studied for six weeks to prepare for his first, successful sermon.

In his mother's life, Yoder saw another powerful example of obedience and submission to the will of family and community. When her foster mother Elizabeth Yoder married Bishop Shem Yoder around 1850, teenaged Rosanna was forced to abandon her dreams of becoming a country schoolteacher because the pursuit of "worldly wisdom" would be inappropriate for a member of the bishop's household. The bishop's rule on this matter must not have reached beyond his own home, however, or perhaps Yoder overstated the case. According to other sources, beginning with the 1834 institution of the Pennsylvania Free School Act, some Amish people in Mifflin County were very active in public education, with men serving as public school directors and both men and women teaching. Jonathan K. Hartzler, president of the Mifflin County Teachers Association, wrote an article in 1866 for *The Lewistown Gazette* to rally support for local country schools:

> We are a firm believer in the doctrine that every child born into the world has as much right to knowledge and culture as to sunshine air, food, and drink. As the public schools seem to be the cheapest and best agency that has yet been devised to promote the universal diffusion of knowledge and culture, therefore it is the duty of every man and woman to contribute a mite toward fostering and improving our public schools.[21]

But for nearly all Amish children of this era, formal education still ended at the eighth grade in the local, country school. Although she loved learning, Rosanna was compelled to stop attending classes when she chose to join the Amish Church at age sixteen. While Yoder depicted these limits on her learning as heart-breaking disappointments in *Rosanna of the Amish* and *Rosanna's Boys*, he portrayed his mother as a person who chose to be deeply devoted to Amish belief and practice, partly out of love for her foster mother.

CULTURAL RESISTANCE

Yoder attributed any departures from Amish simplicity and obedience in their home to Rosanna's Irish heritage. A striking example of such a departure was the family's graceful evasion of the church rules that forbade singing in four-part harmony. Both Crist and Rosanna were musically inclined, and Yoder's oldest brother, Yost, aimed to become a song leader like his father. Because the chant-like tunes of Amish "slow songs" are unwritten and extremely difficult to learn, Crist and Rosanna often invited an elder singer and his daughter to help practice the tunes in their home.

Among Yoder's first and fondest childhood memories are these impromptu "singings." After one of these gatherings, when young Joseph was about three years old and still wearing a dress, he astounded his family with a perfect imitation of a young woman's voice. When Levi and John realized that their baby brother could sing soprano, they taught him songs in German and English, and the three boys formed a trio. Vocalizing in "parts," or harmony, violated the *Ordnung*, which permitted only singing in unison. Nevertheless, Crist and Rosanna "winked" at their sons' transgression, a concession Yoder attributed to the mitigation of a light-hearted Irish influence in their family.

Throughout the *Rosanna* books, Yoder traced complementary differences between his merry milkmaid Irish maternal line and his austere Amish plowman fraternal one. These extremes sharpened his definition of Amish culture and located his own hybrid position between Amish and Irish ancestors. To establish the contrast early in *Rosanna of the Amish*, Yoder dramatized the differences between Rosanna's immigrant mother, Bridget O'Connor McGonegal, and Rosanna's foster mother, Elizabeth, when they lived in together in Half Moon Valley:

> Bridget was a buxom Irish girl with quick wit and fluent speech; Elizabeth was tall and rugged, plain of dress and slow of speech. She always wore a white cap tied beneath her chin, a kerchief folded tightly about her waist and breast, a plain dress and an apron. She generally spoke in short sentences but when she spoke she always seemed to say something that stimulated Bridget's courage or deepened her confidence. Bridget was very happy in this quaint, unadorned home where simplicity and sincerity were natural forms of religion.[22]

With the voluptuous Irish, Yoder associated quick wit and fluent speech—qualities that he developed as a young man and exploited as an adult; to the Amish, he attributed brevity but sincerity of speech and plain appearance. In the friendship between his grandmother and foster grandmother, he demonstrated the ways in which these two temperaments complemented one another: "Bridget's Irish sunshine shed a ray of joy into Elizabeth's somber life, while Elizabeth's calm reserve gave Bridget poise and assurance."[23]

When Bridget died shortly after Rosanna's birth, Patrick left the infant in Elizabeth's keeping, intending to return. Killed in a quarry accident, he never saw his daughter again. Thus, what Yoder called Rosanna's "Irish" nature was entirely inherited or biological, as was his own. Both books celebrated Rosanna's innate Irish qualities as identified by Yoder: swiftness, verbosity, and joy expressed by the Irish lilt in her laugh.

Rosanna's older siblings eventually managed to locate their sister, living among the plain people in the mountains and valleys of central Pennsylvania, and they visited her in hopes of taking her back to Philadelphia. A young teenager by then, Rosanna chose to remain with her foster mother, but retained contact with her siblings for the rest of her life. Visits from the Irish-American, Catholic aunts and uncles from the city are rendered in vivid detail in both of Yoder's books. His attention to the Irish side of his family prompted notice from an unnamed reviewer in the Lewistown *Sentinel* who wrote,

> *Rosanna of the Amish* might well have been titled, *Rosanna of the Irish*. . . . Joe is just as fulsome of his praise of both races and it is hard to say where one begins and the other lets off. And this you can't protest, because the author is just about 50-50, his mother having been 100 per cent from the Auld Sod and his pappy completely Big Valley. There's fully as much Irish brogue in the book as there is Pennsylvania Dutch, which only goes to show what you really can do when you get to stirring around in the melting pot of America.[24]

As this review shows, even by the middle of the twentieth century, the cultural and religious differences of both Irish and Amish peoples were generally regarded by white, Protestant Americans as *racial* differences. Within this climate, Yoder chose not to pursue assimilation into the mainstream but to identify with two minority groups, never fully following the absolute extremes of the stereotyped Amish/Irish dualism he created.

Although he found Amish life to be a matter of "obedience and endurance," it was never portrayed in the Rosanna books as joyless drudgery. Considering the Irish temperament to be a complement to Amish sobriety, Yoder often tempered his critical portrayals of Amish life, admitting that there is something desirable about belonging to a disciplined and coherent community. He attributed the tendency toward depression among the Amish to their life of hard work and obedience to the church, yet found these excesses to be less harmful than the madness that befalls the wastrel:

> The stern rules of the church and the hard daily toil, while leading to piety and religious devotion, is too much sometimes for the endurance of the body, and a deep despondency overtakes some, which they called "*schwermüthig*," (heavy minded) commonly called melancholia. But the melancholia that comes from hard work and religious devotion is decidedly to be preferred to the mental derangement that too often comes from the other extreme, dissipation and social excess.[25]

Amish, Irish, and English

Rather than set the identities of his grandparents in opposition, Yoder forged connections between them while using their differences for didactic purposes in his books. Visits from the McGonegal aunts and uncles provided opportunities for cross-cultural comparison. Rosanna's sister, Margaret, for instance, observed that Amish teachings about nonconformity in dress and obedience to the church leaders parallel the Catholic nun's habit and her obedience to the parish priest. On another visit, Rosanna's brother, William, was reminded of the Catholic liturgy during an Amish worship service, which he attended in good conscience because he could not understand the German language. Although Amish and Mennonite people may harbor an anti-Catholic bias rooted in their memory of sixteenth and seventeenth-century persecution, Yoder portrayed his family as a model of ecumenical tolerance:

> May it be said to our everlasting credit that while all our city relatives were devout Catholic and we were devout Amish, we never had a word of controversy about religion. We looked upon them as good Catholics and we knew the Lord would reward them as he rewards good Catholics and we were not for dictating to God as to how He should treat them. They looked upon us as good Amish . . . and they were not meddling in His affairs.[26]

Late in life, Yoder corresponded with Benedictine monks in an attempt to trace similarities between Amish culture and the practices of that Catholic order devoted to rural life, physical labor, and prayer. Drawing further connections between the two worlds, he mistakenly believed that the Amish slow songs were derived from Gregorian chant.

Whatever its basis in fact, constructing a dualistic Irish/Amish identity provided for Yoder an expression of his own contradictory desires: both to belong to the Amish community and to stray beyond its boundaries. Moreover, it reflects the American habit of selecting and creating a story of one's ethnic identity, sometimes with very little historical evidence. In fact, the 1870 and 1880 Census records of Union Township in Mifflin County, Pennsylvania, cast doubt on Yoder's story. In 1870, Yoder's mother did not indicate that her father was foreign born. In addition, she listed her name as "Anna" rather than "Rosanna," perhaps to claim a more Amish-sounding identity. For the 1880 census, she actually wrote that her father and mother were born in Pennsylvania.[27]

Although research into Rosanna's background is not yet complete, these discrepancies suggest that Yoder had other, more personal bases for his claims. Writing autobiographically, he often attributed to "his Irish" all qualities that did not conform to expected Amish demeanor, from his restless ambitions for education and career to an early taste for finely tailored clothing—even when the tailor had to follow the plain cut of an Amish suit. He recalled one occasion from early childhood when he had not yet learned to obey his mother, and his Irish temper collided with Amish restraint:

> Then she gave me a little spank and commanded me a little more sternly. That spank seemed to offend my dignity, and I continued the disobedience. Then mother gave me a couple spanks and commanded me to stop doing what I was engaged in. But that light spanking raised my Irish to the boiling point, and still not willing to obey but angry as I knew how to get, I ran out to the pump standing in the yard, seized the handle, shook it with all my might and yelled for very rage. I would have sworn but I did not know any swear words, so I just screamed. My mother took in the situation, came out to the pump where I was exuding wrath, seized me by the arm, laid me over her knee, and said in good plain Amish words, "I'll teach you to act like this," and then she paddled me severely. When she was through, I was through, in

fact I was all in, but from that time on I knew that I was not boss, and there were certain liberties which young gentlemen at the age of five were wise not to espouse. [28]

The Irish identity opened a space for Yoder to express emotions forbidden by Amish culture, such as anger, ambition, and pride, and he understood that his "half-breed" status named the source of and granted permission for his transgressive behavior. Many of the things he called "Irish" may simply be marks of education and assimilation into Protestant American culture—what the Amish call "English," in fact. Ironically, the Anglo mainstream longer ago regarded Irish immigrants as part of another race that was brutish, loud, and overly given to drink, sentimentality, and fights—an assessment that likely would not surprise the demure Amish folk of Yoder's imagination. For him, the unruly identity provided an excuse for Amish and Mennonite people to permit or at least explain his flamboyant personality and lifestyle. He is said to have once shocked audiences by offering a rousing solo rendition of "When Irish Eyes Are Smiling" after a performance of sacred songs by his singing school pupils in an eastern Pennsylvania Mennonite meetinghouse.[29]

Individuals in his own community believed that Yoder's foreign blood made him strange, and they still attribute to his Irish heritage his grandiose comportment and style, which they describe variously as loud, articulate, egotistical, argumentative, arrogant, or, in short, "like a banty rooster." By contrast, the Amish count humility of spirit and simplicity of speech among the highest virtues. Identifying a man in terms of his ethnicity seems natural for people who understand themselves in terms of ancestry and community, and it also diminished the possibility that Yoder may have consciously chosen to deviate from their norms.

He was thus excused, or at least understood to be foreign, and therefore unable to help being what he was, even as his cultural contributions have become legendary in the local area. For instance, a Big Valley man recently claimed that Yoder once played a violin solo with the Pittsburgh Symphony in Heinz Hall. When a lively but elderly, plain-dressed great nephew of J. W. Yoder was asked why his famous uncle was so *uncharacteristic* for an Amishman, Yost Zook winked a bright blue eye and immediately replied, "It was his Irish, of course. I've got a little of the Irish in me, too, don't you think?" Then he described the pleasures of his first automobile ride, during the 1920s, in a stylish car owned by J. W. Yoder.

Rather unusual for an Amish family, the Yoders had only four children. Because Joseph trailed his closest brother by seven years, he was the only child at home during the school months, with his Newfoundland dog, Porter, as a sole companion. By the time he started school, his oldest brother, Yost, had already married and moved away. From a very young age, therefore, Yoder was cast in conversations with adults, especially his mother. Rosanna's stories about her childhood and growing up impressed themselves on his imagination so vividly that he was able to write a narrative of her life more than forty years after her death. Close identification with Rosanna is evident throughout Yoder's writing; repeatedly, aspects of his own personality seem to blend with hers, among them, a special insider/outsider status in the community, a love of singing and learning, and a gregarious personality.

In addition to Rosanna, Mary Ann Carson was an important adult presence in Yoder's early life. Twice he attributed his fluent English to this Scots-Irish Presbyterian woman hired to help Rosanna with domestic work after the birth of her second son. Although Mary Ann understood the German dialect, as did many non-Amish Pennsylvanians in those days, she refused to speak it, and, according to Yoder, all of Rosanna's children learned to speak English along with Pennsylvania German. (It is more likely that Yost, the oldest son, would have spoken only the dialect during his early years.) Yoder described himself and his brothers as "two-language children right from the beginning."[30] Elsewhere he wrote, "We never ceased to be grateful to Mary Ann . . . for helping us to speak English so clearly that no one ever detected any German accent in our speech."[3]

Given that he wrote these memoirs at a time of anti-German sentiment in America, it is important that Yoder stressed his own bilingualism as a sign of dualistic identity. Although some English words have entered Pennsylvania German, the dialect remains the Amish mother tongue and marker of distinction; children are still expected to use the domestic and communal language before acquiring English for the public purposes of education and trade. In an article printed in *Blackboard Bulletin*, a newsletter for Amish school teachers, Joseph Stoll delineated the uses of the English and German languages in an Old Order community:

> As Old Order Amish, we associate German with church services
> and our home life—the religious and deeply moral part of our

lives. German in a sense represents all that we have for centuries been trying to hold—our heritage as a nonconformed people, pilgrims in an alien land. It represents the old, the tried, and proven, the sacred way.

The English, by contrast, we associate with the business world, society, worldliness. English in a sense represents everything outside our church and community, the forces that have become dangerous because they make inroads into our churches and lure people from the faith. Therefore, the English language, though acknowledged all right in its place, becomes suspect when associated with the lure of the world.[32]

The Amish call all non-Amish others "English," highlighting the way that language use distinguishes the faithful community from the world. Consequently, for an Amish child who learns English *at the same time* he learns Pennsylvania German as Yoder did, the linguistic hierarchy that traditionally serves to reinforce clear distinctions between the world and the religious community becomes unstable.

Early fluency in English enabled Yoder to understand and join in conversations between his family and their non-Amish acquaintances. Rosanna—a two-language child herself—readily opened her home to non-Amish people. In a gesture much like her own beginnings, she informally adopted a three-year-old Lutheran child whose father had been killed in a fire, and she often welcomed vagrants who stopped at their farm. Yoder recalled talking with a wandering German immigrant who became a regular visitor in their home for many years. Before her death, Mary Ann Carson, the beloved hired hand, walked four hours through snow banks to reach Rosanna's house, where she died a few days later. Members of the Presbyterian church told Rosanna that Mary Ann had wished to die in the Yoder home.

The Yoders also maintained a longstanding friendship with Martha and Robert Maclay. For ten years, the boys helped Little Crist farm the two-hundred-acre Maclay homestead "for shares," without a written agreement. According to Yoder, the boys fell under "the benign influence of Robert Maclay the Scots-Irish Presbyterian, Christian gentleman," whom they called "Uncle Robert." When the older sons began to pursue their own interests and the Yoders could no longer manage the Maclay property, their departure was experienced "almost like leaving home."[33]

Although he must have received a considerable amount of attention from adults, Yoder longed for companions his own age, and therefore found school to be "a great joy." As early in the morning as his mother would permit, he walked across the winter fields from their farm to the village of Mechanicville, where he met his playmates in the yard of a small, brick school house. In those days, school for rural children lasted only four months of the year, and the Amish in Pennsylvania freely participated in public education, even serving on local school boards, which had the power to elect their own teachers.

Besides providing playmates, public school gave Yoder his first exposure to a non-Amish world that was not tolerant of cultural difference. One bully enjoyed provoking fights by encouraging other non-Amish students to call the Amish boys "Long-haired Dutchmen" or to pull their hair. When Yoder's seatmate called him "that unbearable epithet," the bully taunted,"Now, if you take that, you steal sheep." This was more than the "Irish" in young Yoder could handle, and his Amish nonresistance receded long enough for him to engage in "jungle tactics" on the way home from school, in what he called a "grab 'em, down 'em, and pound 'em brawl."

Interestingly, Yoder invoked "the shades of . . . Patrick McGonegal" to summon the courage to defend his Amish identity: "I'm not the worthy grandson of his that I am, if I take an insult like that," he noted. Later, though, he reflected that "On that day I was hardly a worthy grandson of Lame Yost Yoder, for the Amish are non-resistant to the nth degree."[34] This episode prefigures Yoder's later literary attempts to rescue the reputations of Pennsylvania German and Amish people from the "dumb Dutch" stereotype, while also demonstrating how uncharacteristic it is for an Amish person to act or speak in his own defense. In other words, to defend them, even in a schoolyard quarrel, Yoder ceased being one of them. This paradox forever troubled his literary and musical work.

Yoder wrote briefly but nostalgically of his school years, recalling outdoor games and sledding, but mentioning little of the classroom, probably because his most powerful models for learning were at home. During Yoder's early grades, Crist was often indoors studying the German Bible to become a preacher. Yoder attributed the financial success of the family farm to hard work and his parents' self-taught, practical learning. Crist gleaned lucrative secrets from "the horse doctor book," and Rosanna handled unscrupulous butchers and butter dealers by memorizing the 24 x 24 multiplication table from the back of the farmer's almanac. The boys were also encouraged to succeed in useful, academic endeavors. For instance, Crist enrolled his sons in a correspondence course in penmanship to cultivate a skill that had both practical and cultural value in the nineteenth century. Although Joseph was too

1.2 Marginalia from a 1938 letter suggests that Yoder continued to perfect his penmanship, and his signature, c. 1950.

young to take the class with his brothers, he also received special pens, ink and paper, and was encouraged to practice the required "arm movement." His distinctive oversized and decorative signature is still remembered in the community and found on numerous extant copies of his books.

Levi, the second son, exhibited a special talent for arithmetic, which Rosanna attributed to her study of the multiplication tables while he was *in utero*. Yoder, ten years Levi's junior, watched with admiration as Levi and one of his school mates worked late into the evenings on complex arithmetic challenges created for them by the school master. When Levi finished the eighth grade, he took courses at a summer normal school and passed the county examination to become a school master himself.[35] While Yoder was still enrolled in the primary grades, Levi was assigned to teaching posts at the Zook School, then the Sample School, close enough to home that he boarded with his family.

Church Affiliation

Around this time the bishop invited Levi to join his parents' church, and Levi refused. The bishop argued that Levi violated the first commandment with a promise, "Thou shalt honor thy father and mother." Levi claimed that he did honor his parents by working hard on the farm and behaving well, but he would not comply with the church's *Ordnung*. Seven-year-old Yoder was greatly impressed by this conversation and a later dispute between Levi and their father:

> I remember hearing this heated argument from the outside, and I remember with what heartbreaking grief I heard father talking to Levi with broken voice through tears of anguish, pleading with him to "obey." I could hardly refrain from rushing into the "Room" and saying, "Levi, why don't you obey?" but then Levi was generally on my side, so I didn't dare desert him now.[36]

In this scene, the painful parting of ways between father and sons was not so unlike the division that separated Yoder's parents from their grandparents in the church schism before his birth. But in the case of a church split, individuals in both groups retain a sense of belonging to a fragment of the community. It is more difficult for an individual to stand alone. Both Rosanna and Crist had subdued their own desires to remain part of the community, but their sons did not follow their example. When Levi discarded his Amish clothes and got his hair "shingled" (layered), and donned a derby hat, the Amish brethren looked at him and shook their heads, saying, "*Er is en stährköpficher Buh.* He is a disobedient boy. If he was my boy, I'd chase him away from home."[37]

Although Yoder seemed to have distanced himself from Levi's rebellious spirit in this scene, he admired this older brother very much and eventually followed Levi, both in declining to join their parents' Old Order (Peachey) church and in his decision to become a public school teacher. Even before Levi was the example of Patrick McGonegal, whom Yoder always invoked for courage when he sought to stray from Amish norms. For instance, at the age of sixteen, when Amish youth are considered old enough to "run around," he enrolled in a singing school taught by tenor John Hooley at a country school near his home.

Because singing in parts and learning to read music defied the customs of his parents' church, Yoder recognized this to be an exciting infraction of the rules. Nearly fifty years later, he described in elaborate detail the evening of his first lesson. Arriving a bit late, he found class already in session and so paused to listen outside the Milltown country school filled with "strangers," and he was transported "into the realm of ecstasy" by his first encounter with formal four-part harmony. Yet he stalled outside the door, confounded by feelings of delight and a painful sense of his own ignorance:

> As I approached the door, mostly strangers inside, and heard that singing, I paused. That was the most beautiful music I had ever heard,—bass, tenor, alto and soprano. Most of the singing I had ever heard was the Amish type, one part only, so is it any wonder that the four-part harmony just about lifted me into the realm of ecstasy. I was there, ready to go in, wanted to go in, but when I reached for the door knob, I hesitated. Those people in there were so far ahead of me. . . . With my hand on the door knob hesitating, too bashful to go in as an Amish boy, I suddenly seemed to hear a voice saying, "You're no worthy grandson of Patrick McGonegal if you turn back now," and in I went.[38]

In this context, Yoder saw himself as backward, behind those people who are "so far ahead." Yet, by summoning his Irish immigrant heritage, he overcame Amish timidity and taboo and entered the room. There he made his first, illiterate encounter with musical notation and was determined to "catch up" with the rest:

> Someone handed me a book; they might just as well handed me the tablets of the Medes and Persians. Of course, I could read the words they were singing, so I knew when they got to the end of a stanza, but so far as the notes were concerned, "Dey all looked alike to me." Fortunately, Bert Yetter was leaving for Kansas and he wanted to sell his singing book, and I wanted to buy, so when he said he would depart from his book for twenty-five cents, there was no dickering; I produced the cash, and went home with my first singing book. For the next six months, my intellectual diet was mostly keys, signatures, sharps, flats, quarters, eights and sixteenths. Those people had a two-year start on me, but by close application by spring I was singing with the rest of them. [39]

Part singing and a desire to teach school placed Yoder in sympathy with the Amish Mennonites, and at sixteen, he followed Levi in joining the progressive Church House Amish at Belleville. As a consequence of the Amish schisms during the 1860s, this group had become aligned with the Amish Mennonite movement and erected its first meeting house at Belleville in 1868.[40] Although this choice reflects an important shift toward a more individualized religious practice among the Amish during the late nineteenth century, Levi and Joseph were probably drawn to Belleville by more immediate manifestations of change. Joining this group meant that the Yoder brothers no longer needed to conform to the strictest dress codes of Old Order *Ordnung*. Nor would church rules prevent them from pursuing higher education or non-farming vocations. By the time Yoder joined in 1888, the group had for five years opened its meeting house to a Sunday school previously held in a country school. Largely imitating Protestant models, Amish Mennonite Sunday schools encouraged devotional reading and biblical interpretation by lay people, and offered opportunities for women to become involved in church leadership, because they were permitted to teach all-female classes. Both Joseph and Levi Yoder served as teachers and superintendents in the Belleville Sunday school program.[41]

EDUCATION

At age twenty, Yoder decided to take the "peripatetic test" to become a public schoolteacher. In August 1892, with his singing school instructor and friend John Hooley, Yoder walked to McVeytown, about twelve miles on a rutted lane that crossed Jack's Mountain, to attend a four-week normal course which concluded with an oral and written exam administered by a traveling school superintendent. Yoder found the grammar and arithmetic sections easy, but struggled to retain the historical dates needed to pass the test; he did pass, and was assigned a school at Milltown, only two miles from his parents' house. Yoder believed that ever since his mother had been prevented from becoming a teacher, she had harbored a hope that one of her sons would attain that status, and the thought of fulfilling her dream compensated for his own feelings of guilt for abandoning the family farm.

Because all of his brothers had married and moved away by 1892, and Crist and Rosanna could not possibly manage the farm without him, Yoder's decision to become a teacher forced them to sell their livestock, implements, and land. Yoder described that sad day: "We had always been farmers; our horses and cows seemed almost like personal friends. . . . Sale day finally came and we had to see our faithful animal friends sold and led out the lane to their new homes. As we ate our evening meal after the sale, we talked fast,—about other things."[42] The Yoders built a retirement house at their tannery on a piece of their property facing Greenwood Street. While working as a teacher, Yoder lived with them, and in the evenings helped complete finishing details on their new home.

1.3 John Hooley, c. 1894-95.

The two *Rosanna* books contain some discrepancy about when Yoder resigned from his first teaching position. In *Rosanna of the Amish*, he left after the winter holidays of the first year; in *Rosanna's Boys*, after the winter holidays of the second year. Other evidence points to the latter scenario, but in either case, experience in a one-room country school convinced Yoder that he needed to get more education or change professional fields altogether. John Hooley, who happened to be the brother of Sarah, the wife of Yoder's brother John, had already taken some courses at the Brethren Normal School at Huntingdon, and Hooley became Yoder's "educational guide and trail blazer" once again. Both young men aimed to enroll in a bookkeeping and banking course, but J. H. Brumbaugh, the school's president, insisted that they take the Normal English course for teacher training. Brumbaugh may have believed that these Amish-reared young men needed further instruction in English or more foundational work before entering a commercial profession.

For a second time in his life, Yoder left home and crossed a mountain with John Hooley in pursuit of education, traveling about twenty-five miles to Huntingdon, a county seat served by the main line of the Pennsylvania Railroad. Soon to be named Juniata College, Brethren Normal School was the first of seven institutions of higher learning established between 1876 and 1899 by the German Baptist Brethren or Dunkers (later Church of the Brethren), a German-speaking pacifist sect that shared many values and cultural ways with their Mennonite neighbors. Yoder was joining with the progressive side of the Brethren movement. At an annual meeting of the Dunkers in 1831, the question, "Is it considered advisable for a member to have his son educated in a college?" received the response, "It is considered not advisable inasmuch as experience has taught that such very seldom will come back afterward to the humble ways of the Lord."[43]

During the 1880s, however, the Dunkers endured two major schisms, and leaders of the prevailing progressive faction favored education. Increased access to America's universities and fear that education would lure young people into other churches or beyond belief altogether compelled the Dunkers to establish normal schools and colleges. Like many American colleges founded in this era, Brethren Normal School was created to secure religious and cultural identity while training workers for church service and missions.

Resisting higher education of all kinds, the Old Order Amish forbade attendance of even religious schools. A speech prepared for an 1862 national meeting of Amish ministers expressed this sentiment and placed it within the context of the humble, Godly lifestyle that was not so much articulated as simply demonstrated by the lives of previous church leaders:

> Firstly, they have taught us to strive earnestly for work, industry, and honesty, as well as for humility in outward conduct, and have taught this and themselves led the way in doing this. Their way of life was simple, as were their clothing, homes, and food. They warned against pride. Tall flouncy hats, suspenders, buttons, were in part opposed. Multi-colored and striped clothing were opposed, and also having "Kerpets" [carpets] was opposed. . . . Their occupation was work and farming. The merchant business was considered more dangerous, even though at times there was buying and selling. Higher education in schools of higher learning was opposed.[44]

Speaking of himself, Yoder wrote, "When he went away to school many good Amish people were truly sorry." Local education and reading were not discouraged, but to leave the Valley and pursue "higher education" signified a threat to self and community. Deacon Jonas Peachey, a friend of the family, tried to persuade Yoder to abandon his plans out of fear that higher learning would cause him to "lose his soul."[45] But the loss of material comforts bothered Yoder more.

When he arrived at the campus on the hill above Huntingdon on a raw day in January 1894, it was raining "pitchforks and sawlogs," and he recalled,

> Had it not been for my Amish aceticism, I think I would have walked home, twenty-five miles, but I had been taught to "grin and bear it" at least to bear it, and grin if possible. Everything was strange. The buildings seemed enormous to me. When I went to class I could not find my way back to our room, and when I was in our room, I could not find my way to class. Fortunately for me, Hooley had been there before and knew the ropes.[46]

Yoder, the only son at his parents' table for many years, found that "many things were disappointing" at school: he missed his mother's cooking and hated both the gong that woke students and the bolt that "locked tardy ones out of breakfast at 6:35. But in time, the discords died away" as he made friends with the Brethren Normal students and found a hero and mentor in Martin G. Brumbaugh, distinguished educator, historian, and author.

In January 1894, just as Yoder arrived, Brumbaugh had become the first Dunker to earn a doctorate, and had become president of the Brethren Normal School. Only ten years older than Yoder, Brumbaugh graduated with distinction from Brethren Normal School with a Bachelor's degree in English in 1881, and returned to teach literature, grammar, rhetoric, and natural sciences. In 1892 he earned an MA in English literature at Harvard; at the University of Pennsylvania, he wrote a pioneering dissertation on the religious poetry of John Donne—a poet who did not become a usual topic of scholarly studies until the 1920s. In an English class, Yoder recalled being nearly undone by Brumbaugh's discussion of "the beautiful in literature":

> His lecture to the class that day was so profound, so facinating, and so absorbing that when we were dismissed, I simply did not know where to go or what to do. I had my attention so riveted on his lecture that I fully believe I was hypnotized. I saw the others leave the room, so I arose and left too, but I did not know what came next nor where to go. I backed up against the wall, watched classes go by in both directions in the hall, but I was lost. Finally,

1.4 *Normal English Class of 1895. Joseph W. Yoder is third from right in the third row; John Hooley is third from left in second row. M. G. Brumbaugh is fifth from left in second row. Behind them, Students Hall (built 1895) was located at 18th and Moore Streets on the Brethren Normal campus, and contained a gymnasium in the basement, the college library, class-rooms, science laboratories, and rooms for 25 men on the top floor.*

> I thought that if I knew what time it was, I would know where to go. I looked at my watch,—Two twenty, and that was the time for geometry, and geometry, which I did not like, brought me to my senses with a disquieting thud.[47]

In hindsight, Yoder claimed he decided to prove to his community that learning would not cause him to "lose his soul," a move that prefigures later efforts to modify Amish attitudes about education. "Soul" he interpreted to mean his Amish cultural identity, which he reduced to four elements—religious devotion, the Pennsylvania German language, the work ethic, and an attitude of sociability and communality—and he resolved

> to live as fine a Christian life as possible, and in addition to retain his ability to speak the Pennsylvania German language fluently, harbor his muscle and strength and be able to do manual labor of the heaviest kind rapidly and well, and lastly, speak to everybody on all occasions if possible and always in Pennsylvania German if they were Amish.[48]

Because he had departed from the community and transgressed its norms, Yoder assumed the burden of winning back its members' approval, but he failed to recognize that a self-conscious effort to retain emblematic aspects of Amish culture was already proof that he no longer fully belonged. Nor did he seem to see that the means by which he attempted to retain these cultural features, because they were borrowed from the world beyond the culture that valued them, subtly served to further distance him from his community.

In an attempt to "live as fine a Christian life as possible," Yoder took part in religious activities at the Brethren Normal School. As he became acquainted with the other students, he found them to be more "devout" than he, with their devotion expressed in formal and informal speech and through audible prayers at daily chapel, compulsory Sunday worship in town, and a mid-week student Bible study. In contrast, faith in Old Order Amish culture is expressed mostly through a life of quiet righteousness and obedience to the community, and concepts such as a crisis conversion, spiritual testimonies, improvisational spoken prayer, and frequent worship services are largely unknown. Following the pattern of a spiritual testimony, Yoder described his encounter with the students at Brethren Normal in terms of a spiritual conversion: "an inspiring harmony filled my soul, and the Brethren's Normal School became a never-ending source of joy and inspiration."[49]

The pietist spirit at Brethren Normal School was further enlivened by the nineteenth-century Evangelical movement, with its emphasis on missions and service. The school's Volunteer Mission Band eventually became affiliated with the national Student Volunteer Movement, whose motto was "The evangelization of the world in this generation." A year before Yoder arrived, the Young People's Missionary and Temperance Society was named, and it seemed to count the entire school among its membership.[50] A longtime supporter of the cause, Yoder remained a devoted member of the Women's Christian Temperance Union into the 1950s.

Back in the Valley, temperance was one point of conflict as tensions increased between progressive and conservative factions within Yoder's Amish Mennonite church at Belleville. Yoder recalled wine being served at his brother Yost's Old Order Amish wedding, but he testified in court against "the liquor evil" and "the saloon," probably in 1896. This daring excursion into the civil legal system could not go unnoticed, and the following Sunday, the bishop preached a sermon denouncing such behavior, concluding, "We will not excommunicate those who testified . . . if they will stand and confess a fault." By his own account, young Yoder sprang to his feet and replied, "I am one who testified against liquor: I feel I did right, and I will not confess a fault for anybody." A number of congregants responded with "Amen."[51]

This and such other marks of assimilation into progressive Protestantism as part-singing and the use of English as the language for worship, become so controversial that the church officially divided by 1898—but by then, Yoder, bent on making his own progress, was no longer living in the Valley.[52] Yoder was so impressed by Brethren classmates who shared his ethnicity but enjoyed more cultural "liberty" and expressed more religious piety, that he wanted to join the Church of the Brethren congregation at Huntingdon during his tenure at the Normal School. However his mentor, M. G. Brumbaugh, admonished him, "Joseph, stick to your people." [53]

PHYSICAL CULTURE

Yoder heeded Brumbaugh's counsel, at least in some sense. To retain the Amish work ethic, he took part in athletic training and physical culture, or body building. When he arrived in January, men's indoor gymnasium exercises would have included calisthenics and drills with dumbbells and Indian clubs, pins weighing four pounds or more, which were manipulated in each hand to increase upper-body strength. At that time, gymnasium work was still fairly new on the university scene, although from the middle of the nineteenth century, eastern intellectuals like Henry David Thoreau, Calvin Stowe, Lyman Beecher, and Thomas Wentworth Higginson had expressed anxiety that academic and urban life was making American men effeminate, pale, and bookish. In 1878, Harvard built a gymnasium, as much to lure its young men from the taverns as from their books. In 1885, West Point introduced calisthenics in its forth-year training and completed a new gynasium in 1892.[54] By 1890, A. B. Brumbaugh had successfully lobbied for formal physical education instruction and facilities at Brethren Normal School.[55]

In 1894, the physician-trustee continued his campaign to increase exercise on campus with an article in the *Juniata Echo* tracing the history and praising the virtues of various nineteenth-century European physical culture movements, adding that Brethren Normal drew elements from all of them. He wrote, "The Grecians believed that the mind could not possibly rise in culture to the proper limit of its power unless the body was in a highly developed healthy state. Hence the adage, 'Mens sana in corpore sano'" [strong mind in a strong body]. Brumbaugh railed "against football—the brutal exercise of wallowing in the mud, disfiguring and injuring the image of God,"—and outlined the dire consequences of neglecting the "noble manly sports": "A feeble, consumptive body is not the one that leads in any great movement for the good, advancement or liberation of the world."[56]

The notion that well-toned bodies are essential agents in the effort to advance and redeem the world was becoming common on many campuses at this time, even those not associated with military training. In 1858, Thomas Wentworth Higginson used the phrases "physical culture" and *mens sana in corpore sano* in a popular *Atlantic Monthly* essay that made the case for physical education in American schools, especially for the clergy and the learned.

Following the arguments in Emerson's 1837 essay "The American Scholar," Higginson despaired of fainting saints, effeminate preachers, frail poets, and the esteem granted to "mental precocity." Instead, Higginson pointed to the physical, mental and spiritual rigor of New England's Beechers and Stowes and the manly games played by authors and clergymen at Cambridge University. He argued for a distinctly superior American physical culture that would unite German gymnasium work, English sport, and Indian paddling and running in the interest of advancing the individual and protecting the nation: "Guaranty us against physical degeneracy, and we can risk all other perils—financial crises, Slavery, Romanism, Mormonism, Border Ruffians, and New York assassins: 'domestic malice, foreign levy, nothing' can daunt us."[57] Thus, Yoder's attempt to remain Amish by means of dumbbells and Indian pins placed him neatly within a popular movement of the dominant American culture.

In addition to the gymnasium work, Yoder's interest in physical culture led him to join the Washington D.C.-based Ralston Health Club with John Hooley and another Brethren Normal classmate, Kenton Mumaw. This organization promoted health through exercise and a special diet, aimed at developing "glame." Wrote Yoder, "Just what Glame is I could never quite find out, but it was a sort of spiritual and physical

1.5   *A typical room at Brethren Normal School during the era of Yoder and Hooley. Note the double bed and evidence of athletic involvement and school spirit.*

well-being developed through certain exercises which had to be taken with great rhythm, poise and self-control."[58]

During his second year at Huntingdon, Yoder and his clubmates moved off campus so that they could maintain the dietary requirements of the Ralston plan. Thanks to "glame" and the gym, Yoder returned to the Valley no weaker than when he left, and to prove this, he offered to help with the heaviest labor when on the farm, loading manure and forking or pitching hay onto the wagon. On an especially warm June morning, he shocked his darkly attired Amish co-workers by striding across a hay field wearing athletic gear—white shirt, trousers, and tennis shoes. Clearly he was not an Amish field hand, but one of the educated elite returned from college, where physical exertion is more a matter of choice than necessity, and where exercise serves to prime the mind and advance culture.

That morning Yoder pitched against the largest Amishman, because, he reasoned, "The idea was to make the Amishman say, 'I don't see how that Joseph Yoder can pitch hay like he does. Why he goes to college, and when he comes home, it takes a mighty good man to keep up with him in the hayfield.'" As news of his strength traveled, Yoder "felt that he was winning his point—the respect and friendship of the Amish people." He believed that his efforts surely succeeded when Crist Hooley, a former Big Valley resident, was talking on the porch of the Hill Store to a preacher in the Peachey Amish church, "Nancy" John Yoder. Crist noticed Joseph Yoder's stylish attire and asked who that young man might be. The preacher replied, "That's Little Crist Yoder's son . . . he goes to college, but Joseph is not like other young men who go to college. It does not spoil him at all. He is just as common as ever he was, and he's one of the best workers in the valley." This conversation was later reported to Little Crist, and it greatly pleased his son. At least in his own telling, Yoder had managed to appear in possession of the cardinal Amish virtues of humility—being "common"—and industry, although he performed these virtues by self-conscious, conspicuous, and even competitive means.[59]

When Yoder graduated from the Brethren Normal School in 1895, he was selected to give an "oration" at commencement's closing exercises. His topic, "the humble birth" and "noble life and character" of Dr. J. G. Holland, traced the rise of a common man to a station where he could "strengthen and elevate" popular thought. This narrative, offered as inspiration to the students from farms and small towns in Pennsylvania, underlined the school's mission to educate for enlightenment and the improvement of religious and public life.

Like physical exercise, elocution and oratory during this period were believed to equip students with the skills they would need to succeed as individuals and to change the world. It is no coincidence that A. B. Brumbaugh, ardent promoter of physicial culture on the campus also promoted oratory and elocution—not for homiletics, but for verbal combat and persuasion. He wrote,

> But no argument should be raised against the study of oratory by those whose duty it is to present arguments, and lead the thought of the world. All are leaders or nothing, and without preparation for the work, how can any one be successful in leading? The work of the age is preparation, then conquest; and those without the preparation are lost to sight and influence.[60]

Although commonplace in more secular settings, this view of rhetoric seems deeply at odds with Yoder's Amish background, for even his

1.6 Normal English Class of 1895. Hooley is second from left in the third row, and Yoder is fourth from left. The photograph, taken by Kleine Studio in Huntingdon, may have been printed in reverse.

preacher father composed sermons mostly by weaving together memorized passages of Scripture. Usually the Amish believe that the less said, the better in times of disagreement. "Conquest" and public speech for the purposes of worldly influence and personal promotion have as much place in the Amish community as white duck trousers and gym shoes had in a hay field. And yet, toward the end of his life, Yoder challenged the Amish bishops of his parents' church to public debates on doctrinal issues, invitations which they naturally ignored.

Progressive High School Principal

Maintaining a delicate negotiation between worlds, Yoder returned to the Valley in summer 1895 and noticed that his mother seemed weak and her breathing labored. In fact, Rosanna was suffering from an undiagnosed, advanced case of tuberculosis, and this is probably why Yoder decided to apply for work nearby rather than continue his studies. Rumors of his prowess as a hay-pitcher landed him the job of high school principal in Milroy, a factory town at the easterly end of the valley.

The board was concerned because the school had become unruly through lack of discipline, and they hoped that Yoder's physical stature

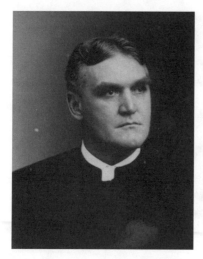

1.7 Martin Grove Brumbaugh in Dunker clerical garb, which he rarely wore, c. early 1900s.

and strength could put things in order. Little did they know that the new teacher had learned a different approach to discipline at Brethren Normal School, under the guidance of his mentor, M. G. Brumbaugh. A progressive pedagogue, Brumbuagh had been elected Pennsylvania's youngest county superintendent of schools in 1884, and after great success in reforming the local country school system and leading statewide teacher institutes, he developed a post-Reconstruction public education program in Louisiana and wrote many popular textbooks. He would also serve as Commissioner of Education in Puerto Rico and as a reform-minded Superintendent of the city schools in Philadelphia.

Brumbaugh stressed child psychology, wholistic education, and student-centered curriculum, introducing art and music as core subjects in the rural schools which he served as county superintendant. He frequently referred to education as "holy work," insisting that teachers must be accountable to both society and God. In one speech he argued against corporal punishment, citing Jesus (Matt. 18:6), "Whatever we do to these little ones we also do to him, who loved them. . . ."[61] According to Yoder, Brumbaugh instilled in his Normal School students a theory of "Christian pedagogy and psychology," an approach both liberal and humane, based on the belief that each soul is unique and sacred: "if you must punish, give the pupil a chance to defend himself, and give his opinion as to whether the punishment is just."

As principal, Yoder never resorted to corporal punishment, following Brumbaugh's advice to, "govern with your eye and not with your voice. Cultivate absolute self-control" and practice "sympathetic consideration."[62] Even the most notorious Milroy students were converted by respect and patience "after being whipped and regarded as a pestiferous mischief" by former schoolmasters. Although he nowhere explicitly

1.8 Christ and Rosanna's retirement home along Greenwood Street. The porch was enclosed kater, but the house and out buildings are original. A buggy dimly visible at left under tree belongs to the house's current owner, part of the Amish church Crist and Rosanna attended in their day.

contrasted Brumbaugh's approach with the child rearing practices of his Amish background, Yoder concluded, "In discipline whether school or home, the most effective and constructive method is couched in those two magnificent words,—sympathetic consideration."[63]

The school at Milroy was twelve miles from Belleville, so Yoder boarded there during the week and traveled by horse back to spend weekends at his parents' home. On one of these Friday evenings as he approached the house on Greenwood Street, he was met outdoors by a young niece who warned him that his mother was gravely ill. When Yoder determined that Rosanna had been poisoned by strong medicines prescribed by her physician, he dismissed the doctor and concocted his own tonic from cracked corn, propelled by the desperate determination that Rosanna must have felt to save his life, twenty-three years earlier, and also perhaps by knowledge from the Ralston Health Club. With his brothers, Yoder nursed their mother for a few days until she died.

As word of her death traveled through the community, church members arrived to make arrangements for the funeral and meal. In keeping with tradition, family members and friends watched over the corpse throughout the night in the Yoder home, and during the day, many came to view the body and to offer food and words of comfort. The funeral was also held in the home, and "Nancy" John Yoder was chosen to preach the main sermon.

Yoder felt apprehensive about the service because he feared that, following custom, the Amish preacher might take advantage of this opportunity to make an example of the three youngest boys and give them "a thorough lacing" for not joining their parents' church. However, this did not happen, and instead of scolding the sons, the preacher praised them: "It is a high compliment to any young man to go away to college as one of these sons has done and then come home with increased loyalty and devotion to his parents."[64] According to Yoder, the preacher distinguished between obeying one's parents' church and honoring one's parents. This idea echoes Levi's emotional argument with the bishop that made such an impression on young Yoder: "I do honor my father and mother. . . . but I'm not going to join your church and promise to obey your *Ordnung*"[65] This was not a distinction that all Old Order Amish people were willing to make, however, and Yoder was criticized into old age for not honoring his parents by joining their church.

Unlike his brothers who married and left home, Yoder established a pattern of constantly leaving and then returning. Although he refused to work on the farm, he boarded at his parents' house, a favorite bachelor uncle to his brother's children. Even when he moved away for study or weeklong stints of teaching, he returned to his parents, who remained his primary family. Along with the care he showed his mother during her illness, these visits were recognized as signs of filial devotion or "honor," highly valued in Amish culture. With her passing, Yoder experienced a great loss and wrote, "I felt as though I was on the threshold of a sorrow I could never overcome. Mother was my confidant."[66]

Shortly after her death, Yoder applied to Hahnemann Medical College in Philadelphia, as if to continue Rosanna's work as a healer and to explore his own concerns for health. An interest in scientific medicine and alternative healing endured throughout Yoder's life, but he did not enter medical school. In a 1954 letter to L. Ron Hubbard requesting permission to audit classes at the Dianetic Research Foundation, Yoder mentioned that application, adding that it "was side tracked by a call to teach in a new college for the Mennonites, Elkhart, Indiana."[67]

This was actually the second invitation from Elkhart. In 1894, while he was still studying at Brethren Normal School, Yoder had been offered the position of principal at the new Elkhart Institute of Science, Industry and the Arts, in northern Indiana. At that time, Yoder was tempted to accept, but wrote that he feared he might "attempt to fill a position beyond [his] ability" as well as being "mindful of [his] being needed at home." He expressed the hope that instead of accepting the invitation immediately he might obtain a four-year degree and join the Institute faculty eventually: "The more I think about the matter the more I am convinced that it would not be a good move for me to ever accept your high position with my education. The stronger your principal the better the reputation of your school. You should have a Ph.D."[68] In April 1897, during his second year as principal at Milroy High School, Yoder was once again contacted by John S. Coffman; this time in person, and this time, Yoder could not resist.

Coffman was admired by many of Yoder's generation, who were among the first in their families to venture beyond local farm communities in search of education. The son of a well-known Mennonite bishop from Virginia, where Mennonites already used English for worship and were not as self-segregating as those in Pennsylvania, Coffman showed that one need not lose one's heritage in order gain worldly learning. C. Henry Smith, who later claimed the distinction of being the first Amish Mennonite to earn a Ph.D. at an American university and remain in the church, recalled that in contrast to the simple-minded, German sermons he was used to hearing, Coffman "preached an English sermon in our church in which he showed himself thoroughly at home in the fields of literature and history and other subjects I had been studying in school. He seemed a kindred spirit, so unlike our own uneducated preachers."[69]

Coffman was a soft-spoken, pious man who earned the trust of local communities even as he introduced progressive innovations, and he became the first traveling evangelist to be accepted by the Mennonites. According to one historian, Coffman "preached a revivalistic call to conversion yet tried to fuse it with doctrine and some of the spirit of an older Mennonitism."[70] A personal invitation to join Coffman at the new school in Elkhart left Yoder "very drawn between two duties." He could hardly resist the opportunity to join the few Amish Mennonites qualified to teach in the new school, nor did he wish to refuse Coffman, whom Yoder described as a man of "pious persuasion" who impressed upon him the obligation of the Christian educator.[71]

On the other hand, Yoder felt he owed the public school at Milroy another year of service, because they had taken a risk in hiring him when he had little experience. Moreover, the school board was divided along political lines between nominating Yoder and another local candidate, whom Yoder regarded as unpopular and unqualified. His Republican patrons threatened to take the case to the courts if the Democratic man were chosen. At the end of June, Yoder wrote to Coffman, "under the circumstances I do not see how I can leave honorably." But it seems that he truly wanted to go to Indiana. When the school board's vote drew a tie, he threatened to withdraw his candidacy if the next election were indecisive. On July 12, he sent a telegram to Elkhart stating, "Will send a definite answer Thursday morning." Three days later, he announced, "I have now decided to come."[72]

Having finally settled his fate, Yoder requested lodging "with good, educated refined people, if possible, and also prefer to room alone." Although eager for the job, "studying up on . . . Latin Literature and History," he also confessed his timidity at the prospect of the journey: "Can you give me any directions in regard to the trip? How long does it take to go out? Had I better start on an early train or not? I have never traveled much so I don't know much about it. Where all do I change cars?"

This letter he signed, "Your obedient servant." The words *obedient* and *servant*, though perhaps used here as a conventional epistolary closing, point to concepts that had great significance in the world that Joseph Yoder was preparing to leave. As he observed in *Rosanna of the Amish*, obedience was among the first things he had learned as a child. And "servant"—an allusion to Jesus and his selfless sacrifice—is the model of Anabaptist virtue. In fact, however, since attending Brethren Normal School, Yoder was well on the way to becoming neither obedient nor a servant in his community's sense of those words, but what he *would* become remained uncertain. He left the farms and mountains of Big Valley in the spirit of his Irish great-uncles, ambitious potato farmers determined to emigrate because "there are no family rules, nor trade rules, and a young man may choose any work he fancies."[73]

CHAPTER 2

THE BODY
AND SPIRIT OF PROGRESS

Then men shall stand up with no sickness in the body and no taint of sin in the soul. My hope for the human race is bright as the morning star, for a glory is coming to man such as the most inspired tongues of prophets and poets have never been able to describe. The gate of human opportunity is turning on its hinges, and the light is breaking through its chink; possibilities are opening, and human nature is pressing forward to meet them.
—Ralph Waldo Emerson, quoted by J. W. Yoder in "A Thing Worth While," *Juniata Echo*, 1903

ELKHART INSTITUTE

When the Lakeshore and Michigan Southern locomotive pulled into Elkhart, Indiana, at just past six o'clock on a Saturday morning in late August 1897, at least one passenger was filled with both hope and apprehension. Having traveled almost twenty-four hours from the Lewistown station in Pennsylvania, Joseph Yoder was about to step into a bustling city of 15,000 people served by three weekly and two daily newspapers, situated at the juncture of three railroad lines, just 100 miles from Chicago. In a landscape that was flatter than any he had seen in the east, possibility must have seemed limitless to the twenty-four-year-old hired to teach language and literature at the Elkhart Institute of Science, Industry and the Arts.

Three years before, the *Elkhart Truth* had announced the school's inception under the headline: "This Enterprise. What Progressive Elkhartians Have Done." The article made no mention of religion, but praised founder H. A. Mumaw, a homeopathic physician and member of the Prairie Street Mennonite Church, along with "a number of progressive Elkhart citizens" who with him envisioned "distinctively a Hoosier Enterprise" inspired by "Armour, Drexel, Franklin, Pratt, Cooper, and other industrial and technical institutes."[1] By the time Yoder arrived, the Institute had expanded its educational agenda to include course work in history, languages and literature, chemistry and physics, as well as farm accounting, teacher training, short-hand, typing, penmanship, and business. A promotional pamphlet from the 1897-98 academic year listed Yoder among a faculty of seven men and proclaimed the school's eclectic offerings "a thorough training in art, science, and literature under religious influences."

The Institute was part of broader nineteenth-century efforts to elevate the material and spiritual lives of all men and women through the related influences of religion, education, and a concern for health. Reforms such as the abolition of slavery, women's suffrage, temperance, Protestant revivals, and the improvement of sanitation and working conditions in the cities were all propelled by progressive attitudes and technological advances. An 1897-98 pamphlet for the Institute was decorated with quotations that link the school to progressive concerns. Among them, advice from abolitionist novelist Harriet Beecher Stowe: "No young lady could have a better safeguard against adversities of fortune or a better resource in time of need than a knowledge of Bookkeeping and business affairs."

Especially pertinent to Yoder's interests were the words of educational theorist Johan Heinrich Pestalozzi, proponent of physical education and follower of Rousseau:

> Education relates to the whole man, and consists in drawing forth, strengthening, and perfecting all faculties with which an all-wise Creator has endowed him, physical, mental, and moral. Education has to do with the hand, the head, and the heart.
>
> Furthermore, the pamphlet announced the school's mission of providing equity and opportunity for all: "All classes and

——THE——

Elkhart Institute,

ELKHART, INDIANA.

FOUNDED A. D., 1894.

2.1 The new home of the Elkhart Institute, built in 1895-96 on Prairie Street in Elkhart, Indiana.

grades of students are equally welcome at the Institute, and made to feel at home. The poor boy from the humble cottage receives the same care as the boy from the costly mansion."[2]

When Yoder arrived, the Institute was attempting to integrate its progressive agenda with a closer relationship to the tradition-conscious Mennonite church. The previous winter, in February 1896, the Institute had moved into new facilities built largely through stock bought by Mennonites from across the country, and located across Prairie Street from the Mennonite church. At the opening ceremony, J. S. Coffman, the respected evangelist who had used his influence to gain financial support for the school, offered the famous speech, "The Spirit of Progress," in which he articulated a concern for serious scholarship, international affairs and peace, and Christian service.

Noting a connection between the theme of the 1893 World's Columbian Exposition in Chicago and the title of Coffman's address, Susan Fisher Miller has observed that "it must have taken great courage for a leader of the staunchly sectarian Mennonite church of that time to embrace progress by name, instead of dismissing it in favor of tradition."[3] In fact, Coffman had attended the world's fair, taking in an international peace conference and sermons by Dwight L. Moody and Cyris I. Scofield.[4] This judicious consumption of both worldly progress and piety was unlike most attitudes toward culture that Yoder would have encountered among Amish in the East, and his first impression of the Institute was that it was "a new sensation," yet "definitely a religious school."

"New sensation" could also describe the busy Mennonite community at Elkhart in those days. When Yoder arrived, it was the center of what mid-twentieth century historian H. S. Bender called "the Great Awakening of the Mennonite Church." Borrowing a term from America's Protestant revivals to name an era marked by the rapid creation of charitable institutions, Sunday schools, mission work, publications, and institutional church boards, Bender acknowledged the source and inspiration for many of those activities.[5] His father, George L. Bender, was among the circle of bright, young Mennonites and Amish Mennonites who had gathered between 1890 and 1910 to work with John F. Funk at Elkhart. Most of those men were former schoolteachers like Yoder, well-educated by late-nineteenth century standards; and like Yoder, they were energized by conversations between their sectarian backgrounds and the spiritual and intellectual movements stirring in America's social and religious spheres.

At the center of this community was John F. Funk and his printing press. A Mennonite from eastern Pennsylvania, Funk had been converted in a Presbyterian revival in Chicago. He went home to be baptized in a Mennonite congregation, but returned to the city, where he was active in a Baptist Sunday school and worked in circles that included Protestant evangelists like Dwight L. Moody. In 1864 he began publishing the first church-wide periodical for Mennonites, *The Herald of Truth/ Der Herold der Wahrheit*, in English and German editions. Founded during the Civil War, the newspaper bore a motto from Romans 10:15, which blends a spirit of evangelism with Mennonite pacifism: "How beautiful are the feet of them that preach the gospel of peace."

In 1867, Funk moved his printing operation to the city of Elkhart, a short train ride from Chicago yet in an Indiana county that contained Mennonite farm villages. Under Funk's direction, the Mennonite Publishing Company produced Sunday school materials and other literature that introduced Mennonites to American Protestant thought, along with texts that preserved their Anabaptist heritage, such as *Martyrs Mirror* and *The Complete Works of Menno Simons*. Funk also founded the urban Mennonite congregation at Prairie Street and introduced new programs for congregational development and training lay teachers.

For Yoder, the most influential figure in the Elkhart community was probably the man he described as a "devout Christian minister and gentleman" who was responsible for his being there, J. S. Coffman. Drawn to Elkhart by Funk in 1879, Coffman had served as an associate editor at the Mennonite Publishing Company and as a minister at Prairie Street before turning his energy to directing and raising funds for the Elkhart Institute. When Yoder arrived as a boarder, the Coffman home housed five of the seven Coffman children along with their mother Elizabeth J. Heatwole Coffman and a longtime member of the household, Anna Sowers.

Although he had requested to board alone, Yoder greatly enjoyed his year at the Coffman house on Eden Street. "From young manhood, I had always lived in a family where I was the only young person, and now to live in a family of three lively young men and two charming daughters was a joy I had never experienced before," he wrote.[6] J. S. Coffman had been a singing school instructor in Virginia, and all the Coffman children were "fine singers," according to Yoder. They often gathered to sing from a repertoire of gospel songs and hymns, and they welcomed Yoder's strong bass voice into their circle. By contrast, that year a conservative faction of 118 people withdrew from Yoder's Church House Amish congregation at Belleville after nearly a decade of disagreement about many issues, part-singing among them. The desires and ambitions that Yoder had managed to consign to the outlaw "Irish" aspects of his personality

2.2 The 1898 cast of the Messiah Chorus, Elkhart Institute. Joseph W. Yoder appears in second row, fourth from right.

2.3 Tickets from the Messiah performances.

in Pennsylvania were suddenly acceptable, and even affirmed by the Mennonites in Elkhart.

Whether in the Coffman parlor or in public, Yoder's greatest pleasure that year was singing. From late September until May, he met weekly with the Institute's Philharmonic Society to study and rehearse Handel's *Messiah,* under the direction of Abram B. Kolb, a seasoned musician and editor of Funk's *Herald of Truth.* For Yoder, mastery of this great classical work was so gratifying that it stands out in his memoir as the single mention of academic life at Elkhart. He missed only three rehearsals in seven months, and probably sat during practice and performances beside his housemate, Daniel J. Coffman, an Institute student seven years his junior.[7] In February and May, oratorio "reditions," were offered to the public, with organ and piano accompaniment, four soloists and a chorus of ninety-two voices. A photograph of the full cast was taken to commemorate the Messiah productions, which were highlights of the 1897-98 academic year, rating even the suspension of Institute Literary Society meetings.

Yoder also participated in the Institute's Literary Society, which staged weekly programs for the edification of school and town folk. These meetings followed parliamentry procedure and typically opened with a musical piece—such as Yoder's solo, "Come to Jesus"—followed by a recitation, essay or paper, and extemporaneous speeches. The climax of each meeting was a formal debate adjudicated by three observers. Daniel Coffman was president of the Society, and Yoder was elected to the office of "Critic," responsible for assessing the weekly performances. A survey of the debate topics for the 1897-98 academic year reveals that students were interested in issues ranging from psychology and human development to national and international affairs. Although many of the Amish-Mennonites came from communities where their members did not participate in the political process, the students learned through the debates to think critically, formulate their opinions as arguments, and to conduct themselves in a public forum. According to Literary Society minutes, the more progressive positions generally prevailed in these debates:

> That the home has more influence in the development than associates.
> That the young man raised in the country has a better chance for success in life than the young man raised in the city.

That environment has more to do in forming character than heredity. [In this question, Yoder debated the negative position and won.]

That hope of reward is greater than fear of punishment.

That the elective franchise granted to the Negro at the close of the war was premature.

That S.F.B. Morse deserves more credit for the invention of the telegraph than Stevenson for the locomotive.

That legislation is the means for the annihilation of the liquor traffic.

That the dismemberment of China is justifiable.

That Germany has a better system of government than the U.S.[8]

In November 1897, the Institute's public lecture series featured A. S. Zook delivering a speech titled, "Shun the Corduroy Road through Inebriation." Temperance, a passion of some progressives, remained one of Yoder's concerns at Elkhart. In April he led a special meeting of the Literary Society that showcased speeches on the topic by twelve males, likely his students. There is evidence that health-consciousness and the physical culture movement—which Yoder would later follow with great zeal—also influenced some in the Funk circle at Elkhart. "Physical Culture" was the title of an extemporaneous speech delivered at a Literary Society Meeting in spring 1898.[9]

By the end of the summer term, looking toward his twenty-sixth birthday, Yoder believed that he had finally discovered his life's path. In Elkhart, he had found homes—both within the Coffman family and in Mennonite church institutions—where his musical and oratorical abilities were appreciated and nurtured, and where he could develop a career in the company of forward-looking men who shared his background and vision. In this regard, he longed to gain the "respect of educators, even a position in the Elkhart. Institute."[10]

At the same time, he realized that he needed more education if he were to contribute in any significant way to the school. Guided by Henry C. Heasley, the Institute's Episcopal principal, Yoder decided to continue his education at Northwestern, the Methodist university north of Chicago where Heasley had taken his degree. In late July, Yoder rode the train back to Pennsylvania to visit family and friends, but his thoughts remained in the Midwest. By early August, he sent a four-page letter to J. S. Coffman in which he asked after "Mother Coffman," confessed that he thought of the family daily, and chided young Daniel for not answering his letters. There at home with his father, Yoder complained, all he did was "keep the bread from molding . . . and keep the horse from getting wild."

He also explained he had been corresponding with Ansel, an elder Coffman son studying music at Northwestern, and laid out his own plans to take a year of preparatory school, then four more at the university at Evanston. "In my limited means, I can hardly think of going to school five years," he wrote, "yet that is the way things look just now." The plan was for Yoder's brother-in-law, John M. Hooley, Yoder's classmate at the four-week teacher-training course in McVeytown and his roommate at Brethren Normal School, to accompany him.[11]

That summer, Yoder visited friends and Institute students in Lancaster County, Pennsylvania, in an effort to promote the school and advance the cause of higher education in that old Amish and Mennonite settlement. Like his progressive contemporaries, Yoder believed that proper education could improve the body as well as the mind and soul. In a letter to Coffman, he mentioned meeting a former Institute student whom he had urged to return to Elkhart so that he would reform certain unnamed "bad habits," predicting, "I am afraid he'll be as bad as ever if he stays at home." Elsewhere in the letter, Yoder marveled at the backwardness he encountered in the rural, conservative community and urged Coffman to uplift them with his preaching. "It is wonderful the amount of barbarity there is among the Christian people yet. The people would like to have you come to Lancaster Co. Go, enlighten them." In a particularly telling paragraph, Yoder expressed his desire to be identified with the Elkhart Institute and to take on the delicate task of promoting higher education among the Amish Mennonites, but he feared that one year of teaching did not qualify him to lay claim to a place in the Elkhart circle. He seemed torn between his own ambition and the need to behave in a humble manner for the sake of piety. Perhaps most worrisome was his fear that he may have had more in common with Pennsylvania's barbarian farmers than the "Christian gentleman" he was addressing:

> You may be assured I painted the school in a beautiful manner whenever I had an opportunity to ply my verbal brush. So far as I could learn, the people think well of the school and are becoming more favorable to education in general. I think if we stick to-

gether humbly "preferring one another in honor" our school will be [*sic*] grow and do much good. I say *our* school because I feel that I have a hand in making that school go. Maybe I should not feel so much that way; is it selfish I just feel that I'm about to make a five year sacrifice to prepare to boom education among our people. Have I a right to feel that way? If I have not tell me and *I'll go to the farm. Be candid!*[12]

Coffman's response to this letter has not survived, but it must have assured Yoder, because shortly thereafter he spent several days visiting with the Coffman family on his way to Northwestern. Just before Yoder's departure, John Hooley decided to remain behind and continue his coursework at Juniata College (formerly Brethren Normal School). Hooley's desertion disappointed Yoder because it meant that he would have to set off without his "educational guide and trail blazer" for the first time. But he wrote to his mentor in Elkhart, "I remain steadfast for Evanston and the advancement of education among our people."[13]

NORTHWESTERN UNIVERSITY

When he arrived in the fall of 1898, Yoder felt "lost and very home-sick," and he wrote, "Had it not been a reflection on my self-control, I think I would have come back to Juniata." He enrolled in Greek and other preparatory subjects at Northwestern Academy, floundering and alone without Hooley until he found his way to the Young Men's Christian Association (YMCA). He wrote, "those boys treated me so well, that I soon had many friends and I became very fond of Northwestern and my homesickness vanished."[14]

+Active on American campuses since the mid-1800s, the academic branch of the YMCA was approaching its peak influence when Yoder joined. By century's end, it would count 32,000 student members in 623 college and university chapters; by 1920, 94,000 students in 731 chapters. Patterned after the urban Ys which were designed to divert working men from the saloon and other vices, university-based programs offered a range of services to help students adjust to college life, particularly those like Yoder who were first-generation college-goers. In addition to providing reading room and gymnasium facilities, the YMCA sponsored school handbooks, book-exchange programs, employment bureaus, tuition loan programs, tutoring, and Bible studies.

Y's also promoted intercollegiate interaction though summer conferences that emphasized evangelism, social justice, international peace, and ecumenicity.[15]

By this time, the YMCA had become firmly associated with muscular Christianity, a literary, religious, and social movement imported from Victorian Britain that thrived on American soil.[16] By the 1880s, muscular Christianity influenced the culture that surrounded and supported Christian revivalism and evangelism in the United States. Sharing a belief in cultivating the "whole man"—the mind/body/spirit connection symbolized by the Y's red triangle insignia—muscular Christians sought to develop strength of character through sport. Drawing on values associated with chivalry and honor, military training and self-discipline, virtue and manliness, the muscular Christian was religiously sure, physically fit, and mentally strong enough to be master of both self and circumstances.[17] Lessons learned on the playing field or gymnasium, it was believed, would enable men—and in some cases, women—to build an enlightened society or triumph on the battlefield. When the YMCA opened a new gymnasium in New York City in 1869, the *New York Times* noted that

> This concession to the muscular Christianity of the time has been made, we are glad to hear, almost without dissent, nor can any one who appreciates the moral force of the *sana mens in sano corpore* find fault with the athletic character it is proposed to give the young Christians of New York. If the association succeeds in drawing to its gymnasium a large number of the young men of the City, and in giving them sound bodies and muscles of iron, as well as healthy religious principles and moral characters more enduring than steel, it will deserve and receive a double commendation. We may then hope for a next generation of New Yorkers fully equal to the occasions of an advancing civilization.[18]

That Yoder remained active in the international YMCA movement throughout his life is suggested by a 1950 letter to the Huntingdon, Pennsylvania, Justice of the Peace, in which he begged to be excused from paying a fine for having driven through a stop sign: "Why did I not come to a complete stop? I was taking the National Sec. of the Y.M.C.A. of Korea to the Mennonite church just east of Allensville, and I wanted to get him there to hear the singing at the beginning of the service."[19]

Having found a home with the young men at Northwestern's Y, Yoder thrived in the classroom, literary society, and gymnasium. During his first year at the Academy, he studied formal debate and in June 1899 represented the Euphoria Society, which he served as secretary, in a contest sponsored by the Academy Literary Societies. According to a school publication, his speech "sounded a warning to America to live up to her highest ideals and predicted that, should she do so, the title of his oration, 'Shall history repeat itself?' might be answered in the negative."[20] Yoder won the first place prize of ten dollars. That spring in honor of the Academy class of '99 he also delivered a Class Day speech, which reflected his forward-looking philosophy as well as the ornate diction of the day, as the printed text reveals:

> Our ship of study has been sailing steadily and persistently onward, through the orange fragrant zephyrs of the sunny southland, though the dark and storm-cast billows of the frigid northland, climbing up the ladder of fame, round by round, until today, she sits confident and triumphant up on the very apex of the zenith of glory. As I look down from this dazzling height of intellectual acquisition, upon this sea of upturned faces, I am reminded of the instability of man, of the metaphysical attainment of the class of '99 and that the end of life is death.[21]

Yoder studied elocution with Dr. Cumnock, one of only two faculty members mentioned by name in his memoir: "one of the best, if not *the* best reader in the United States, and he cheerfully admitted it." Yoder admired the thespian's skill and demeanor, and reported hearing the master boast, "If I knew of anybody that can read the English language better than I can, I would go anywhere in the world to hear him."[22] In class, students observed Cumnock's performances and learned by example. Yoder found especially memorable the impact of a tear-jerking traditional Irish story:

> When he came before the class sometimes, he would say, "Children [young men and women from eighteen to thirty] what shall I read for you today?" Some freshman villain would call out, "Read Connor," and at once the girls would wail, "Oh Doctor, please don't." They knew that they would have to weep too audibly for comfort in polite society, if the accomplished doctor read "Connor."[23]

2.4 *The Euphronia Literary Society, Northwestern University. Yoder is seated
front and center; hereafter he always assumed this position in group photographs, suggesting one implication of his years in Evanston.*

2.5 *J. W. Yoder at
Northwestern, c.
1899-1900.*

Cumnock's classroom nurtured Yoder's flair for performance and doubtless influenced his career as a dramatic and charismatic lecturer who, though greatly respected for his oratorical force, was also judged to have a "proud" demeanor by many in the Amish and Mennonite community. The only other Northwestern faculty member who merited mention in Yoder's memoir was Hollister, a professor of physical education. Building on his earlier efforts at Brethren Normal School, Yoder was already "much interested in gymnasium work and track work" when he got to Northwestern. Although he excelled in these areas, he had not yet gained the confidence he so admired in Cumnock. At some point during the academic year 1899-00, Professor Hollister did not feel like changing into his gym suit for class and asked for a volunteer to lead exercises that day. As he tells the story, Yoder was nominated by "some good Samaritan" for this task he wanted but was too timid to claim.

From then on, Yoder led class frequently, with or without the professor, and this responsibility both pleased and "emboldened him."[24] It cast him before the class in a position of leadership, working at a task in which the primary instrument was his own body—a position he would assume in various forms for the rest of his life.

TROUBLES IN ELKHART

After two years at Northwestern, Yoder returned to Elkhart in the fall of 1900 to teach English and Greek, but he did not find the "new sensation" that had inspired his allegiance just two years before. J. S. Coffman, Yoder's fifty-year old mentor, had died of cancer during summer 1899, after seeking treatments at the sanitarium of John Harvey Kellogg in Battle Creek, Michigan. Dr. Heasley, who had encouraged Yoder to go on to the university, was no longer on the faculty. Nor did A. B. Kolb continue that year what had become an annual tradition of performing Handal's "Messiah" and "Creation."

Trouble was afoot in Elkhart. Coffman had been a powerful yet gentle mediator between change-minded young people and the Mennonite church, and after his death, school-church relations became increasingly tense. In the fall of 1898, Heasley, the Episcopalian with a Bachelor of Arts degree, was replaced by a twenty-five-year old Mennonite Ph.D., Noah N. Byers. Characterized as brilliant and progressive, educated at Northwestern and the University of Chicago, Byers was active in the

YMCA and missions movements, and he instituted a chapter of the Young People's Christian Association (YPCA) during his first semester as principal at Elkhart. When student representatives returned from intercollegiate conferences in 1899, they were eager to institute new ideas from the broader Protestant world, without much consideration for Mennonite values or traditions.[25]

When Yoder returned in the fall of 1900, tensions between the school and church had reached a breaking point, and some of the institute's students and faculty were about to withdraw from the Prairie Street congregation and its bishop, sixty-five-year-old publisher, John F. Funk. School and church parted ways that year for reasons that must have felt hauntingly familiar to Yoder, who from childhood harbored a distaste for schism and authoritarian bishops. Years later, Yoder assessed the situation simply, "When Bishop J. F. Funk could not dominate the Institute, he did everything he could to hinder it."[26]

Although personal conflicts between the school's founder and later administrators had simmered for some time within the church community, the immediate reason for the break was framed mostly in terms of change and tradition: some Prairie Street members disapproved of the Institute students' worldliness, as exhibited in their fashionable dress, social activities, and the proliferation of literary societies and athletics.[27] One of several new men's debating clubs called "Coming Men of America"was organized in 1898 under the unequivocal motto: "Progress." A notable point of contention for the conservatives at Prairie Street was men's sport, and Yoder—fresh from Northwestern's gym and YMCA—was the driving force behind that.

Early in the fall of 1900, a group of male students elected Yoder to organize and preside over the new Elkhart Institute Athletic Association. They immediately built a track and baseball diamond and bought equipment for field work, and already that fall, they were competing in outdoor contests of running, shot put, hammer throw, pole vault, and jumping. When the weather was warm enough, the men also swam and dived in the Elkhart River. In winter, Yoder instructed them in light gymnastics—body building with dumbbells, bars, and Indian clubs—at the Elkhart YMCA, although some students eventually outfitted a barn on Prairie Street to practice their gymnasium work.

The transformation of the barn into a gym nicely paralleled the transformation from farm hand into athlete that Yoder first experienced under the discipline of physical culture when he was a student at Brethren Normal School. However, years later he traced his passion for the gymnasium to a spring board his older brothers John and Levi had laid over a straw-covered manure pile, and to the trapeze they had rigged in the hay mow of their father's barn, inspired by a circus that had come to Belleville some time in the late 1870s:

> To take a running start, jump onto the springboard, leap high into the air, turn a somersault or "flipper" as we called it, and light on your feet in a standing position, was a feat not all could do. Our springboard and trapeze brought boys from town to practice and observe, and it really gave us social standing in the boy community. . . . While I was too little to perform well on the trapeze, I did learn to turn a flip, and turn a hand-spring and walk on my hands.[28]

Visits from the traveling circus are described repeatedly in Yoder's memoirs, and the spectacle of human stunts, showmanship and "the boy community" became enormous elements in his life.

A formal portrait of coach Yoder, in a black turtle neck, surrounded by the twenty-seven gym-suited members of the Elkhart Institute Ath-

2.6 *The Elkhart Institute Athletic Association, 1900-01. J. W. Yoder (black turtle neck), John S. Umble (row 1, left), Jonathan M. Kurtz (Row 3, left of Yoder), H. Frank Reist (Row 4, 5 from left), J. E. Hartzler (row 4, 5 from right), Frank S. Ebersole (row 4, 3 from right).*

letic Association captured the spirit of muscular Christianity that must have pervaded the Association that year. It is no wonder that the sensibilities of conservatives at Prairie Street were offended. These immodestly dressed, shapely fellows were not only hard-working farmer's sons—although many of them may have been—but self-conscious and body-conscious men whose physiques were defined and elevated under Yoder's careful coaching. A practitioner of physical culture from the days he claimed that exercise kept him "common" in the eyes of the Amish, Yoder aimed to integrate mind and body, transforming brawny boys into poised men of distinction. Among the young fellows emerged many outstanding individuals: J. E. Hartzler and H. Frank Reist, presidents of Goshen College; Frank S. Ebersole, prominent Goshen business man and mayor; and Jonathan M. Kurtz and John S. Umble, Goshen College professors.

Yoder's model for masculinity was less the defenseless, suffering Savior—or even his own father who humbly yielded personal gain to minister to the community—than the disciplined soldier or athlete. Although the ideals of self-control and right action are central to both muscular Christianity and Anabaptism, the consequences of these two ideologies are quite different as they are embodied in the demeanors and behaviors of individual men. The aim of the former is service through domination of selfish desire, and the consequence of the latter is more an "art of the body," which makes a man more skillful, powerful, and publicly esteemed, even as he becomes more highly disciplined.[29]

Yoder's commitment to muscular Christianity is most evident in his "Elkhart Institute School Song," written during the 1900-01 academic year. These verses are preserved in a booklet printed by the Institute's alumni association; and, as if waiting to be found by posterity, a typed copy remains in Yoder's personal papers with a note in his hand: "written by J. W. Yoder to be sung by chorus at services." The song maps the progressive Mennonite pupil's journey from Anabaptist "fathers of old" to "eternity's shore." Between reverence for history and hope for heaven are chivalric sentiments typical of period alma mater songs, such as pledges of devotion to one's school and friendships from student days. The text includes images particular to the experiences of Yoder and other Amish Mennonites who left "field and the farm" seeking a progressive education that would elevate and civilize their raw "brain" and "brawn" toward "knowledge and culture and art."

Our fathers of old wrought with patience and prayer
To leave us a heritage dear;
Now with gratitude deep for their kind loving care,
We their names and their memories revere.
From the field and the farm with our brawn and our brain,
They have sent us to learn wisdom's ways,
And in knowledge and culture and art to attain
That which brightens and cheers all our days.

Verse three employs a list of allusions to ancient intellectuals and warriors that would seem peculiar in any sense other than the muscular Christian's conflation of these roles. The sound mind in a sound body ethic is explicit in "sages in class, athletes in play," and the purpose of *sana mens in sano corpore* is a defense of "the right." A possible reference to pressure from the Mennonite conservatives optimistically asserts that it *is* possible for scholar athletes to be "gallant and brave" while also honoring their elders.

Here with Euclid we reason, with Ceasar we fight,
And with Homer we lay siege to Troy;
With Demosthenes' power we stand by the right;
When grave questions our talents employ.
We are sages in class, but we're athletes in play,
Our motto is "gno-the-se-au-ton;"
To be gallant and brave and our elders obey
Is our object in duty or fun.

The song's final verse, however, departs from that obedient posture. Here the manly Institute graduate sets out to meet his destiny as an educator, missionary, or community leader. Although he carries the zeal of his Anabaptist ancestors, he is also inspired by classical heroes and intends to influence "church and state," abandoning humble, separatist enclaves for action in the public arena.

Fair school of our boyhood, the pride of our youth,
Thou hast launched us on destiny's sea;
In our manhood we'll toil to teach others thy truth,
And lead their young footsteps to Thee.
O Alma Mater, with our ancestor' zeal
Long may we thy precepts adore,

That in church and in state we the influence feel,
Till we meet on eternity's shore.

Females were conspicuously absent from Yoder's song, although official Institute literature of this time asserted that "Ladies are admitted to all the departments, and are afforded the same advantages as gentlemen."[30] In April 1901, as one of his final contributions to the Elkhart Institute, Yoder helped Leila G. Munsell to organize the Elkhart Institute Tennis Association for "the social and physical development of young women." Two courts were marked, equipment was bought, men were admitted as associate members, and tennis became the rage at Elkhart that spring.[31] Newly imported from Britain, the game was more genteel than today's version, with women chasing the ball in toe-length, white dresses—and doubtless conservatives saw in it yet another unnecessary, worldly and frivolous innovation.

When the 1901 year concluded, Yoder was anxious to resume his studies so that he could continue teaching on the faculty. Although he was hired to teach Greek and English at Elkhart, he had came from Northwestern with only two years of coursework in the language. A former student recalled that Yoder brightly announced at the close of the semester that spring, "Now you know all the Greek that I know."[32]

Tensions surrounding the fledgling Institute that he had once called "our school" would only increase, however, and Yoder's dream of obtaining a permanent teaching position at Elkhart—later Goshen College— never came true. By 1913, conservatives forced Noah Byers to resign; in 1918 Yoder's friend and Athletic Association mate, J. E. Hartzler, resigned from the presidency, and four more presidents quit within the next five years. Before the school gained firm footing, withdrawal of financial support from the East closed its doors from 1923-24, partly influenced by the modernist/fundamentalist debate raging in broader Protestant culture.

When Goshen reopened, that first generation of professors, trained at some of the best universities in the country, had found work and worship elsewhere. More of the students and faculty wore plain dress; and, mindful of the power of its Mennonite constituency, the school never fully regained the worldly innocence and freedom of its progressive Institute days.

JUNIATA COLLEGE

Although he was "thoroughly sold on Northwestern," Yoder accepted an appointment as Athletic Director at Juniata College for the academic year 1901-02, returning to Pennsylvania because he needed to save money and because he believed he should "be near home for one year . . . on account of mother's passing."[33] Rosanna had died in 1895, nearly six full years prior, and although Little Crist lived alone with the help of a hired girl, he was only sixty-four years old, fourteen years from his grave. Moreover, Yoder's three brothers were all married and living in the Big Valley community at the time, and presumably they could have easily cared for Little Crist. Perhaps Yoder was feeling other losses—of Coffman and the progressive Elkhart community that had once promised an alternative home—as much as those in his own family that year.

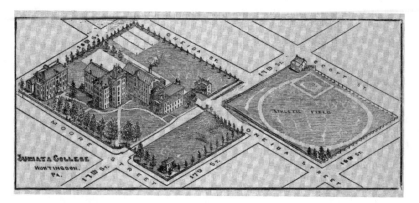

2.7 Juniata College campus, 1900.

Despite his determination to graduate from Northwestern, Yoder never returned to Evanston to study. For what seem to be financial reasons, the one-year commitment expanded into three and a permanent departure from the Midwest. After the end of his first year, Yoder was enticed to remain at Juniata in exchange for full tuition and board, leaving him responsible only for an annual seventy-five cent library fee during his last two years of college. Popularity among the students, gained through his energetic leadership of athletics and other extracurricular activities, may have also kept him in Huntingdon.

In 1901, Yoder—characterized in the official college history as "a sports-minded Amish freshman"—was poised to succeed as the school's first paid Athletic Director. A bit older than many of the undergraduates, "emboldened" through his previous experience at Northwestern and Elkhart, Yoder arrived at a time when enthusiasm for sport was high at the college and in the nation. In 1899 Juniata had created a new athletic field; in 1900 the Boys and Girls Athletic Associations on campus merged to form a co-ed organization that helped to raise nine thousand dollars to build the school's first free-standing gym, a large brick building with a 50x80-foot floor, that was dedicated in 1902. By 1902, 270 colleges nationwide had adopted physical education; 300 city school systems required some form of exercise; 500 gyms had been built by the YMCA, and 100 more had been created on military bases and in health facilities.[34]

Across the country, new wealth was financing the construction of country clubs and health clubs; progressive educators embraced physical exercise, believing it strengthened the mind and developed character and citizenship. On September 14, 1901, just eight days before Yoder's 29th birthday, Teddy Roosevelt—the robust New York governor who had been shunted into the vice-presidency in an attempt to blunt his rigorous political reforms—suddenly became the youngest president in the nation's history upon the assassination of William McKinley.

Tony Ladd and James Mathisen have identified in Roosevelt a "secularized version of muscular Christianity"—a heroic man of action who embodied moral, physical, and intellectual ideals without exerting an overt religious witness.[35] The YMCA movement would also follow this course, and this attitude best describes Yoder's position in these years. His piety was often less evident than his zealous commitment to promoting individual success through the strong mind/strong body ideal, as described in one *Juniata Echo* report:

> Great enthusiasm prevails in all forms of athletics, and it is gratifying to note the splendid spirit and manly qualities which participation in such manly sports develops. Everyone seems to recognize that a "sound mind" goes hand in hand with a "sound body." They are both necessary to each other. Joseph Yoder, the physical director, has the respect of all the fellows and is doing good work. [36]

In December 1901, a committee of students and faculty—Yoder likely among them—petitioned local church elders and college trustees for permission to form a chapter of the YMCA on Juniata's campus. The

*2.8 Joseph W. Yoder,
c. 1900-01.*

request was declined because Church of the Brethren officials opposed the community Y movement on the grounds that it provided members "with amusements."[37] This decision—reversed in response to student pressure just three years later—must have frustrated Yoder, who worked tirelessly to develop athletic culture at the college. During his first year, he introduced competitive track and field events and coached the team, as well as continuing to develop the men's gymnasium program.

During his second year, he tried to convince acting president I. Harvey Brumbaugh to admit athletic attire onto campus. Until that time, track uniforms were completely unknown, and Yoder recalled his efforts to win their approval:

> "What are track suits?" I tried to explain and describe "shorts" and sleeveless shirts, but he [the president] could not quite get the idea, and he was not bringing anything to this Brethren College that was going to arouse scandal. To protect himself he said, "Do you have one of these track suits?" When I told him I did, he said,

"Suppose I bring Father [Elder H. B. Brumbaugh] and Professor Swigart to your room. You don a suit and we'll have a look." I put on my track suit, and covered up with my bathrobe, so as not to make the first shock too great. When they arrived and were seated, Professor I. Harvey said, "Well, Joe, we came to see that track suit, are you ready to demonstrate?" I arose, threw off my bathrobe, and stood in my track suit, turning around so it could be seen from all sides and angles. Professor Swigart broke the silent inspection with his usual little sniff and then said, "I don't see anything particularly offensive about that. At commencement time the girls go about with sleeveless dresses and low necks, and I confess, I rather like to see it." Professor I. Harvey could hardly suppress a little snicker, and Elder H. B. said, "I don't see any objections to it, if you confine their use to the athletic field."[38]

2.9 Brethren Normal School founder Elder H. B. Brumbaugh and his son, I. Harvey, a Juniata president and longtime friend of J. W. Yoder.

Thus, in spring 1902, track suits were used for the first time at Juniata College, and the following year, Yoder led the team in its first intercollegiate meet against Susquehanna University. As well, the baseball team began intercollegiate play during Yoder's tenure.

That year, Yoder pushed another athletic issue with, or perhaps behind the backs of, Juniata authorities. According to the college history, trustees forbade the playing of football—the more manly American form of British soccer, which had during the nineteenth century become associated with both higher education and war.[39] In 1902 Juniata's trustees decided that football was too dangerous even for intra-mural play,[40] yet the college's archive contains a professional photograph of a football squad, with mussed hair and muddy cheeks, piled in a heap at the feet of coach Yoder, as if after a game. The numerals "02," chalked on the soles of one boy's shoes, confirm the date. Although this picture captures a seemingly casual moment, it appears to have been carefully composed, an artful record of a deliberate infraction of the rules.

2.10   Football squad, c. 1902 with Athletic Director Yoder at center, back.

In his more official capacity, Yoder developed the annual men's gymnasium exhibition into a two-hour public performance. Excitement must have been high in spring 1903 as student and faculty spectators crammed Juniata's new gymnasium to watch more than fifty young men dressed in white duck trousers, white shirts and black bow ties vault on the horse and flip around the horizontal and parallel bars. Some lifted dumbbells or juggled Indian clubs, while others performed stunts of tumbling and built elaborate pyramids of human bodies. That spring, the *Juniata Echo* reported that "A very steady increase in gymnastic and athletics has been in evidence all along under Mr. Yoder's energetic direction."[41]

In addition to coaching and teaching athletics, traveling by train to inter-collegete athletic contests, and offering public exhibitions on campus, Yoder led the Health Club during his Juniata years as Athletic Director. In his memoir, he connects interest in health and alternative healing to his mother's work as a pow wow practitioner and to her folk and herbal cures that saved his life as an infant: "But that determination to build up my strength implanted in me a never-ending desire to be strong and well."[42] As a child, he often accompanied his mother in her work as a *Braucherei* practitioner, well known for her special abilities to stop bleeding and relieve pain. When he was fifteen years old, Yoder studied physiology and began to doubt the power of sympathy healing—until he ran a dung fork into his foot and the wound became infected:

> Now Joseph knew that his mother could powwow and stop that pain in a minute if he would ask her, but he had posed with the educators who did not believe in powwowing; so he was ashamed to ask her to powwow for his foot. Finally the pain became so severe that he could scarcely endure it. When the pain had overcome his pride, he said, "Mother, could you powwow for this pain in my foot and take it away?"
> "Yes, I can, if you want me to."
> "Well, I wish you would."
> Rosanna stroked her hand across the wound three times, repeated the words (or formula) that allay pain and in about two minutes the pain was gone and Joseph fell asleep. That was a lesson to him; he never pooh-poohed powwowing again.[43]

Distrust of doctors and a struggle between scientific medicine and alternative cures were significant themes throughout Yoder's life, and he was not alone in viewing health as an arena for the contest between modern and traditional ways. Scientific or "heroic" medicine came under attack from all sides during the late nineteenth and early twentieth centuries: advocates of homeopathic medicine from Germany asserted that disease was as much mental as physical; some religious re-formers preached that Christ's second coming would be delayed until people obeyed the healthful laws of nature; others believed that if spiritual and physical perfection were possible in the next life, they could also be attained in this one. Cracker inventor Sylvester Graham rejected medicine in favor of whole-grain foods and sexual abstinence; others advocated health through water cures, fasting, dietary reform, and the liberation of women's bodies from organ-crushing garment stays.

Together with the YMCA and progressive pushes for physical and moral education, health fads were mostly middle class movements, sometimes fueled by a fear that bulging cities and the influx of foreign immigrants would contribute to white "race suicide."[44] Into this atmosphere came Bernarr MacFadden, sickly child of poor Ozark farmers, brawny champion of physical culture, pulp magazine publisher, and personal hero of Joseph W. Yoder.

Macfadden's *Physical Culture* set the agenda for Juniata College's Health Club under Yoder's leadership. The magazine promoted exercise of the entire muscular system and fasting cures; it attacked organized medicine and vaccination, denounced "the white bread curse" and promoted a diet of raw or partly cooked vegetables, plenty of water, and little meat. (In this, MacFadden was more than half a century ahead of his time, for most scientific nutritionists recommended foods high in calories in those days.) He considered tobacco, caffeine, and alcohol to be deadly poisons.

Through his magazine, MacFadden publicized the stamina-building habits of physical culture practitioners, such as eating live grass, taking ice cold baths and sleeping outdoors—a practice Yoder maintained most nights into old age. MacFadden celebrated sexual vigor, endorsed monogamous marriage and sex education, and was among the first to publish frank discussions of venereal disease, claiming that prudery was the source of prurience and immorality in America.[45] In 1901, he also began publishing a women's magazine that promoted healthful living and denounced the constraints of fashion and cultural convention under the slogan, "Ugliness a Sin, Health is Beauty." According to a recent biographer, MacFadden made physical culture a religion: "health and strength not only contributed to character but to discipline of will, success in business and in marriage, to courage, morality, virility, and happiness."[46]

Want to be a man, a woman, with superb power, energy and beauty? If so, read

2.11 *Advertisement from a Bernarr Macfadden publication, 1900.*

Physical Culture magazine first appeared in 1899. By February 1900, its slogan, "Weakness a Crime. Don't Be a Criminal!" was blazoned on every issue. This memorable phrase—the title of an editorial in the premier March 1899 issue—echoed in Theodore Roosevelt's speech agitating for U.S. intervention in the Philippines after the war with Spain, a speech delivered one month *after* Mcfadden's magazine appeared:

> We must send out there only good and able men, chosen for their fitness, and not because of their partisan service, and these men must not only administer impartial justice to the natives and serve their own government with honesty and fidelity, but must show the utmost tact and firmness, remembering that, with such people as those with whom we are to deal, weakness is the greatest of crimes, and that next to weakness comes lack of consideration for their principles and prejudices.[47]

Like MacFadden, Roosevelt was a weakling as a boy and a dandy in his youth, and so his mythic exploits as a western rancher and Rough Rider charging San Juan Hill were as impressive as the sinewy, nearly nude photographs MacFadden often published of himself. Mcfadden admired Roosevelt, considering him "the best president of the United States, barring none," and a "physical culturalist to the core," a "strenuous, open-air, rugged President" who served as a model for a new kind of robust American man.[48] Similarly, Yoder—who idolized both MacFadden and Roosevelt—described his own frail beginnings as "Irish stamina" in a "wobbly little frame,"[49] and he passionately strove, through exercise and clean living, to embody and promote in others strength and the vivacious, confident affect that he called, simply, "LIFE."[50]

To generate enthusiasm for health and fitness, in 1903 Yoder published a heavy-handed essay that followed MacFadden on most points, sometimes even raising the stakes. "The motto of a certain health magazine is 'Weakness is a crime,' and to this might be added sickness is a sin." Yoder believed that every illness could be traced to "some violation of nature's law—too much eating or drinking or abuse of the body in some form either by the subject or his ancestors."

This seems particularly punishing in light of Yoder's own losses, including that of Rosanna to turburculosis and J. S. Coffman to cancer, but the belief that one might *control* one's body and live to be one hundred, as Yoder would later claim, was not far from other notions of mastery and domination that accompanied the muscular Christian world-view. Echoing the complaint of Higginson's *Atlantic Monthly* article, "Saints and their Bodies," Yoder continued, "A weak body, sometimes, contains a beautiful soul; but it is the exception, else Stoicism and Asceticism would still prevail." He praised "the new college spirit for better physical development," but scolded bookworms who found no time for the gym. For them, he predicted "anywhere from invalidism to death." And, on a slightly more encouraging note, he thundered,

> If weakness is a crime, let's not be criminals! At college we should learn the art of living. If we are not stronger, handsomer, healthier boys and girls when we leave college than when we came, we have missed one essential feature of college training. Penny-wise and pound-foolish students never take time for lectures, exercise, and social culture; hence when they return to their homes from college with nothing but book-knowledge to show, their friends are disappointed because they still have the same listless walk, the same stupidity in company, and probably a worse complexion than when they started. Book learning does not "stick out" perceptibly, but vitality, vigor, enthusiasm—LIFE does.[51]

In another article, "College Life," Yoder borrowed a phrase made popular by Roosevelt's speech, "The Strenuous Life." As Roosevelt defined it, "the doctrine of the strenuous life" was the hallmark of American character: never to shrink from labor, hardship, striving, or conflict; for men to bravely embrace work or war, and women to face maternity without fear. Roosevelt denounced "slothful ease" and "weaklings," associating them with the international peace movement. Rather, he advocated "clean, vigorous, healthy lives" of hard work. For the nation, he prescribed a stronger army and swift confrontation of American "responsibilities" in Hawaii, Cuba, Purto Rico, and the Phillippines, as well as the construction of the canal in Panama, following England's example in India and Egypt. Thus, the imperative of individual strength and courage translated into polices of national military expansion and imperialism. By 1900, "The Strenuous Life" was published in a small volume by that title. The work ethic resonated with Yoder's experience of Amish life, but Roosevelt would have included Little Crist among the "prattlers who sit at home in peace" during wartime. Nonetheless, Yoder embraced Roosevelt's "doctrine" and adapted it to the college setting:

The "strenuous life" can be practiced nowhere better than in college. Work hard during study hours. When college interests are at stake wake up and get into the current and help make it go. Meet men and women. Be able to talk and act without embarrassment, and college life to you will mean a preparation that prepares.[52]

Elsewhere in the essay Yoder complained about the bookish "plodder" and the lazy "idler," two student types who refrain from extracurricular activities because they have not discovered that "There are lessons to be learned in college that are not found in any text book." Casting sports and debate in terms of military contests, Yoder called the students to expressions of school spirit, as if they were preparation and analogous to acts of patriotism or religious witness:

> The student who is not sufficiently interested in the success of his own College to sing her songs or yell her yells when a great crisis is on; when victory or defeat in debate or athletics is pending, will not likely be moved to action by any righteous movement in his own community when, as a man, he takes his place in the ranks of men.[53]

In February 1903, the *Juniata Echo* noted one of the extracurricular activities Yoder promoted: "Our physical culture enthusiasts are doing their stunts on the ice and snow instead of in the Gymnasium at present. There is nothing like out-door sports in the winter."[54] The unnamed stunts probably refer to a "snow bath" inspired by *Physical Culture* magazine, which Yoder described in some detail many years later. As he recalled it, the Health Club boys heaped several feet of fresh snow onto the tennis court one wintery day; then late that night, they met in the gym, stripped off their clothes, and rolled in the snow.

> It was a clear, cold night with the stars fairly sparkling and when we struck that snow with our bare bodies, we found that snow was a mighty sight colder than cold water. We rolled in it, and threw it over ourselves and each other, and rubbed it on our bodies, but NOT for very long. We soon scampered back into the gym, rubbed our bodies with turkish towels, and strange to say, in a very few minutes our bodies reacted so strongly that the cold air in the gym seemed very comfortable. . . . But for some reason, we never tried it again.[55]

Yoder noted in his memoir that the snow bath took place "after study hours"—later than half-past ten—a slight reminder that he was also a full-time student during his tenure as Athletic Director, but never the bookish sort he despised.

Although he was an English major, Yoder had neither language nor literary history and analysis at the center of his coursework, which according to the college catalogue focused on "recitations, declamations, and essays." Tall, handsome Yoder, with his deep, booming voice, was perfectly suited to the demands of the English curriculum of those times.

A passionate and experienced public speaker who seemed especially to enjoy verbal contests, Yoder organized Juniata's intercollegiate debate team under the auspices of the Lyceum Literary Society in 1902. The team consisted of two men, with Yoder as captain, and one alternate. The first contest against Susquehanna University addressed the question, "Resolved, That the United States Should Hold Permanent Possession of the Philippines." Following Roosevelt's policy of temporary intervention, Juniata upheld the negative and won the debate unanimously. The following year, they triumphed again on the topic of "Trade Unionism." And during Yoder's senior year, the team returned once more to the Selinsgrove Opera House to debate Susquehanna on "Resolved, That Education will Solve the Negro Problem." Juniata took the negative position, resting its argument on the proposition that the Negro problem—the political and economic disenfranchisement of African-Americans—is a moral problem, and education is an intellectual problem, and they once again prevailed.

The triumphant thespians were met at the Huntingdon train station by a local car dealer, who drove them to campus in a new Cadillac, one of only five automobiles in town—honking and bedecked with college colors. As was the custom, students celebrated Juniata's victory with a bonfire on the athletic field and a spirited rally of college songs and yells.[56]

If Bernarr Macfaddan shaped Yoder's body and Teddy Roosevelt inspired his spirit during the Juniata years, then another brilliant, burly man nurtured his imagination and mind: Martin Grove Brumbaugh, Juniata's longtime, absentee president. When Yoder arrived in the fall of 1901, Brumbaugh was about to resign from his post as Commissioner of Education in Puerto Rico. Although he returned to Philadelphia the

2.12 *The Lyceum Literary Society with the three members who represented Juniata at the first intercollegiate debate in April 1902. The debaters were
Joseph Yoder (front, center), Jacob M. Blough, (Yoder's right) and Joseph D.
Johnson (Yoder's left). John H. Cassady, Church of the Brethren evangelist
with whom Yoder later worked, stands in the back row, second from right.*

following year to teach pedagogy at the University of Pennsylvania, his
influence was never far from Yoder or Juniata. Brumbaugh retained a
house on the edge of campus in Huntingdon and was reappointed president for the fall of 1902, even as he continued teaching at Penn.

About five years before, Brumbaugh had counseled Yoder to remain
with the Amish Mennonites rather than joining the Dunkers. "Dr. M.
G. Brumbaugh, my first college president, said to me several times,
'Joseph, stick to your people.' I took his advice much against my own
wishes," Yoder recalled somewhat bitterly years later. [57] Although he remained, Yoder constantly resisted the constraints and conventions of his
birth community; in this, he followed Brumbaugh's example as well. In
fact, it may be that Brumbaugh's famous advice said as much for his own
career as it did for Yoder's.

Although he became one of the most influential educators of early
twentieth-century America and was the last clergyman and pacifist to be

elected governor of Pennsylvania, Brumbaugh tried to maintain ties to his Pennsylvania German and Dunker roots. He repeatedly used the education and talent that made him an exception within his own group to reinterpret and represent their experience, both to themselves and to the broader culture—a path that his protégé would also follow. By the time that Yoder first met him, Brumbaugh had joined the Pennsylvania German Society, a group of descendants of early German or Swiss immigrants who promoted preservation and research of a history that they believed had been neglected and maligned by historians focused on New England and Anglo-American culture.

In the 1890s, Brumbaugh also began working on *A History of the German Baptist Brethren in Europe and America*, a scholarly history of his sect which aimed to portray the Brethren as cultural, educational, and religious leaders on both sides of the Atlantic. "What he sought to do," writes Brumbaugh's biographer, "was to give back to the Brethren their lost educational consciousness."[58] Grounded in historical research and published in 1899, the work aimed to reconstruct the past and direct Brethren culture toward a progressive agenda.

This spirit of historical reconstruction can be seen in the 1898 speech that Brumbaugh gave in the Bellefonte, Pennsylvania courthouse on his inauguration as president of the Pennsylvania State Teachers' Association. Titled "An Educational Struggle in Colonial Pennsylvania," the speech celebrated William Penn's holy experiment of founding a colony tolerant of religious difference, and argued that German-speaking citizens saved this vision from being destroyed by Benjamin Franklin and William Smith, rector of Philadelphia's Christ Church (Anglican) and provost of the College of Pennsylvania, later the University of Pennsylvania.

Among understandings Brumbaugh drew on in offering the speech were these: Tolerating what he called the "swarthy masses" of German-speaking immigrants little more than he tolerated African slaves or Indians, Franklin saw in their language and sectarian religion a threat to Anglo culture and devised a plan with Smith to educate German children in charity schools partly funded by the crown. Christopher Sauer I, a Dunker publisher in Germantown, exposed the cultural and religious chauvinism of this plot in his German language newspaper, and the Pennsylvania Germans continued to run their own church-related schools. (When the colony faced Indian skirmishes along the Susquehanna, Sauer's paper also vexed Anglo-Pennsylvanians by turning out the German vote to fill Assembly seats with pacifist Quakers.)

Amid such factors, Brumbaugh concluded that Pennsylvania Germans had wrongly been represented as ignorant and hostile to education. In his Brethren history, he further argued that the Franklin-Smith ploy incited so much anti-education sentiment in his group that the next generation would mistakenly reject education altogether.[59]

In 1904, during his senior year at Juniata College, Yoder undertook a project that was smaller but quite similar to Brumbaugh's effort to revise Brethren history and change their views of education. The case can be made that all of Yoder's later literary work springs from this period and from Brumbaugh's influence. A full five years before the appearance of C. Henry Smith's revision of a University of Chicago dissertation, *The Mennonites of America*, Yoder published a long essay interpreting Amish history and culture. Perhaps written for a senior project and later adapted for publication in *Juniata Echo*, Yoder's essay represents his people and explains their ways to a non-Amish academic community. The major concerns, themes, and even fragments of wording from this first essay appear in the *Rosanna* books of the 1940s and 1950s—work which earned Yoder a commendation from the Pennsylvania German Society, to which Brumbaugh was elected president in 1927.

In his essay, Yoder traced the group's origins to the French Waldensians, following an early erroneous theory. He then described Amish dress and worship services in great detail, with special attention to singing. He noted that although Amish men never lift their hats to women, "women are highly respected" in the culture. Among Amish virtues, he listed temperance, honesty, hospitality, and simplicity, describing them as a modest and quiet people who are nonetheless good farmers and "anxious to drive a close bargain."[60]

In a paragraph devoted to attitudes about education among the Amish, Yoder advanced an argument precisely patterned after Brumbaugh's: the ancestors were learned, but persecution from outside authorities thwarted educational efforts, and subsequent generations mistakenly came to resist schooling. The university-trained Anabaptist leaders were the predecessors of contemporary progressives, such as those in Indiana. Yoder described the school established at Elkhart, Indiana, by the Amish-Mennonites and Mennonites, and later moved to Goshen, called Goshen College. Many young people attend this school, he reported, but some conservatives still look upon it with a degree of suspicion.[61]

A blurring of the distinction between Amish and Mennonites in this essay may partly reflect a turn-of-the-century social reality in Yoder's home community, where the boundaries between Amish and Amish Mennonites were still being negotiated. Yet, "a degree of suspicion" is highly euphemistic for the blunt resistance Yoder encountered from the Old Order deacon when he choose to go to college. Running short of funds during his last year at Juniata, he borrowed either fifty or seventy dollars from his father, and years later he bitterly wrote, "Had the bishop known that father loaned me money for college, I think the church would have excommunicated him, but they never knew it, and now he is beyond their persecution."[62]

But writing in 1904 for an audience of outsiders, Yoder was optimistic about the possibility of cultural change and education, and his essay concludes, "the more progressive factions . . . have discarded many of the old customs, especially in dress, and social conduct, and are taking on modern American ideas instead."[63] Yet even as he celebrated cultural assimilation and change in his essay, Yoder worked to rescue Amish traditions from obfuscation and shame—already embodying the paradox that lies at the center of much of his work and life.

During his final year of college, an "epidemic attacked" Yoder, causing him to brood on the personal losses that had come with his educational gains. In a spirit of nostalgia and genuine ambivalence, he described his early school days, family life, and the death of his mother in a Pennsylvania German poem titled "*Noch Denke*" (nostalgia or looking back), which was printed in the *The Belleville Times*, Yoder's hometown newspaper. In *Rosanna of the Amish*, Yoder cited publication of this poem as proof of his sincere effort to retain ties with the Amish community, but it probably did not serve that purpose. Although he may have composed the poem in Pennsylvania German, usually a spoken language, Yoder *wrote* it, perhaps improvising orthography based on the standard German he was studying in college.

Likely Yoder's Pennsylvania German verse was part of his new pride of heritage, inspired by Brumbaugh. An account in the college newspaper of this period reports that Yoder's translation and recitation of the legend of William Tell—the nationalistic story of Swiss resistance to Austrian rule—was the longest, most impressive piece in a performance of the Juniata German Club. Moreover, writing dialect German verse was fashionable among many non-Amish, educated Pennsylvania Germans at the turn of the century, and Yoder's verse is quite typical of that genre.

In the mid-1800s, ten major German newspapers operating in the Pennsylvania Dutch triangle between Philadelphia, Harrisburg, and Easton began publishing letters and poems written in dialect. By the century's end, dialect poetry regularly appeared in both English and German papers. The poets who composed these pieces were often educated people who considered their dialect writing to be American literature, sometimes arguing that Pennsylvania German is no more the language of Germany than English is the language of Britain.

In response to disruptions of local life caused by westward and urban migration, dialect poets expressed nostalgia for home, parents, school days, nature, and folk culture in a language that seemed to be losing ground every year. (In 1911 English was made the official language of public school instruction, although grammars for bilingual education were published at Kutztown State Teachers College for at least another decade and until World War II silenced Pennsylvania German almost completely in all but the strict sects.) Earl Robacker has designated the years from 1861 to 1902, "The Language-Conscious Period" in Pennsylvania German literature, and this is precisely when Yoder was completing his studies in English, occasionally writing in local dialect, and translating from High German.[64]

Among his many activities at Juniata, singing had remained a personal priority, although Yoder did not take advantage of opportunities for classical training and performance. Instead, a 1904 photograph of the college Glee Club depicts twenty-four young men in identical dark suits and tiny, bow ties surrounding Yoder, who appears to be their leader—older than the rest, already bald.

During his sophomore year, he organized the college's first Varsity Quartet, in which he sang second bass. The group gave two inaugural concerts in Yoder's native Big Valley at Allensville and Belleville, probably in the Amish Mennonite meetinghouses. They then traveled "extensively over the state" during the Fall and winter months, earning a "splendid reputation as the sweet singers from Juniata College."[65] Their program lists edifying readings and popular numbers along with the "Temperance Song." Of the four solos on the program, Yoder sang

2.13 *Juniata Glee Club. Row 1 (l-r) L. R. Holsinger, E.A. Zook, W. C. Werz, E. W. Long, F. M. Miller, H. E. Shaffer, J. H. Wright, C. S. Brumbaugh. Row 2 (l-r) J.H. Fike, J.C. Detwiler, L. L. Brenneman, G.K. Walker, J. W. Yoder, J. S. Furry, Brown Miller, N. J. Brumbaugh. Row 3 (l-r) C. E. Fahrney, W. B. Mikesell, E. R. McClain, H. F. Sanger, Walter Peoples, D. B. Little, G. A. Early, J. S. F. Ruthrauff.*

three. It was during this time that Yoder probably became known at Juniata College as "the Sweet Singer from Big Valley," and among Amish and Amish Mennonites in Big Valley, simply as "Singer Joe."[66] The Varsity Quartet performed during commencement celebrations when Yoder graduated in 1904, a detail he rarely omitted from even brief biographical summaries.

In the wake of his dazzling and strenuous school days, Yoder was left with no clear plans about what to do with the rest of his life. Marked by a pledge to progress and not especially devoted to scholarship, he was not called back to teach at Goshen College. Leadership, singing, debate, and athletics all involved performance, charisma, and an ability to persuade or motivate others, and yet Yoder was unable to imagine a *career* that used these talents—except perhaps the ministry, which he never seriously considered. His poem "Do Something," probably published during his senior year of college, reiterates the industrious spirit of the early twentieth century with a certain wide-eyed awe at the accomplishments of the great men: Rockefeller and Astor's wealth, Roosevelt's reforms, Moody's evangelism, Longfellow's verse, Burbank and Edison's advances in science and technology.[67]

Swept up in the period's spirit of success and promise of limitless personal achievement, Yoder had rigorously preached "the life that prepares" throughout his college years. Yet by the age of thirty-one, indebted to his father, with no clear job prospects, he had no choice but to move his possessions back to his father's house and pick up work as an itinerant singing school instructor, searching for his own path.

CHAPTER 3 THREE

THE SINGING BACHELOR

When you are married
and living at your ease
Remember that I am single
yet doing as I please.
—Abram Y. Byler, Belleville, Mifflin County, Pennslvania, January 23, 1889, from the autograph book of Thomas J. Peachey (1872-1939)

W hen asked what he remembered of J. W. Yoder, one member of the Mifflin County Amish-Mennonite community replied, "Only one of those boys stayed in the Amish church. It was Yost." Before this elderly man could reminisce about Yoder's booming baritone voice, signature black bow tie, or striking physique, he drew the most important line, and placed the Yoder brothers in relation to it.

As Yoder understood it, "The Amish Church is a sort of Family Circle organization, and the ideal Amish family is the family where all the children and grandchildren belong to the same church that father and mother belong to."[1] Crist and Rosanna's family church circle had been broken twice: first by a congregational schism in the 1860s that divided them from their parents, and again by the progressive moves of three of their four sons. In her study of the fragmenting consequences of cultural change in the late-nineteenth century among several major Anabaptist groups, Beulah Stauffer Hostetler has observed in each group a shattering of the community into three distinct factions: conservative, modernizing and moderate.[2] This pattern is also apparent in Yoder's family.

Representing the conservative position, oldest son Yost followed his father as horseman and farmer, joining the Old Order church of his parents and marrying Barbara E. Peachey, the bishop's daughter, in 1881. If Yoder portrayed Yost as wealthy by Amish standards, owning two or three farms at a time, his life was ordered by simplicity and tradition. Viewing him from a more worldly perspective, Yoder in *Rosanna's Boys* projected onto his older brother a rule-based spirituality in which submission to the *Ordnung* earned salvation. Humility and obedience, expressed through self-sacrifice and refusal to acquire material possessions, were the marks of a respected Amish man, and Yost abided by community standards, led singing in church, and provided for his family.

Second son Levi, Yoder's favorite brother, represented the modernizing position and typified the nineteenth-century's heroic self-made man. For about fifteen years, Levi taught school in the winter and worked as a carpenter during the summer months. In 1887 he married Amanda Anna Hartzler, and in 1896 began to manufacture carpets at Belleville. From a cottage industry, his enterprise grew to employ about 100 workers in a factory built entirely with his own hands or under his supervision. He introduced and sold the first automatic washing machines in Big Valley, ran an automobile showroom, and acquired expensive tracts of farm land on the outsikrts of Belleville, Burnham, and Lewistown—where he created the area's first subdivisions for residential and commercial use.

An early twentieth-century history of the region described L. M. Yoder as the model of self-reliant manliness: "a capable energetic man of business, and varied as are his interests, he is easily master of every detail and always the master of every situation occurring in any department of his affairs."[3] When the rules of the most forward-thinking Amish-Mennonite congregation in the Valley did not coincide with his desires, Levi simply ignored them; when musical instruments were forbidden, he bought a piano for his daughters without facing serious repercussions from the church. Members of the congregation recall that Levi and his wife stood out in their elegant dress, he with a mouthful of flashy, gold-capped teeth and she, wearing face powder to church. Several of their six children attended the Mennonite college at Goshen, and at least one of his sons-in-law served in World War II. The large brick mansion Levi built for his family in Belleville now houses the local Veterans of Foreign Wars post, and for many years it held the Valley's only tavern, to the frustration of many Mennonites.

John, the brother closest to Yoder in age, represents the moderate position and also best embodies the nineteenth-century's Christian gentleman ideal, a man whose ambitions were tempered by his moral character. (Among Yoder's role models, both J. S. Coffman and Robert Maclay, the Presbyterian landowner who hired Little Crist to work his fields, are called "Christian gentlemen.") John married Sarah Emma Hooley in 1887 and began farming, like Yost, but eventually acquired a planing mill and worked in the lumber and house-building trades like Levi. At age forty-four, he was elected to the ministry of the Amish Mennonite church at Belleville. Having only a country school education, he sold his business and, with his grown son, enrolled in Goshen College to gain the education he felt he needed to become a successful preacher. John did not adapt to academic life, however, and finally abandoned the call to the ministry, choosing to become a successful businessman rather than a mediocre preacher, according to his brother. He eventually became president of the milk condensing plant at Goshen, where he lived with his family and belonged to the Mennonite church.[4]

Reflecting on his brothers' lives some years later, Yoder succinctly expressed the conservative/modernizing/moderate scheme: "Being in love with the bishop's daughter, Yost obeyed the *Ordnung* to the letter, having 'worldly ambitions,' Levi refused to obey the *ordnung* and went liberal, but John was a happy medium."[5] The very different life stories of Yost and Levi merit individual chapters in *Rosanna's Boys*, but the lives of John and Joseph merge together into one, although Yoder had little in common with his "happy medium" milk condenser brother. In the swing from conservative to modern, John occupied the middle ground, but there seemed to be no place for a fourth son. Similarly, in the range of nineteenth-century masculine styles—from traditional agrarian, to self-made achiever, to the Christian gentleman—Yoder fitted no place.[6]

"HE WAS A BACHELOR"

By the time he graduated from Juniata College at age thirty-one, his brothers had established thriving families and prosperous careers, and he had few prospects for either. There is no local memory or record of special friendships with young women during Yoder's college years, and his most ardent youthful relationship—with John Hooley—seemed to dim with Hooley's last-minute desertion before Yoder enrolled at Northwestern, and Hooley's subsequent marriage to Myra B. Longenecker in 1901.

"He was a bachelor," several older people in the Valley have said of J. W. Yoder. Pressed to explain the meaning of that word, one woman added, "You know, a bachelor! He was a teacher, a singer. He wrote about his mother. He never should have married. He was a bachelor." Yoder's single status was regarded not so much as a stigma or shame as a fact that had a name and some legitimacy, at least to the extent it freed him to pursue his work as an itinerate teacher, singer and writer. Thus the term *bachelor* seems to say as much about who Yoder was, as it does about what he chose or did not choose. Until he married in 1932 at age sixty, he belonged to a large group of single men particular to his time.

Yoder's adult life coincided with what historian Howard P. Chudacoff has named "the age of the bachelor," 1880-1930. In 1880, unmarried males over age 15 constituted 41.7% of the American population, dropping only slightly to 38.7% in 1910, and to 34.1% by 1930. During that period, the average marriageable age for men also dropped from 26.1 years in 1890 to 24.3 years in 1903.[7] The proportions of single people did not reach these levels again until the 1970s, due to an increasing social acceptance of co-habitation.

During Yoder's youth, Chudacoff's work reveals, a recognizable subculture of bachelors emerged for the first time in America as families, churches, and local communities exercised less control over young men's lives, and urbanization, mobility, and jobs drew them to cities where the saloon and YMCA provided alternative, male-only homes. Some of these bachelors are known to have been gay men, but most were heterosexuals who chose to delay or avoid taking on the responsibilities associated with family life. Rooming together in urban boarding houses, group residences, or with married siblings, they were sometimes seen as selfish or as a dangerous threat to the social order. Although Yoder never moved to a major American city where bachelor life thrived during this era, his choices expressed many of the values cherished by the bachelors of his day: autonomy, male-oriented sociability, and stylishness.

The emergence of the bachelor occurred at a time when the nature of masculinity itself was changing. In the latter half of the nineteenth

century, industrialization, mechanization, bureaucratization, and urbanization altered the ways that middle class men worked and related to
their families. For instance in Yoder's family, three of the four men chose
to leave family farms and take employment that removed them from the
home. At the same time, women were gradually entering public and political life. These moves created anxiety about the meaning of masculinity during the Progressive Era, designated 1900-1910. During this time,
renewed emphasis on what might be called "family values" drew men
into domestic roles and focused on their responsibilities as providers and
leaders in the home. At the same time, a contradictory consequence of
this anxiety was the new spirit of manly "primitivism"—which pervaded
most of Yoder's college passions—expressed through the glorification of
the male body; the popularity of athletics, especially rough and competitive games like football, and the doctrine of the strenuous life.[8] These
virile pursuits stood in contrast to feminized "civilization," associated
with matrimony, the nurture of children, and religion.

During the early nineteenth century, the word *manly* was understood to mean the opposite of "childish," but by the turn of the century,
it had come to mean the opposite of "feminine."[9] Especially in athletics,
"the sustained values of boy culture merged with the bachelor subculture of the saloons and clubs to create a new concept of manliness," according to Chudaoff.[10] Throughout his college days, Yoder remained
largely within a male world, excelling in public exhibitions of sport, verbal combat, and musical performance—all activities associated with
bachelor culture at the time. But whether his college successes would
translate into manly accomplishments seemed a source of some anxiety.

Just before graduation in spring 1904, one of his Juniata classmates
asked Yoder to take his place teaching a music class at New Enterprise,
near Bedford, Pennsylvania. That opportunity came like "a rope to a
drowning man," and Yoder quickly added three additional classes in
nearby communities. By July, he had earned enough money to repay his
school debt to his father, and by the summer's end, he felt like "a free
man."[11] Freedom—from both tedious work routines and family responsibilities—was the mark of a true bachelor, and Yoder reveled in his
independence. His next opportunity came with an invitation from the
superintendent of schools in Huntingdon County to lead singing at the
Fall Teachers' Institute. Compared to farm labor, Institute work paid a
fortune—and all he had to do was sing:

Twenty-five dollars for one week's work! I had never heard of the like. I knew plenty of strong men who were working on farms for fifteen dollars per month, and now to receive twenty-five dollars per week and board and room at a good hotel, that was really a financial opportunity for a young Amishman. But if I have one institute, why not have two?[12]

Almost immediately Yoder approached the superintendent of schools in his home area and secured an additional teachers' institute appointment in Mifflin County. His charismatic personality together with his philosophy, "Keep 'em smiling, keep 'em singing" proved highly successful. As early as summer 1905, Yoder began mailing circulars to school superintendents advertising his availability to lead singing at county teachers' institutes throughout the state. The initial mailing brought four invitations, and as he describes it, "as the years came, I was called to more and more institutes until I had as many as ten or twelve in each year."[13] These five-day conferences were especially popular in rural areas and influenced the professional growth of teachers more than anything else in the early twentieth century. They were so favored by teachers and regarded as so effective by school superintendents that state legislatures generously allocated public funds to underwrite the programs and even paid teachers to attend.

Institute work eventually took Yoder as far away as Ohio, Virginia and Illinois, and it was quite lucrative. During those years, he raised his initial *weekly* fee of $25 to $100 or $125. By comparison, the average *monthly* income for a public schoolteacher at this time was $70.75 for men and $54.19 for women.[14] Yoder eventually became part of an elite circle of men who were standard teachers' institute lecturers and musical directors, M. G. Brumbaugh, foremost among them. Wrote Yoder, "In my music work in Teachers' Institutes I met some of the finest men in the nation . . . not only instructors but teachers whose friendship I regard most highly."[15] This work was perfect for a single fellow who enjoyed the company of articulate, educated males and who did not mind boarding week to week in small town hotels, but Yoder continued to search for a more appropriate career.

In spring 1905, M. G. Brumbaugh replied to a verbal query with advice on the two career paths that Yoder was then considering: scientific agriculture and education. Concerning the former, Brumbaugh romantically mused about the possibility of covering the banks of the Juniata River with vineyards, so that central Pennsylvania would become "the second Rhine Valley," but not for wine production, of course. His primary reservation was that Yoder—like the progressive educator and thinker Brumbaugh—might be perceived as a visionary so far ahead of the common agricultural practice as to be dismissed:

> The one real difficulty in that seems to be the fact that the man who fits himself to do this kind of work scientifically by his very fitting puts himself out of touch with the great army of farmers whom he wishes to know. His activities are so different from others, his processes are so radical that they question both the value of his activity and their own ability to carry them out. It's the old story which always bobs up when people are asked to follow a leader.[16]

At Brumbaugh's suggestion, Yoder immediately sent an inquiry to L. H. Bailey, director of Cornell University's College of Agriculture. Although Yoder's letter has not survived, Bailey's reply indicates that he must have inquired about the financial viability of the field. His advice: "If money-making is the ambition of one's life then I should not go into agriculture or agricultural teaching or any professorship, but into some line of trade or commerce."[17] Moneymaking was a major concern for Yoder, who characterized the century's first decade as a period when "self support, success in business and personal attainment was the main ambition."[18] His older brothers, both plain and fancy, had already achieved considerable wealth and Yoder felt left behind. He envied Yost's fine horses and farms, and described Levi and John's manly competition for financial dominance:

> In wrestling, and boxing, and working each tried to surpass the other, and in manhood this rivalry still existed. When one had a business the other tried to have a little larger business; when one built a fine house the other tried to build or buy one just a little larger and nicer, when one bought a diamond ring, the other bought one just a little larger.[19]

With regard to himself, Yoder wrote, "School teaching was very attractive to me, but then came the whisper from somewhere, not much money in it, and like the other boys, I, too, wanted to make money."[20]

3.1 "When you get rich, lend me your horse, J. W. Yoder." Undated, unpostmarked photograph post card given to Anna Mellinger in Ronks, Pennsylvania, in the first decade of the twentieth century. A nearly identical photograph post card was given to Clarence Mellinger in Ronks, Pennsylvania, with the inscription, "This is what I call real pleasure. J. W. Yoder."

Nor did Brumbaugh predict financial rewards for Yoder in education. Noting a trend toward administrative positions that depended as much on political acumen as intelligence and expertise, Brumbaugh advised, "All the higher places in teaching are resolving themselves into executive functions, and mere scholarship and mere experience as a teacher will not guarantee success in the larger places."[21] Given what he knew of his former student's "equipment" and experience, Brumbaugh was not overly encouraging about education. Nonetheless, he left Yoder at the age of thirty-two with a sense of urgency about his decision. He warned that it no longer mattered so much *what* he decided but *that* he find a specific goal if he intended to make anything out of himself:

> You have reached an age when if you are to be anything more than what moral growth indicated you must drop everything else

and focus your efforts upon one special thing, after that it is a matter of persistent effort, hard work, patient planning, and unswerving resolution.[22]

At last, Yoder chose to pursue studies in journalism at Harvard University, where Brumbaugh had also taken a master's degree. In a richly detailed scene of *Rosanna's Boys*, he described packing a trunk in his old bedroom at his father's house in Big Valley, probably sometime during the early fall of 1905. As he folded his clothing, he was frozen in a mystical episode that recalls biblical stories of dramatic life reversals, Saul on the road to Damascus or Jonah defying the call to Nineveh:

> When the time came to go I went to my room to pack my trunk to go to Harvard, nothing daunting. As I began to lay out my clothes, some mysterious influence seemed to flood my mind with the thought, "Don't go." I tried to brush it aside, but the impression became stronger and stronger. I tried to fight it by saying to myself, "You're just afraid; don't be a mamby-pamby." When I determined to fight off this idea of not going, the influence seemed then to attack my body. I became so weak I could scarcely go on with my packing. I stopped to rest and think. I seemed never to have had such a weight on my shoulders. It came to me finally that maybe "There is a destiny that shapes our end." I went downstairs and told father. . . . He said very quietly, "If you feel that way, you had better not go." I decided that at least journalism was forbidden to me, so I decided to go to Lancaster County and organize music classes and wait for further guidance. I took the same train for Lancaster that I had intended to take for Harvard, and the burden which weighed me down while packing for Harvard rolled off my shoulders entirely. I felt like a man who tried to go into a room but bumped his nose against a closed door, but the moment I decided to go out and teach music, I seemed to face an open road illuminated by some supernatural sunlight.[23]

To go to Harvard would have represented Yoder's final step into "the world"—completing a forward motion that began with his hesitation outside the country singing school when he was a boy of sixteen. But this time, the spirit of his Irish immigrant grandfather did not urge him to turn the doorknob and take his place in that roomful of accomplished strangers. Instead, Yoder felt his Amish nose bump against a door that remained closed to him. Although worried that he was being fearful or effete, "mamby-pamby," Yoder finally claimed his own fate. His anxiety about going to Harvard, described as "a weight on my shoulders," used terms identical to those in his portrayal of Little Crist's dread of accepting the call to preach in the Amish church. Determined neither by the traditional community nor propelled by capitalist ambition, Yoder chose a path directed by a vague sense of divine fate that coincided with his own desire to sing and teach.

In this way, he began his work as a singing school instructor in Lancaster County during winter 1905-06. Founded in colonial New England to sustain the Puritan tradition of psalm singing, singing schools were very common in rural areas of the northern South and Midwest during the nineteenth century. In Pennsylvania, during the years following the Civil War, itinerant singing masters criss-crossed the state introducing musical literacy to the smallest rural communities. Although four-part a cappella harmony is now regarded as a quintessential element of Mennonite tradition, it was largely a twentieth-century practice grounded in the singing schools of the mid-nineteenth and early twentieth centuries. Before then, "part-singing" was forbidden in many communities because it was regarded as too "worldly," signifying an individualistic and proud spirit, whereas unison singing expressed humility and congregational unity.[24]

Associated with Sunday schools, English preaching, revival meetings, gospel songs, and other progressive innovations, musical notation and harmony were among the issues responsible for church schism during Yoder's youth. In Mifflin County, part-singing was a factor in the Church House Amish division of 1898. By 1900, part-singing was practiced by Yoder's Amish Mennonite church at Belleville, and a few years later the more conservative break-away group at Locust Grove also accepted it.[25] Sadie Byler, of that congregation, recalled feeling great pity when, as a girl, she watched a young man forced to stand up during a Sunday morning service and publicly confess the sin of having sung bass.

In 1898, one year after he directed the choral society that included Yoder at Elkhart Institute, Abram B. Kolb cautioned progressive, turn-of-the-century Mennonites against spending too much money on piano and voice lessons, which only prepare individuals for solo performance.

Instead, he wrote in *The Herald of Truth*, "give us back the old-fashioned singing school, that teaches the young people of the community to read music, and to sing it together."[26] Vocal training strengthens congregational singing, Kolb argued, whether one sings old-fashioned hymns or the great choral works of Haydn, Handel, and Mendelssohn. Yoder took up Kolb's argument and continued throughout his life to advance congregational and choral singing with the zeal of a missionary. In letters promoting his singing schools to church leaders, he argued that his schools built unity in the congregation, complemented preaching services, and provided wholesome social activities that kept young people from "rowdyism."

In Lancaster, Yoder's work quickly established his reputation in the Mennonite community. Denominational periodicals with national readership, the *Gospel Witness* and *The Herald of Truth*, reported enthusiastic attendance of the Lancaster singing schools and praised Yoder's abilities as a teacher, while testifying to the general usefulness of music instruction in the religious community. Both papers described audiences overflowing into churchyards during the schools' final performances, and both expressed the community's desire that Yoder continue his singing school work.[27]

The report of a local writer in the *Herald* stressed a collective acceptance of the schools following performances of 310 students from five classes. At the close of an afternoon program given for older people in the community, Bishop Isaac Eby of Kinzer granted his approval. The author added that "all went home rejoicing from the fact that the pupils showed very plainly that they had acquired a great deal of knowledge and skill in vocal music while under the training of Bro. Yoder." The same writer reported that a two-hour evening performance at the Mennonite church at Paradise was "filled to its utmost capacity and many on the outside were eagerly waiting to hear the sweet strains." Once again, at the close of this concert, "all expressed themselves well pleased and many wanted that the work be continued." The article concluded with a pious endorsement for the project that was unanimously embraced: "There is no better way of expressing our gratitude to God than to render him prayer, praise and thanksgiving by the sweet melody of human voices. We hope that Bro. Yoder may be able in the near future to come back to us and continue the good work."[28]

Central State Normal School and Singing Master

At the conclusion of the Lancaster classes, Yoder returned to central Pennsylvania to take a position on the faculty at Central State Normal School at Lock Haven (later Lock Haven State University). Hired primarily as a mathematics professor, Yoder also taught logic, English, vocal music, and penmanship, as well as coaching baseball and basketball. Immediately, he introduced college songs, glees and yells to the students at Lock Haven, much in the spirit of his boisterous Juniata days. In another repetition of his own college experience, Yoder advised the debate team and organized Lock Haven's first inter-collegeate match with West Chester Normal School.

The manly association between verbal contest and athletic competition was not lost on one observer, who reported, "this friendly contest of brain instead of brawn aroused the *esprit de corps* as never before, as those who heard the glees, cheers and school yells will heartily agree." Before the debate, the article reported, Yoder had led the audience in songs and yells that he had composed; the chorus of one song named the individual debaters and outlined their argument in favor of a constitutional amendment to provide for the direct election of U.S. senators:

> So come on now and cheer for the Normal,
> For Merrick and Cochran and Smith;
> We want all voting by the people,
> The old constitution is a myth;
> And no doubt that this famous battle
> We'll count among our latest joys;
> We'll shed no tears, but will loudly cheer,
> We are proud of the Normal Boys.

While the judges deliberated their decision, Yoder treated the crowd to a solo which "completely carried away the audience," and when the Lock Haven team was finally pronounced victorious:

> What a wonderful cheer greeted the decision! We cannot depict the scene which followed. How hearty the congratulations! How spontaneous and infectious the enthusiasm! The victorious debaters were mounted high on stalwart shoulders and carried from the rostrum, and the vanquished were not forgotten, but West Chester was cheered over and over again.[29]

Yoder remained at Lock Haven through the end of the spring semester in late June, performing several solos at commencement and the final meetings of several student literary societies. A review of his first year's efforts concluded, "Since Professor Yoder's connection with the school, the chapel and class singing has greatly improved. He is now endeavoring to compile for next year a Normal Song Book that will properly represent C.S.N.S."[30]

At the end of the semester, after a few weeks' visit with his father in Mifflin County, Yoder returned to Lancaster County in July 1906 to organize summer singing classes for the Mennonite congregations of Kinzer, Paradise, Stumptown, New Providence, and "the Brick" (Willow Street). Singing schools traditionally were held in the winter, when farm work slows down, but when Yoder appeared, "although it was a busy season and some predicted failure, more pupils were enrolled than ever before, and the interest and zeal for music grew as the term advanced," according to a report in *Gospel Witness* submitted by an individual identified only as "Pupil."

From five congregations, 345 students enrolled in this session, with the largest class containing 108. In a 1953 account, Yoder recalled offering 12 sessions in six locations in Lancaster during 1906: 72 classes in all. As was his policy in communities where he offered multiple sessions, Yoder permitted pupils to attend as many classes as they wished for the price of a single registration. Amos Meyer, who later became a minister in the area, attended 71 sessions, thereby singing with Yoder every night of the week except one for 12 weeks, and he scored 99% on the singing school's written examination. The final concert, held on September 6 at the Mennonite meetinghouse in Strasburg, attracted an audience of 1,000 or 1,200, including those gathered on the lawn. It was described by a witness:

> There were nearly three hundred singers in the class at that time, and the music which went out from that body, as they arose to sing was thrilling and inspiring. The class sang beautiful hymns and choruses, and for want of books, and for a little variety, a few hymns were sung by only a few voices.

The writer referred to the chorus as a *body*, perhaps alluding to the biblical metaphor of the church or religious community as "one body," a concept central to early Christian and Anabaptist understanding. In keeping with this value, Amish and conservative Mennonites made a case against the fragmenting effect of "part-singing" in church services and insisted that the religious community sing in unison. By this time, most Mennonite worship services included a cappella congregational singing in four parts, yet they still forbade "special music," such as quartet or solo performances, which could encourage individual pride and self-aggrandizement. Yoder's inclusion in the Lancaster program of quartets or octets—numbers sung by "only a few voices," whether for an unlikely "want of books" or for aesthetic reasons—suggests a progressive move on the part of the singing teacher. This innovation did not attract unfavorable response from most people, and again the reception he received was overwhelmingly positive. He was praised for his ability to get *his people*—the Mennonites—to sing:

> Many persons express the hope and desire that Bro. Yoder may return and continue his work, for it is much needed everywhere, and we believe that much good comes from it, and we can also say that those of us who were in the class have learned something more about music. Bro. Yoder is a leader of unusual force and enthusiasm, and has no difficulty in getting his people to sing. We hope if he comes back many more will join the class.[31]

The pattern he established in Lancaster became Yoder's standard: twelve weekly classes over three months offered in multiple sessions held in several church meetinghouses throughout the community. According to a former pupil, Yoder was a rigorous but engaging instructor who emphasized literacy: reading both notes and words with precision. He called his singing students "singing scholars" and required that they take written examinations. In 1938, thirteen-year-old Percy Yoder of Mifflin County learned to read music and sing in the prescribed manner, using his arms to beat the tempo of the song, breathing from his abdomen, and holding his torso erect so that the tones did not seem "raw or uncovered" and "placing the tone far back in the throat." Singing required physical discipline and exercise, like athletics. Following Yoder's instruction, Percy practiced singing the scale thirty times a day, and he remains a respected song leader in his congregation.

In addition to teaching what he called "the rudiments of music"— scales, rhythm, and solomization, the do-re-mi-fa-so-la-ti-do system of sight singing and notation—Yoder introduced his singing school pupils to the literature of classical composers. Many farmers and children of farmers learned in his schools to perform music that was beyond the grasp of most sectarian, rural people, and that they would never have heard in concert or even through professional recordings. In southeastern Pennsylvania, where Yoder's influence was especially strong, Bishop John E. Lapp recalled in a conversation with John Ruth that he learned to sing Handel's "Hallelujah Chorus" and Haydn's "The Heavens Are Telling" at Yoder's singing school at Deep Run. When young John Lapp mentioned this to his public schoolteacher, she found it impossible to believe that a Mennonite bumpkin could know such things: "No you didn't," she insisted, "You just thought you did."

In summer 1906, while he was still working in the singing schools in Lancaster county, Yoder received a letter from his mentor, M. G. Brumbaugh, warning him against wasting his time on secular music that did not serve "his people"—perhaps in response to a bit of alumni news in the *Juniata Echo* that reported Yoder's new position at Lock Haven, noting that he was leading chapel singing and teaching the students "college songs." Scrawled on letterhead from his new post as Superintendent of Public Education in Philadelphia, Brumbaugh wrote,

> Dear Yoder: I still say, "Stick to your people." I am not at all inclined to change my view. It is your time given to music other than for your people and your delay in getting your bearings for the real things that led me to raise the query. And always, I do this because you are one of the Juniata boys and I want all of them to get on to the best that is in them. You have only my best wishes and my continued concern for your success.[32]

It is difficult to determine whether in Brubaugh's estimation Yoder ever got his "bearings for the real things." That he calls Yoder "one of the Juniata boys" here hints at the problem of the bachelor who is regarded as eternally boyish, because he fails to prove his masculinity and maturity by providing for a wife and family. Men of Yoder's time found themselves caught between the conflicting images of Victorian "domestic masculinity"—marked by professional achievement and support of home and family—and "virility," associated with independence and self-assertion.[33] A member of the Big Valley community described Yoder as a "free man, someone who just couldn't be bound by church or family or anything." And yet, Brumbaugh's "Stick to your people," collided with that spirit. Years later, Yoder blamed his mentor's advice for his own refusals:

> When I first went to Juniata College Dr. M. G. Brubaugh said to me, "Joseph, stick to your people!" Owing to our great confidence in him, his words made a lasting impression on me, so that when my voice would have justified me in going into Grand Opera, something held me back. Later, when I made preparations to go to Harvard to study Journalism, again something held me back.[34]

Although he was not responsible for supporting family or employed by a church institution, Yoder was informally bound to his community of origin. Unable completely to part with the values and expectations of his background, he established lines of departure and return, as if he fully belonged neither among the school masters of Lock Haven or the Teachers Institutes, nor among the Mennonites in Lancaster or the Amish in Big Valley. More likely, he belonged a bit to all of those places and could not lose his hold on any of them. During these years, his temporary but regular employment in several communities set patterns that finally shaped his vocation. "He went to the world," one Big Valley man identified the central paradox of Yoder's life, "so why did he keep coming back to us?" This man was not ungrateful for Yoder's contributions to his community, just puzzled. Another former singing student from Mifflin County summarized the ambivalence with which she and many Mennonites in her community regarded J. W. Yoder, recognizing that his transgression may have also been the source of his gift to them: "Well, he went to the world, but he sure taught Mennonites how to sing!"

When he returned to Lock Haven in the fall of 1906, Yoder fit in as "a regular member of the faculty . . . doing splendid work."[35] In addition to teaching courses at the Normal School, he served as music director at the County Teacher Institutes in Cameron, Bedford and Huntingdon that fall—districts that hired teachers from Lock Haven, so that he conducted alumni reunions as part of the Teachers Institutes. During winter 1907, he accompanied the debate team to another triumph at West Chester and coached the men's basketball team.

At the semester's end in summer 1907, Yoder returned to Big Valley to continue a project he had begun while still at Juniata College. With the help of his father, his older brother Yost, and neighbor Reuben Kauffman, he had recorded musical notation for three "slow songs" or

3.2 Coach Yoder wearing a bowler hat with the 1907-08 basketball team of Central State Normal School atLock Haven, Pennsylvania.

Langsame Weise tunes preserved through oral tradition and sung in chant-like unison during Amish worship services. Lacking rhythm all together, these hymns are melismatic, one syllable extending for more than five or six notes. St. Augustine, in about 400 CE, commented on the expressive power of melisma. By transcending the one-to-one relationship between syllable and note, he wrote, this ancient singing expresses "a joy too deep to describe."[36] As a sensitive child listening to this music, Yoder found, "The slow upward and downward swings of these heavy strains soon began to tenderize my heartstrings, and the next thing I knew, I was weeping. It was many years later that I was able to see the beauty of this strange harmony."[37]

Mysterious and rhapsodic, the Amish tunes seem somber and alien to the ear accustomed to modern Western music. They are performed by a male *Vorsinger* who intones the first measure of a line, then the congregation follows, singing notes in a slow, continuous drift and breathing at the end of each syllable. The prolonged, somber tones express the spirit of the age in which the hymns were composed. German texts are paired with traditional tune titles in a large volume called the *Ausbund*, first published in Europe in 1564 and in America in 1742. The 140 hymns included in the *Ausbund* refer mostly to suffering and hardship because many were composed by Anabaptist prisoners, and some recount martyrdom narratives from capture to internment, trial, and execution.

Although most members of the community can learn how to follow or *noch singe*, only those individuals who are specially gifted are able to retain the slow tunes well enough to lead them. Thus, as Yoder wrote in *Rosanna's Boys*, "It is considered the duty of every young man who can master these tunes, to do so, that he may do his part in carrying on this religious music."[38] Those who distinguish themselves as *Vorsingers* are esteemed in the community, but even the most talented are rarely able to retain more than five or ten hymns in a lifetime.

Describing his desire to write the Amish tunes, Yoder outlined a rationale for the project that might win Amish support. He recalled accompanying his father to an Amish wedding where a young man visiting from a western settlement was honored with an invitation to lead the "*Wacht Auf*," the first song that is always sung after the wedding meal. The man confidently proceeded, but it became clear to the group that he could not sing the song as they did, and a leader in the Pennsylvania crowd tried to pull the tune back on course. After the wedding, Little Crist confessed to Yoder that the dissonance of the episode was so horrible it made him feel sick to his stomach. Yoder seized this opportunity to suggest that Crist sing the song properly, so that he could write the notes, and they would avoid future stresses of that kind; perhaps the taboo against musical notation could be overlooked to preserve congregational singing. Crist agreed, and Yoder described the painstaking process of catching the tune:

> At our first opportunity we sat down to the table in the living room, and proceeded to write the *Wacht Auf*. He sang a line and I jotted down notes where I thought the pitch indicated. Then he sang it again, and I made corrections. Then I sang the line back to him and he made corrections. By going over a line from five to ten times, we finally got it to where father would say, "Now that's right."[39]

After writing the first line, Yoder was baffled as to how to proceed until he realized that the tune modulates. Before he was done, the tune changed keys seven times, something which became apparent only in writing the notes. Finally Yoder sang it back to his father, and later to old Reuben Kauffman, a respected *Vorsinger* in the community, assuming that if the tune passed their approval, it was "right." Moreover, he believed that if he mentioned to other *Vorsingers* that these two old men had cooperated with the project, he might get permission to write the tunes of more songs.[40]

During summer 1907, Yoder transcribed two more songs, "*Weil nun die Zeit vorhanden ist*" and "*Der Lobgesang*," or hymn of praise. The latter is the most familiar slow song because it is sung as the second hymn in every worship service, about serving the purpose of the "Gloria" in a traditional liturgy. The two tunes, the first from the *Ausbund* ever printed in note form, were published in C. Henry Smith's 1909 volume *The Mennonites of America*. Yoder's project is aligned with the efforts of M. G. Brumbaugh, Smith, and others who sought to preserve the histories and distinct cultures of American ethnic and religious groups in the late nineteenth century. It also would have found parallels in the work of those who were gathering and publishing tunes and words to traditional spirituals and slave songs from the American South. In addition to the two scores which appear with directions for performance in Smith's 1909 volume, Yoder collected four other tunes between 1907 and 1910 with the help of his father and Reuben Kauffman.

Like the gifted young Amish man who feels compelled to "do his part" for the community's musical tradition by learning to carry the tunes, Yoder felt obligated to do his part by writing them. Although he learned to sing before he learned to read, the ability to participate in vocal music had always been associated with literacy in his mind. As a child, he longed to learn to read so that he could sing with his brothers: "singing made me want to learn to read, because, thought I, the only reason that people do not sing is because they cannot read the words."[41] Forty-one years later, he disregarded the Amish prohibition on musical notation, so urgent was his desire to record the oral tunes.

Similarly, Yoder longed to take a photograph of his father and regretted that he never managed to capture an image of Rosanna. (As with written music, the photography taboo forbids the use of technology to preserve the memory of a living thing in inanimate form.) Eventually Yoder and a friend convinced Little Crist to sit for the snapshot in front of his house by claiming that they would focus on the vines and flowers growing

3.3 Little Christ, taken by his son, J. W. Yoder., early twentieth century.

around the porch. Wrote Yoder, "if the picture included father sitting on his chair, well, we just couldn't help that, but we got his picture anyway."[42]

During the academic year 1908-1909, with another professor from the Normal School, Yoder joined the Hospital Charity Minstrels, a troupe of forty-seven white men, including the Clinton County judge, who performed black-faced minstrel shows in one of the town's opera houses. The February 1909 performance was the sixth in an annual series that raised funds to buy equipment for the town hospital. For material, several of the men traveled to New York City to gather the latest jokes and songs from minstrel acts on Broadway. On performance day, the costumed men paraded through town playing instruments in the fashion of the traveling troupes of the day. Yoder was one of two white-faced soloists in a ninety-minute program described by the local paper as "coon songs, the funniest stories, brand new jokes, witty cross-fire and clever local hits." In addition to vocal and instrumental performances, including several songs by Stephen Foster, and skits, the show featured acrobatic and clown stunts, balancing, tumbling, and juggling of illuminated Indian clubs. Afterward, the cast and ten-piece orchestra retreated to the local armory, where they joined the audience, dressed in ball costumes, for dancing that lasted until past midnight. The newspaper account concluded, "As the sweet strains of the dreamy home waltz were finally struck, the numerous spectators reluctantly arose and the dancers, dead tired, but unwilling to miss a step, danced on until the last note died away."[43]

The *Clinton Republican*'s description of one of the players speaks to the nature of minstrelsy: "the ideal personification of the ample girthed, down south darky." From the middle of the nineteenth century, these shows depicted slaves in the South or ex-slaves for mostly northern audiences. The most prevalent and influential form of live entertainment in America during this era, they were also exported and became hugely popular in Britain. Relics of the shows persist in our language through phrases like "hamming it up," a reference to the mixture of ham fat and burnt cork that actors smeared onto their faces; "Dixie" as a name for the South; and "Jim Crow," who was a popular, shuffling character. The skits reinforced images of African-Americans as happy-go-lucky, irresponsible children, and audiences assumed that the shows accurately represented their speech, singing, and dancing. The Lock Haven show enacted another non-white stereotype in an act titled "Macaroni Non Gratin," that featured "the 'dago,' both in makeup and acting."

Around the time Yoder was involved with the Lock Haven minstrels, Lithuanian-born Asa Yoelson was gaining fame as Al Jolson, best known for his performance and recording of "Mammy." For this immigrant, minstrelsy must have been a means of assimilation into white American culture. Likewise Yoder, who complained to J. S. Coffman about the "barbarity" of the Lancaster County Amish and Mennonites, must have gained a sense of belonging to the broader culture through his work with the minstrel singers in Lock Haven. It is unknown what significance, if any, can be attached to the fact that he remained a white face among the black-faced minstrals, or whether he saw a connection between this kind of exaggerated and damaging racial representation and the stereotypes of the Amish in literature that he fiercely resisted less than twenty years later. Certainly his involvement with the troupe was

3.4 Hospital Charity Minstrals, Lock Haven, February, 1909. J. W. Yoder sits second from the right in the second row.

part of a much larger set of assumptions and biases pervasive in American society at the time.

With the close of the spring semester 1909, Yoder resigned from his position at the Normal School, although he insisted on using the title of "professor" for the rest of his life. The circumstances of his leaving Lock Haven are unclear. Likely his popularity as music director for teacher institutes had already reached the point where, as in later years, he could spend August through December on the road. The institutes would have garnered more money, and a life of singing on the road was likely more attractive than classroom teaching. Together with his summer singing schools and song leading work, Yoder managed to earn a good living, but he still had no home of his own.

According to the census of 1910, Yoder was living with John and Meribah Cassady and their four young children in Johnstown, Pennsylvania. In a brief mention of his work as music director for this successful Church of the Brethren evangelist, Yoder recalled that the burly West Virginia farm boy preached with "tremendous zeal." He wrote, "Those were the days when Billy Sunday was conducting his great city campaigns, and it looked as though the Rev. Cassady had gotten some of his inspiration from Billy Sunday."[44] A National League baseball player with Chicago, Pittsburgh, and Philadelphia, with an 1891 record of ninety stolen bases in 116 games, Sunday was converted by a female minister at a Chicago mission in the 1880s and eventually left baseball to become a muscular Christian evangelist.

3.5 *Joseph W. Yoder, music director, with John H. Cassady, Church of the Brethren evangelist, who wears the traditional clerical frock coat, c. 1910.*

Sunday dared men to "have enough grit" to convert, and threw up his fists to box with Satan at the pulpit. A staunch temperance man, he declared, "Whiskey and beer are all right in their place, but their place is in hell."[45] It may be no coincidence that in 1909, around the time Yoder began working with Cassady, Sunday also began using a soloist and song leader in his ministry. Cassady probably become acquainted with Yoder when he was a student, debater, and minister at Juniata College during the years when Yoder served the school as athletic director and captain of the debate squad. In addition to the work in 1910, Yoder later joined Cassady for a short stint in 1917, the year of Sunday's great ten-week, systematic campaign that brought 98,000 souls to the altar in New York City. A portrait of Yoder and Cassady, taken to promote their work, shows Cassady in the plain Brethren minister's frock coat and Yoder in more conventional attire.

In the early half of the twentieth century, Yoder worked as a soloist and song leader at many Brethren, Reformed, and Methodist Sunday school conventions and evangelistic meetings. In 1915 at Newtown, Pennsylvania, Yoder assisted evangelist Chester Birch, described as "a manly man in figure and face" who came with an endorsement from

Billy Sunday, "I have known him for a number of years and consider him absolutely on the square."[46] In 1918, without the aid of instruments, choir, or electronic amplification, Yoder led singing at the Church of the Brethren Annual Meeting at Hershey, Pennsylvania, where the audience numbered about 10,000. Ever engaging before a crowd, Yoder's solos and song leading were poised to arouse emotional responses, softening hard hearts in preparation for an altar call or binding believers together in song.

His repertoire of stirring gospel hymns stood in blunt contrast to the slow, tunes of his Amish childhood. Whereas the "white spirituals" triumphantly described the moment of conversion as a "happy day, when Jesus took my sins away," and attribute salvation to the "wonder-working power in the blood of the Lamb" and the "wideness in God's mercy," Amish hymns offer praise and advocate individual submission to God's will. The slow, rhythmless tempo and limited tonal range of the Amish tunes reflect an emotional atmosphere and attitude that Yoder abandoned in his youth. His life, nevertheless, drew on several cultures and musical traditions. While Mennonite reporters praised his ability to get *his people* to sing in the early Lancaster singing schools, Yoder considered the Amish—not the Mennonites—to be his people. The Old Order Amish would never attend his singing schools or embrace musical literacy, yet he was deeply committed to preserving their musical practices—even as he performed gospel songs with flair on the evangelical preacher's platform.

"MR. AND MRS. HOOLEY AND MR. YODER"

When he left the Cassady household in early 1911, Yoder was thirty-eight years old, and he still listed as his permanent address the home of his elderly father in Mifflin County. Although he moved skillfully and unfettered among many communities, he must have grown weary of the itinerant life, and finally found a way to obtain a family and home of his own—without marrying. Evidently, Yoder convinced his former singing school master, roommate and "educational trailblazer," John M. Hooley, to purchase with him a farm of about 100 acres with out-buildings and an eleven-room stone house, located on Tanyard Road between the villages of Ivyland and Richboro in Bucks County, north-west of Philadelphia. Until then, Hooley and his wife of nine years had been living in Lancaster County with their baby daughters, Pauline and Marian. John had worked in various jobs: mail clerk, school teacher, and most recently for Park Seed Company's *Floral Magazine*.

According to the local newspaper, "Messrs. Hooley and Yoder" moved together to the farm on March 3, 1911. Two months later, they received a visit from their in-laws and siblings, Yoder's older brother John and his wife Sarah, who was Hooley's sister. In a life that was thoroughly documented in published memoirs and through preserved correspondence, Yoder left no traces of his eighteen-odd years of living with the Hooley family. What is pieced together here concerning the household publicly called "Mr. and Mrs. Hooley and Mr. Yoder" is drawn from brief notes in the Richboro community columns of the *Doylestown Daily Intelligencer* and *Newtown Enterprise* newspapers and from the memories of neighbors.

3.6 *Home of J. W. Yoder and the Hooley family, located about two miles east of Ivyland, Pennsylvania, on a tract of land bordered by Hatboro Road, Alms House Road and Tanyard Road.*

From the start, the Hooleys and Yoder—Amish and Amish Mennonite in background—were active in local society and in Richboro's Addisville Reformed Church; the Hooleys joined the congregation, but Yoder was such a transient, he never did.[47] Hooley served as choir master for many years and directed special Christmas cantatas and occasional musicals, such as his 1913 offering, titled "The New Minister's

Honeymoon." Yoder was usually featured in Hooley's productions and often soloed during Sunday services; the two sang in a men's quartet that regularly performed at the Reformed church and in other social and religious gatherings in the area.

During the 1940s, after Hooley had lost his sight and Yoder was no longer living with the family, "Uncle Joe," as he was known in the family, returned to visit, and the two men sat together and "sang by the hour," their tenor and bass voices blending.[48] During the 'teens, John Hooley also taught music in the Richboro public schools, but throughout the early part of the century, he occasionally left his family for several months at a time to work at jobs in Lancaster and Hershey, a habit that scandalized the neighbors.

Continuing the patterns of departure and return that he had established in his parents' home, Yoder left the farm twice or three times a year for three-month stints of teachers' institute or singing school work, usually in western parts of the state, his travels chronicled in the local newspapers. Within the immediate area, Yoder was known as "The Professor" and commonly regarded as "a cut above" the local folk, "always well dressed and well mannered."[49] When he was home, he regularly entertained the community by offering solos in venues ranging from elegant parlor musicales to Grange Hall meetings; in 1928, he gave a vocal recital on a Philadelphia radio station, accompanied by a pianist from the Richboro area. Yoder even wrote and performed an original anthem as a tribute to the Northampton Farmer's Club, of which Hooley was a member. During the early years, Yoder and Hooley appear to have been gentleman farmers; tax records indicate that they kept one cow and about five horses or mules for transportation and work around the farm.

As early as 1912, the Hooleys and Yoder are regularly included in newspaper accounts of meetings of the local chapter of the Women's Christian Temprance Union (WCTU). Founded in 1883 to shield women and children from the effects of alcoholism, the WCTU was known by its slogan "home protection;" in addition to closing saloons, the group sought reform in issues ranging from prostitution to women's rights. Thanks to the efforts of the WCTU, by the early twentieth century, the phrase *municipal housekeepers* expressed the domestication of local politics and a widening of women's roles in public education, labor, and the neighborhood, as the community surrounding the home gradually fell within the female sphere.[50] Myra Hooley hosted "parlor meetings" of the WCTU in their home, and Yoder and John Hooley often sang for the programs, which sometimes attracted as many as 150 people. An unusually detailed account of a 1913 meeting offers a glimpse into the social and political atmosphere of these events:

> The Richboro WCTU held a parlor meeting at the home of Mr. and Mrs. Edward B. Search on Saturday evening last and notwithstanding the condition of roads and extreme cold, large sledloads and sleighers began to gather at the home and by time for the opening exercises the large and beautiful parlors were filled to the most.

The female president of the local WCTU presided over the evening's program that included piano selections, a solo by Yoder, and recitations of poetry by four women and one man. Then, remarks on "the growing temperance sentiment and the great and good work being done by this organization" were made by Yoder, a clergy man, and two other men. The newspaper account concluded: "Seldom has such enthusiasm prevailed among those interested in this work. This was possibly one of the best parlor meetings ever held by the organization."[51]

Although Yoder had supported the temperance movement since the 1890s when his efforts were aligned with the Anti-Saloon League, his move to eastern Pennsylvania in 1911 probably marked the beginning of his involvement with the WCTU. In 1914, he also served as music director at the state convention of the Loyal Temperance Legion. In 1929 he directed music for the WCTU's production of "The Bottle and the Bell," an elaborately staged and costumed musical pageant that traced the story of drink from colonial times until the passage of the eighteenth Amendment and beyond, "showing . . . ardent defenders and supporters of prohibition."[52] The performance, directed by the play's author and attended by WCTU celebrities from Philadelphia, was staged on the lighted steps of the Reformed church and attracted an audience of over 300 people.

But beyond advancing the dry cause, Yoder's engagement with the WCTU along with his living arrangements with the Hooleys—whose three daughters grew up with Yoder in the house—placed him in intimate contact with women, perhaps for the first time. Well after national prohibition was achieved and then repealed in 1933, Yoder's loyalty to the WCTU persisted, as evidenced by a 1946 letter full of gossip about the or-

PENNSYLVANIA LOCAL OPTION SONG

TUNE—"It's a Long Way to Tipperary."

I

Down from Gov'nor Brumbaugh
    Came an edict clear one day,
Saying, "Local Option, boys,
    Must have the right of way.
Pennsylvania wants it,
    And I'm pledged to do my best,
So frame a law that gives fair play,
    Let voters do the rest."

CHORUS

We will stand for Local Option,
    We will stand against rum,
We will vote for Local Option,
    For we know it's bound to come.
Good-bye, Whiskey traffic,
    Farewell, you're not square;
'Twas a long, long way to Local Option,
    But now we're right there.

II

How the people shouted
    When they heard the gladsome news,
Years and years the rum king ruled,
    No others got their dues.
"Pass this little measure, boys,"
    Said Gov'nor with a smile,
"Or else I'll stump this state myself,
    And you'll be out of style."—*Chorus.*

III

Rally round the Gov'nor, men,
    Our chance is here to win;
Strike a blow at politics
    Long ruled by rum and sin.
Work for Local Option, boys,
    Make Pennsylvania dry.
Let's shout and sing, "Saloons must go!"
    Make this our battle cry."—*Chorus.*

Written by J. W. YODER, Phila., Pa.

3.8 *Text of the song that Yoder drafted in support of M. G. Brumbaugh and the temperance movement in Pennsylvania.*

ganization's national president and other members. He was frustrated that "some refined ladies have such an awe inspiring regard for University professors" that they accepted a Yale School of Alcohol Studies report that moderate drinking was not harmful. "Not so this Irish-Amishman, who begs to remain an ardent worker for Temperance," he concluded.[54]

Sometime during the mid-teens, Yoder wrote "Pennsylvania Local Option Song," which was printed and distributed in pamphlet form. Local option, a provision that enabled any small municipality to declare itself dry, was the primary strategy of Pennsylvania anti-liquor activists in their fight to achieve state-wide and national prohibition. The song may have been distributed in support of the 1914 gubernatorial campaign of Yoder's mentor, M.G. Brumbaugh. Despite the fact that only two years prior the Church of the Brethren Annual Meeting had judged voting and political involvement inadvisable for Christians who owe their loyalty to a heavenly kingdom, Brumbaugh ran for office on the Republican ticket—although his party machine did not support the prohibitionists' strategy.

3.9 Governor M.G. Brumbaugh (second from right) with members of the 53rd Infantry during World War I.

Local option therefore became the most controversial issue of the 1914 race. Before the election, Teddy Roosevelt come to Pennsylvania to campaign against Brumbaugh, calling him a "wooly lamb," in reference to his unruly gray hair and the fact that he was a pacifist minister.[55] Brumbaugh prevailed in the election, however, receiving the most votes cast for a Pennsylvania governor before women's suffrage. Roosevelt's epithet must have haunted him, though. With World War I, a conflicted Brumbaugh was obliged to call the Pennsylvania militia to arms and serve as its figurehead commander, and the troops he summonsed to subdue riots in Pittsburgh killed several strikers—to the chagrin and shame of many in his denomination.[56]

After four years in the governor's mansion in Harrisburg, Brumbaugh declined several invitations to preside over distinguished Pennsylvania universities, returning instead to Juniata College, determined to "stick with [his] people" despite what some Dunkers regarded as a compromised conscience. Likewise, Yoder remained connected with Mennonite communities, even as he worshiped with the Reformed congregation at Richboro.

His first documented singing schools in the nearby Mennonite community of Mongomery and Bucks Counties date from 1912 or 1913, shortly after he moved to that area.[57] A young pupil's diary reveals that Yoder refused classes with enrollments of fewer than fifty students, so that during the spring session of 1913, he offered lessons to at least 250 students at five different locations—Perkasie on Monday evening, Souderton on Tuesday evening, Line Lexington on Wednesday evening, Doylestown on Thursday evening, and Blooming Glen on Saturday evening—all in the days before he had an automobile. With enrollment fees set at $1.25, his income for twelve weeks of work would have well exceeded $300, or $100 a month. During that term, Yoder was called away twice—once to lead singing at a Sunday school convention in his home community and again when his father suffered a stroke. At the news of his father's illness, Yoder traveled to Big Valley to be with Little Crist for two weeks, but then returned to complete the twelve-week curriculum.[58]

This was Crist's second stroke, and his health must have continued to decline until his death in September 1915, four days after Yoder's forty-third birthday. Likely Crist's illness and death contributed to the period of turbulence and uncertainty in the Yoder/Hooley household, for it is clear that they decided to rid themselves of the Richboro property, move back to central Pennsylvania, and live separately. As early as January 5, the *Newtown Enterprise* announced that J. W. Yoder and J. M. Hooley had already sold their farm and were preparing for a public sale of livestock, farm implements and personal property, and that Hooley planned to resume his former employment—probably with *Floral Magazine* in Lancaster.

But on February 6, the same paper printed a bill of sale for Yoder and Hooley, describing personal effects as well as real estate offered for auction. Apparently the sale did not go as well as the men had hoped, for they decided to keep the farm, although tax records for this year indicate that they sold all of their livestock. Hooley resumed his job in Lancaster County, and the May 19 Doylestown paper noted that he had traveled from his home in Lancaster for a weekend visit with his wife and children, who remained on their farm near Richboro.

If the farm had sold, Yoder would likely have relocated closer to family members in Big Valley, in a move that echoes his return from the Midwest after Rosanna's death. Such a move would have also placed him closer to Juniata College, with which Yoder formalized an agreement to work as a student recruiter that year. This position seems to have been created

Closing-Out Sale of Personal Property and Real Estate of Yoder & Hooley,

On the William Crayçn farm, one-half mile west of Richboro, on

Tuesday, February 9, 1915,

at 1 P. M., sharp, to wit:

STOCK—Five horses: No. 1, gray mare, weighs 1450, 12 years old, single line leader, excellent worker; No. 2, bay horse, 11 years old, good, tree worker; No. 3, brown mare, 14 years old, sound, works anywhere; No. 4, gray horse, 11 years old, good leader, quiet and trustworthy; No. 5, bay driving horse, works anywhere, plenty of ginger; cow, good one; 6 brood sows, Chester Whites, will farrow about March 1, some of these farrowed 12 to 14 pigs the last litter; seed hog, 2 years old, Chester White; about 3.01 S. C. White Leghorn hens, thoroughbred, good layers.

WAGONS—Two-horse farm wagon, Conklin, good as new; surrey, falling-top, 3-spring market wagon, good condition; runabout, light.

IMPLEMENTS—Old binder, works well; Osborne hay loader, three mowers, riding plow, walking plow, both Oliver chilled; spring harrow, Clark cutaway; leveling harrow, 2 Iron Age riding cultivators, cultivator, potato digger, hay rake, hay tedder, corn planter, J. I. Case; clover seed sower.

HARNESS—2 sets heavy work harness, set light work harness, 3 sets single light harness, one set Lapp's make, never used; 4 sets check lines, housings, 6 leather halters, 6 work bridles, 2 open do., 3 collars, carriage do.

CROPS—25 acres wheat, 4 tons baled oat straw, about 800 bus. corn, 200 bus. oats, about 500 large bundles cornfodder, some good second crop hay, 30 tons baled hay.

MISCELLANEOUS—2 grindstones, wheelbarrow, 2 harpoons, 150-ft. hay rope, nearly new; 16-ft. ladder, 20-ft. hay ladders, hay cutter, corn sheller, feed chest, forks, rakes, shovels, hoes, mattocks, wheel hoe, pick, saws, pulleys, grain bags, carriage pole, trace and breast chains, lots of 'em; 2 log chains, fifth chain, double and single trees, about 600 feet new boards, 3 35-ft. poles, Cyphers incubator, 400-egg capacity; colony house, 8x8, heated by gasoline; 2 small brooders, other poultry accessories, and many small articles used about a farm. TERMS CASH.

THE FARM will be sold at same time— 101 acres of level, square fields, all tillable, clay loam soil, responds readily to culture. Good 11-room stone dwelling, wagon house with 6 horse stalls, potato cellar, another building suitable for 15 cows or 50 hogs, 3 barracks, hay barn, holding 40 tons baled; 3 wells, one never-failing. Farm to be sold at 3.30 P. M. Terms reasonable, fully explained day of sale.

Jan. 23-3t   Ira H. Cornell, Auctioneer.

3.10 Sale Advertisement listing the household goods, farm implements, livestock and real estate owned by Joseph W. Yoder and John and Myra Hooley, Newtown Enterprise, Feruary 6, 1915.

especially for him and suited his talents perfectly. As with the ongoing singing school and teachers' institute work, the job required that he travel, perform, and solicit his own appointments. A sample of such a letter of solicitation stated his purpose: "to help keep your pupils somewhat college conscious in general and Juniata conscious in particular." He described his half-hour presentations as, "a few solos, a few stories, and a short talk on some educational subject which definitely concerns the girls and boys."[59]

The schools Yoder visited were scattered across Pennsylvania in rural areas and small towns. Until he bought a car in 1921, he traveled by train and was usually able to make only one visit per day. Driving, he could appear at two schools in one day, and remained on the road five days per week. His schedule from 1933 listed 125 school visits in seventeen weeks. Until his retirement in 1941, Yoder followed a rigorous schedule: from about November until June, he visited high schools; from June through August, he offered summer singing classes in Mennonite, Brethren, Lutheran, and Reformed churches; during autumn through the end of the year, he also led singing at the teachers' institutes, choosing the more profitable institute work over high school visits in case of a conflict. According to one pupil, Yoder did not sell Juniata as much as he entertained and inspired the students; he concluded on hight school assembly lecutre, "And now, young friends, as you slide down the bannister of ife, remember me as a splinter in your career.

In 1916 when he returned to the singing schools in the Mennonite community located in Bucks and Montgomery counties, Yoder's popularity had increased; the largest single class enrolled 140 at Blooming Glen. During that term, Yoder was called away to lead singing at revival meetings in Shippensburg, Pennsylvania. According to the diary of his young pupil, "He did not want to do it. But they said he must come or else their meetings would not be much, so he had to promise to go." After the final concert of this session, she wrote,

> On Saturday evening July 15, 1916, we had our final Singing classes altogether at Blooming Glen for the last time. This was the twelfth [sic] night. I was there we were all there and it was full, outside all over. It was nice. On Sunday afternoon was the last time in Deep Run. I was not there but it was full there. The classes are all over now. Mr. Yoder went home again. He read a German hymn.[60]

This student, on her third cycle of singing school lessons with Yoder and apparently fond of him, mentioned as an afterthought that her teacher *read* a German hymn at the performance. That he chose to read rather than sing a solo or have his students perform the hymn is reminiscent of Amish funerals, where the lyrics of songs are read but not sung. Yoder may have wanted to emphasize the German language because the Mennonite community in that area had made a painful shift from German to English some years earlier. Having been raised as a "two-language" child himself, he would have been sensitive to the communal tensions and individual consequences of such a change.

In that community, Yoder maintained a special relationship with the Deep Run congregation, offering singing schools and leading singing services annually until his death at mid-century. Samuel G. Detweiler, chorister at Deep Run since 1908, was a good friend of Yoder's and something of a kindred spirit. According to congregational historian Tim Rice, Detweiler competed with choristers from other churches in the area and had his singers meet between their classes with Yoder to get extra practice. In those days, there were no lights in the meeting house, so the classes were held in the afternoon. Yoder spent the first hour with younger singers working on musical rudiments, and the second hour practicing advanced vocal pieces with the adults.[61]

At the last session of the singing school, all of the area classes gathered at Deep Run for a final concert that drew huge crowds. In August

3.11 *A Mennonite chorus that had performed in the Addisville Reformed Church, gathered on the lawn of the Hooley/Yoder home, Yoder sits front and center, 1925.*

1919, for instance, 1,200 persons crowded into the Deep Run Meeting-house for a singing service with J. W. Yoder, and about 200 automobiles were parked outside.[62] Yoder took the Mennonite singers from Deep Run and Blooming Glen to perform for his community at the Addisville Reformed Chruch in Richboro in 1913 and 1919.[63] Throughout the 1920s, mentions of "Prof. Yoder's Mennonite chorus," "the Deep Run Male Chorus," or "Mennonites" (perhaps men and women) frequently appeared in the newspaper with reference to the Reformed church.

3.12 Sam Detweiler (standing left) leads singing at a Harvest Meeting at the Deep Run Meeting House, 1938. The ministers sit at the bench in front, women sit in the center, and men on raised benches on the side, beneath racks for their hats.

Singing master Yoder was an outsider working within the Mennonite community. According to oral tradition, the Deep Run overseers did not approve of his being so involved in congregational life there. As a remedy, Sam Detweiler arranged for him to join the church and receive communion so that there would be no further objections.[64] At some point, he may have been banned from holding singing classes in the meeting house, so they met in the Hilltown High School building in Blooming Glen.[65] Another time, Yoder wanted to offer some of his books for sale after a song service at Deep Run. Sam Detweiler wanted to make an arrangement for the people to pay for the books the next morning, but Yoder could not stay until Monday and was insistent. Finally, Detweiler said that he was related to Preacher Jake Rush and everybody else at that church, and that if he allowed Yoder to sell books on a Sunday, it would be end of his song-leading at Deep Run. The next day Detweiler went to see auctioneer Irvin Yothers, a fellow-member at Deep Run, and told him what had happened. Irvin said that Sam had done the right thing, although it had annoyed Yoder, and they both agreed that he was "rich" and did not need the money anyway.[66]

These stories of personal and denominational friction provide context for a statement attributed to Yoder in a rare, detailed newspaper account of one of his singing services at Deep Run: "The power of music makes us forget our dislikes and animosities." The reporter was surprised to find excellent singing, although "for several hundred years a tuning fork has been the only musical instrument in the severely plain meeting house of the Mennonite faith." He raved that "everybody seemed blessed with a melodious voice; everybody sang with a sturdy assurance and the precision of a trained choir, even the most difficult of church music, producing volume and harmony like that of mighty organ strains." The unrehearsed group sang in "balanced four-part" (harmony) for two hours, executing a program that ranged from a classical Easter cantata to gospel hymns. The reporter said the "older folks in the audience reflected the training they had received under [Yoder's] meticulous tuning fork," and he noticed that Yoder "only had to whack the fork on his hymnal twice, as a rebuke for the singers' slips in time."[67]

Yoder's famous tuning fork appeared in a local story told to show the depth of his influence. An elderly woman told John Ruth that J. W. Yoder must have been slightly hard of hearing in his right ear because he always hit the pulpit with a tuning fork, then drew his arm across his torso and held the fork to his left ear. Therefore, in imitation of the master, a chorister in the Deep Run congregation always lifted his tuning fork to his left ear when he led singing in church.[68]

Almost from the start of his singing school and teachers' institute work, Yoder began publishing music collections with the Hall-Mack Company in Philadelphia, each year issuing a new songbook. These slim,

6"x 81/2" paperbound volumes of about eighty pages bore his name as editor and typically had simple titles like *The Diadem* or *The Banner*. *The Galaxy*, published in 1912, included a special section of song texts designated "Temperance and Patriotic." *The Crown* from 1913 included Stephen Foster numbers "Massa's in the Cold, Cold Ground," "My Old Kentucky Home" and "Old Black Joe," and for years Yoder listed "Negro Spirituals" as a special selling point in letters soliciting public school subscriptions. *The Victor*, from 1915, featured an antiphonal reading of Scripture verses titled "New Birth" articulating the Evangelical doctrine of salvation. By 1921, *The Lyric* included war-inspired tunes and titles like "The Air Patrol," "The Soldier's Farewell," and "Tramp! Tramp! Tramp!"

Yoder sold the booklets for profit at fifteen cents each, or $12.50 for a hundred during the 'teens and 1920s. By 1938, a larger 128-page book cost fifty cents. The collections included secular and gospel songs and some also featured a section called "rudiments of music." He later published

3.13 The front cover of Yoder's 1923 song book, on the back were music and lyrics to his "Pennsylvnaia."

The Music Reader with choruses and an expanded "rudiments" section. When he tried to revise that book, the Hall-Mack Company, which held copyright, would not permit changes, so he published a simpler book called *The Cardinal Songster*, which became very popular.

By 1920, versions of his "Pennsylvania" began appearing on the back cover of the songbooks. Written in 1912, this three-verse song praises the state's scenic beauty and educational culture and history, offers a devotional petition, and concludes with a pledge of allegiance. Yoder believed that if enough people learned the song through his singing schools and teachers' institutes, it would eventually be adopted by the legislature as the official song of the Commonwealth. In 1925 a version of "Pennsylvania" in waltz-time was defeated in the legislature, so Yoder revised the tune to march time. In 1941, it was pitted against another song in the legislature and neither was adopted. In 1951, a newly revised "Pennsylvania Forever" was again defeated, despite considerable letter-writing and lobbying on Yoder's part. The song was last introduced in 1987 and again rejected. Yoder also wrote a similar song for Mifflin County.

During World War I, he issued a glossy pamphlet with a portrait of himself advertising his services as an institute music director by exploiting American war-time sympathies. "This war gave music a new mean-

3.14 Promotional Pamphlet. Inside it read: "Music is the LIFE of an Institute / The LEADER is the life of the music." And, "I should be pleased to come to your County Teacher's Institute in the near future to lead the music. For twelve years or more I have devoted most of my time to this delightful work in Pennsylvania, Indiana and Illinois, and have been recalled to many counties from four to seven times. I aim to inspire the teachers to sing in their schools; to keep them fit mentally and physically through the music to profit by the Institute Lectures; and to entertain upon occasion with bass and baritone solos. Keep this card for reference, inquire about my work, and if I can be of service to you and your teachers, I shall be very happy. I hope I may hear from you."

The image caption beside the portrait reads: "This war gave music a new meaning / Institute Music" and below the portrait "J. W. YODER / 21st and ARCH ST., PHILADELPHIA"

ing" the flyer declares along with a quote from Major General Wood: "The best singing army is the best fighting army." Comparing teachers to soldiers engaged in the battle of education, the flyer continues, "The best is none too good for YOUR teachers."[69]

Whatever his personal views on the war, this pamphlet would have placed Yoder outside the Amish Mennonite religious community. As the

1893 Chicago exposition was viewed by many Mennonites as "the *world's* Fair," the Great War in Europe was regarded as the *world's* war. In 1917 a Mennonite conference in Indiana articulated a clear statement of the church's position and called for obedience and loyalty from within the denomination: "We hold that Christian people should have no part in carnal warfare of any kind or for any cause."[70] World War I placed pacifists at odds with the nation, and an individual's response to the conflict was a test of membership in many Mennonite churches. Yoder's pamphlets would have been especially offensive to pacifists who suffered at the hands of their patriotic neighbors or were detained in military camps. In the Midwest, several churches, barns and the main building of Tabor College burned to the ground, and conscientious objectors were often treated brutally and imprisoned.[71] In Big Valley, a letter in the local newspaper characterized Amish and Mennonite conscientious objectors as "contemptible milk sops, peace-at-any-price polliwogs, slackers, and Red Cross non-supporters,"[72] but treatment of Anabaptist COs was considerably less severe in the older communities in the East. Only twenty men were drafted from 3,726 members of Franconia Conference near Yoder's home, and only a few more were conscripted from Mifflin County.[73]

During the war, Yoder continued his work as a high school recruiter for Juniata College. The correspondence files of Yoder's old friend, acting-president I. Harvey Brumbaugh include numerous letters, often on hotel stationery, listing Yoder's engagements and tallying his expenses; in one, he complained that the college paid him so little, he was having to live on oatmeal and doughnuts. But beyond news from the high school circuit, these letters occasionally also offered glimpses into life back at the Hooley/Yoder farm. In February 1917 Yoder wrote,

> I have made John Hooley a proposition to set him up in the poultry business. He has not accepted my offer yet as he has a slight chance to get a $1,000 R.F.D. route [rural postal delivery route]. If he accepts my plan, I'll have to build some houses and restock the farm, so I do not know just how much time I can spare.[74]

Evidently Hooley accepted the "proposition" because Yoder built the poultry house; in May 1917 he reported, "The chicken house is about completed and I am getting very tough—physically."[75] The following year, a letter to "Dear Prof. Harvey" suggested that forty-five-year-old Yoder was again about to be without a home, and he had only his alma mater to turn to:

> The Hooleys have suddenly taken a notion to move from the farm to a small house in the village. That lets me without a house for the present. As I shall travel a great deal in music work after the Flu [epidemic] is over, I was wondering whether you could not permit me to make my headquarters at the College for awhile. I think you have a rule against taking boarders, but the fact that I solicit for you at times may overcome that rule.[76]

Whether the difficulties were financial or otherwise, there is no evidence that the Hooleys moved from the farm in 1918; news of the musical and social activities of the parents and two teenaged daughters, Pauline and Helen, persisted in the newspapers, and Yoder continued to use his personal stationery with the Ivyland address. (The Hooleys' daughter Marion had Downs Syndrome and spent most of her life in an institution.[77]) From 1918 through 1922, Bucks County tax records list both men as owners of the farm and their profession as "gentleman." In 1923, running water and electric lighting were installed at the farm house, and that year Yoder must have bought Hooley's share of the property, for thereafter he is named on the tax lists as the sole owner, with Hooley identified as "tenant" and "chicken raiser" or "poultry man." Yoder is designated as "musician," reporting an annual income of $200, which, considering his rates at the time, represented about one month of Institute work or less than one singing school cycle.

Yoder's name appeared in the Richboro neighborhood section of the *Doylestown Daily Intelligencer* one last time December 11, 1929. After describing several engagements in other parts of the state, the column noted that he planed to return to his home near Richboro after the holidays and rest for a time there before resuming duties as the high school visitor for Juniata College. Although that might have been true nearly every winter since 1915, this note had a final feel to it. Likely Yoder was preparing to move to Huntingdon to take up residence near or on the Juniata campus. One month earlier, he had sold the farm to Hooley for $1 through an unpublicized transaction involving a third party.[78] By 1930, Yoder had decamped without a trace, and for the first time the Bucks County tax records list the owners of the farm in a more conventional way: "John M. and Myra B. Hooley, poultryman and wife."

*3.15 a, b
John M. Hooley
(left) and
Joseph W. Yoder
(right) pose in front
of the home they
shared for nearly
two decades,
c. late 1940s*

Perhaps his time with the Hooleys convinced Yoder of the virtues of family life, or more likely, feeling his age, he longed for a companion and home of his own. In any case, a few months after his sixtieth birthday, on February 18, 1932, Joseph Yoder married Emily Lane of Lane's Mills, a small town in the forests of Jefferson County in north-central Pennsylvania. One month later, he bought a home at 1772 Mifflin Street, a couple of blocks from the Juniata campus. News of Yoder's late marriage surprised those in Big Valley who had long regarded him as a confirmed bachelor and "handsome heartbreaker." If any recalled that Rosanna and Little Crist had maintained close friendships with Presbyterian neighbors, they did not associate those individuals with Yoder's new Presbyterian wife. Among Yoder's relatives in the Amish-Mennonite community, Emily remains veiled in myth, an outsider who once lived in Pittsburgh. Some say that he never even knew her real age and that Emily tricked Yoder into marrying her by promising that she could accompany him on the piano, but after their marriage revealed that she could not play.

Emily was a striking, white-haired woman who wore stylish clothes and stood nearly as tall as her husband, so the two of them "cut a fine figure" walking into the Amish Mennonite Church at Belleville. At that time, men and women were segregated in seating sections on either side of the aisle, but Joseph and Emily Yoder sometimes sat together, conspicuously defying convention. Invariably they also sat toward the front, since it was assumed that Yoder would lead singing when he attended Maple Grove. As a former deacon of the congregation explained, "Anyone else was embarrassed to lead singing when Joe was there." Their marriage was unconventional by many measures, from its inception late in their lives to the fact that they maintained independent pursuits and retained church memberships with different denominations.

Although some have described it as a "marriage of convenience," it seems that Joseph and Emily were well-matched companions. A "New Woman"—independent, forward thinking, and interested in health and fitness—she supported temperance and women's suffrage. (Only twelve years before their marriage, Pennsylvania was among the last states to grant women the vote with the national passage of the nineteenth Amendment.) Emily served as superintendent of Sunday schools at the Presbyterian church in Huntingdon—a position that would not have been granted to a woman in a Mennonite congregation then—and was a leader in the local Girl Scouts organization. As well, she enjoyed friendships with female students at Juniata. One older member of the college community recalled that "Mrs. Joe Yoder" gave her and her classmates their first taste of carrot juice and taught them how to make hammered aluminum trays, a popular craft of that era.

Yoder's marriage and the purchase of a home in Huntingdon marked the end of his bachelor days and also signaled a significant turn toward family and heritage. With his move to central Pennsylvania, he began visiting relatives and friends in Big Valley and attending the Amish Mennonite church he had joined in his youth, making the drive of about twenty-five miles once or several times a month. On a 1935 Juniata College alumni survey, Yoder listed "Amish at Belleville" as his church affiliation.

Two years after his marriage, he began a twenty-year term as president of the Pennsylvania Yoder Reunion, a task he executed with the zeal of his athletic director days. For this annual event, he published in 1954 *The Yoder Family Reunion Book*, a scholarly study by Franklin and Marshall College professor and folklorist Don Yoder that traces both Anabaptist and Reformed branches of the Yoder family through tales of colonial American heroics to their roots in Berne, Switzerland. Yoder also published and sold versions of the *Yoder Songbook*, which included thirty-two hymns and popular numbers as well as rousing lyrics he wrote especially for the occasion, such as "The Yoder Family Song" and "The Yoder Reunion Song."

Held at Kish Park in Lewistown, the reunions were attended by hundreds of Yoders, worldly and plain, in a display of tribal ecumenicity that undoubtedly pleased the reunion's president and first lady. Yet some Yoders also stayed away, because they feared that as their charismatic relative became increasingly well-known and outspoken through his publications, he might have a negative influence on the next generation.

3.16 *Joseph W. Yoder with his wife Emily Lane Yoder, who wears a Girl Scout insignia on her lapel, c. 1951.*

FOUR CHAPTER

"BEING AMISH-BORN": *ROSANNA OF THE AMISH* (1940) AND *AMISCHE LIEDER* (1942)

Story writing is an attempt to preserve the life of a certain time and locality with all the accompanyings of local coloring. The personal experience of the writer becomes thus all important as it should. He can testify only of what he knows. —Anthony Wanchope, 1894

Sometime in the late 1930s, Yoder read *Straw in the Wind* by Ruth Lininger Dobson, the book that made an author out of him at the age of sixty-eight. Set in an Amish community of northern Indiana, not far from the former Elkhart Institute, the novel chronicles the demise of an old order and celebrates the dawn of a gentler, liberal era. Given the course of his own life, Yoder might have been sympathetic to such a plot. However, Dobson's unflattering and stereotypical representations provoked Yoder to write a book that set out to fix public perceptions of Amish people.

Straw in the Wind

The novel begins with land-rich and greedy Bishop Moses Bontrager scheming to buy his neighbor's plot of fertile lowland for growing mint. A tyrannical potentate, he hogged food at the table, chose mates for his children according to their wealth, and treated family members like slaves. His meek wife suffered silently, "her whole identity . . . swallowed up by his vigorous, engulfing personality."[1] Moses hated public education laws because they took his children from farm work. When a teacher stopped in to discuss the talents of an artistically inclined son, Moses' face grew reddish-purple, and, calling her "the Devil's own handmaiden," he raged "that is not for God-followin' Amish folk to make graven images."[2] Like himself, Moses' God was all-powerful, all-knowing—but not very intelligent—and poised to strike down sinners with his wrath, the brutal God of Law, as imagined by progressive Christians. Meanwhile his family—especially his wife, Sarah, and their artistic son, not incidentally named Christian—found comfort in their own labors and the beauty of nature.

Dobson's book traces the erosion of Moses' authority. Before the story began, a schism within his congregation had created the "Pinky Amish" (Amish Mennonites) who permitted cars, telephones, lightning rods, and planned to build a meetinghouse. Moses's daughter, Rebecca, fell in love with a young member of this group, who happened to be the son of the man who owned the coveted mint field. The bishop's oldest daughter, Polly, who earned income for her father as a domestic worker, was seen listening to dance music in town. When she tried to defend herself, Moses retorted with scriptural allusions: "Let the women learn in silence with all subjection," and "I suffer not a woman to teach, not to usurp authority over the man, but to be in silence—Notwithstanding she shall be saved in childbearing if she continue in faith."[3]

He then hatched a plan to redeem Polly by marrying her off to an undesirable, old widower after her church confession. When Polly refused to repent during a worship service, Moses grew red in the face and excommunicated her on the spot, calling her a "daughter of Jezebel," shouting "I cast you off still and already to the Devil and all his angels I commit you yet. . . . Burn, burn you will forever, iffen the wrath of the Lord you shall kindle with your hankerin' after pleasurement."[4] After this church service, Polly ran away from home. Moses' grief-stricken wife, for whom "work was the only antidote she knew,"[5] was overcome with the loss of Polly and took to her bed. When the doctor visited, he recognized in Sarah's body all the worn farm women's bodies he had ever been helpless to save, and he angrily told her husband, "You can't work humans like animals, Mose."[6] Sarah died shortly thereafter, and Moses scheduled her funeral for a Sunday, so he would not lose a work day for harvesting mint.

When they went to Goshen to sell the mint oil, Neri, the son most like his father, noticed how "dumb Dutch" Moses appeared negotiating with the Chicago peppermint broker, and after being taunted by "English" boys, he smoldered with a shame that provoked him to steal his father's money and run off to "the world":

> Making fun of him again as if he were some queer animal to be stared at. A fierce resentment rose in him chokingly. It was his clothes, his hair, having to ride in a buggy—being Amish that kept him apart, kept him in a world he hated. The sound of the laughter that followed him bit mortifyingly into his being, cankered his thoughts.[7]

Next morning, when Moses discovered he had lost both his money and his son, he raged out onto his land. Under a scorching sun, he strode through the fields, furiously husking corn for hours, hands bleeding, "tearing, rending, ripping . . . spending his rage."[8] At last, dehydrated and overwrought, "his whole being bursting aflame,"[9] Moses fell dead—having completed a transformation from angry god to devil.

Aside from the helpless, wife and children, the most sympathetic character in the novel is Moses's bachelor brother, Ezra, who also lived and worked on the Bontrager farm. Early in the book readers learn that Ezra committed an unmentionable sin in his youth, from which Moses saved him. Ezra's transgression is not disclosed until the end of the story when he crept into Polly's bedroom to comfort her on the eve of her shunning. As a young man, Ezra had wanted to be a traveling performer. He remembered, "Sing, all I want for to do was to sing still. I dreamed yet that over the hull of the world I should go just singing fur folks."[10] He kept his desire secret and saved his money until one Saturday night a traveling opera company came to Goshen, and he could not resist: "Somethin' riz in me too strong for to fight and I knew I should stay for to hear it. . . . Such music, I hear, it wondered me iffen the angels in heaven could bettern them. Sometimes a workin' in the fields it seems liken I kin hear them yet."[11]

After the performance, Ezra met one of the actresses backstage and confessed his desire. She invited him into her dressing room, where he sang all that he knew—Amish slow hymns—and she was so taken with his talent that she said, "The world will someday come to hear you sing. You must come with us to learn."[12] At that moment, Moses burst into the dressing room, calling the woman a "scarlet Jezebel." He took his brother home, prayed over him all night, and pressured him to confess his sin the next morning in church.[13] After services, the older people regarded Ezra as if he had "the Devil's blood" and the young people laughed at the foolishness of "an Amishman wantin' fur to sing."[14] Concluding his story, Ezra gave Polly a purse of his savings to help her if she decided to leave the community. However, he advised her to count the cost of leaving family and home, "only with such folks strange in our ways you will have to live yet . . . if with loneliness still in your heart, she is heavy, it won't do no good, whatever."[15]

Ezra inherited his brother's farm and children after Moses' dramatic demise in the cornfield. In the novel's final scene, the children freely engaged in the activities they were denied during their father's lifetime: Christian painting a picture; Jacob reading a book that he had kept hidden since the last day of school; and on the porch, Rebecca whispering with her "Pinky" beau about plans to marry and visit Polly and her new husband. Ezra, taking this all in, suddenly became burdened with a liberal epiphany:

> If he could only point out, show them how to keep from making the mistakes he had made; warn them not to let their lives be cluttered with little petty things losing the vision of the whole; teach them to regard as sacred the right of another's dreams; give to them out of his years a feeling of tolerance, of understanding. Anxiously, humbly, he longed to offer the little he had learned so that they might go on from there. . . . [but] His words belonged to age and even now the past was gone, scattering futilely like straw in the wind before the rising future.[16]

A modern American novel in its alignment with progress and emphasis on honoring the pursuit of the individual's dream, *Straw in the Wind* heralded the destruction of old ways ordered by religion and tradition. The death of the patriarch Moses unleashed the redemptive powers of the arts, education, religious tolerance, love, and hope for a brighter future. In light of his own beliefs and experience, it is almost inconceivable that Yoder would not identify with this book. Yet if he saw himself in the character of Ezra, the bachelor uncle who heard opera as "songs of heaven" that "lifted [him] into the realm of ecstasy," as young Yoder had once been transported outside a country singing school, he did not acknowledge this. If he heard in Ezra's voice echoes of his own desire to sing for "the world" or traces of his own pleas for religious tolerance and ecumenicity, he did not say so. Looking back on his life, Ezra wondered, as Yoder must have once wondered, "Iffen the Lord I couldn't have served with singin' as well as farmin'."[17]

Yoder could have recognized his brother, Levi, in the rebellious Neri; or seen in the aging Moses an exaggerated image of Bishop Shem, who forbade Rosanna to continue schooling to become a teacher. In the progressive "Pinkie" group did Yoder see the church house Amish congregation he joined as a young man? In the "flesh wasting" illness of Sarah, did he recall his own mother's fatigue and tuberculosis, or in the gesture of the sensitive, artistic Christian slipping pansies under his dead mother's hand, did he see himself? If Yoder found any parallels between the book and his own experiences, he did not admit them—and perhaps he did not even recognize them. Instead, he attacked *Straw in the Wind* as an inauthentic and unfair representation of the Amish people.

In 1938, he sent a review to *The Middlebury Independent* of Middlebury, Indiana, where the novel was set. Because the paper previously had published criticism by the local Amish bishop, the editor declined to print Yoder's piece, but a copy remains among his papers, a revealing record of his encounter with this book.[18] With a dubious assertion of his own authenticity, Yoder began by claiming his right to comment on the subject: "being Amish born, raised Amish and still belong to the Amish Church, I wish to protest against the many misrepresentations in that novel." This birthright claim would later serve as the justification for much of Yoder's work with Amish material. Like contemporary makers of anything from pickle relish to picnic tables who announce that their products are "Amish made," Yoder depended on his background to authenticate his work in both literature and music, attempting to prove the accuracy of his cultural representations by asserting the verity of his own identity.

His review attempted to discredit Dobson's novel as a misrepresentation of Amish life and culture. Primarily, he objected to the figure of Moses Bontrager; for a bishop "to fly into a rage and thunder at his people is just out of the question," he wrote. "The Bishop is elected by lot, hence the Amish people feel that he is the direct servant of God, clothed with authority, so the Bishop does not need to use coercion, the people follow his leading willingly." Moreover, he added that the Amish are a "quiet people" who value self-control and a "Godly demeanor," and bishops are expected to exemplify these virtues. When they offer reproof, it is in a spirit of "sympathy, charity, and even sorrow." Although Yoder did admit that bishops "sometimes are strong, thrifty men," he could not imagine one dying of rage over lost income. In addition, he objected to the dramatic scene of Polly's excommunication in which "one would think that Amish Bishops are nothing short of madmen."[19]

Among the book's many factual errors, he cited the administration of an oath in a church service and the selection of children's mates by Amish parents—admitting that "one fundamental desire on the part of the parents [is] that they marry someone in the church." He refuted the funeral scene, where women wailed and ministers tried to "out do" each other in their preaching. He was most offended by the tortured English dialect spoken by the Amish characters in the novel. He explained that the usual household language is Pennsylvania German and, although English word-order may become confused because of translation, "the awkward conglomeration used in that book is not spoken by the Amish nor by anybody else." He concluded that "many other fallacies could easily be pointed out," and that if the Amish were not a "non-resistant people" Ruth Dobson might be asked to write a public apology or "appear on a charge of libel."[20]

Yoder and others were especially annoyed that *Straw in the Wind* received national praise. Dobson won the 1936 Hopwood Prize from the University of Michigan, which granted a purse of $1,500 and publication of the book with Dodd Meade and Company of New York. By the end of its first year, the book was into a fourth printing, and reviewers repeatedly recommended it as a reliable representation of Amish culture. R. C. Feld in a 1937 *Books* review wrote, "As a fictionalized study of the manners and customs and speech of a little known religious sect, it is worthy of attention: as a novel it is weak." That same year, Stanley Young wrote in the *New York Times*, "Miss Dobson . . . appears to have full knowledge of this strange, rural cranny of American life."

Both of these comments were cited with frustration by Mennonite critic Elizabeth Horsch Bender in her 1945 essay on local color writing. Because Ruth Dobson grew up on the edge of an Amish settlement, and because she described actual locations, the "unwary reader" would also trust her account of the culture, Bender concluded. Although she granted that descriptions of houses and dress are accurate, the brunt of her critique was similar to Yoder's. In an insightful analysis of cultural stereotyping, she observed that Dobson perverted Amish virtues into vices: the patriarchal discipline of the church was represented as despotism; love of land was selfish obsession; and a commitment to family solidarity became absolute control of one's children. Bender's concern was that these distortions would taint public perceptions of the Amish in America—an important issue amid World War II and on the eve of conflicts between Amish communities and public school consolidation.[21]

Straw in the Wind was not the only popular novel that portrayed Amish or Mennonite people in exaggerated and negative ways. Following similar kinds of regional and dialect writing about New England, the South, the Midwest, and California, stories featuring Pennsylvania Germans became especially popular during the first quarter of the twentieth century. Chief among these were the works of Helen R. Martin, who began publishing short stories featuring Mennonite and Amish characters in *McClures Magazine* in 1902. Among her numerous novels about plain people were *Tillie A Mennonite Maid* (1904), *Sabina A Story of the Amish* (1905), *Martha of the Mennonite Country* (1915), and *Maggie of Virginsburg* (1918).

Tillie was particularly successful; by mid-century it had gone into twenty printings, inspired both a play and silent film, and made the term *Tillie* an epithet in Dutch country. During the 1970s, a Mennonite girl riding a public school bus in Lancaster County was called "Tillie" as empty juice cartons were hurled at her head covering, but neither she nor the bullies had any idea where the name originated or what it meant beyond a negative reference to her religious and ethnic background.[22] Earl Robacker succinctly captured the stereotype created by the character and context of *Tillie*:

> public schools capable of teaching nothing and the . . . children incapable of being taught, the grasping obstinate father; the equally heavy, loutish suitor; the sodden resigned mother or stepmother; and the attractive young girl who in no time at all rises superior to her surroundings and makes a good marriage to an attractive outsider, usually a New Englander.[23]

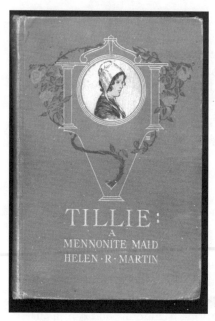

4.1 *First published in 1904,* Tillie: A Mennonite Maid *was Helen R. Martin's most successful novel.*

In Martin's novels, Amish and Mennonite people have hideous names, enact buffoonish behaviors, and speak an almost indecipherable dialect. Contemporary with black-face minstrelsy, local color writing presented exaggerated images of an American subculture that readers believed to be authentic. The presentation of amusing and inferior groups thus established American norms and consolidated the culture and language of the white nation. A feminist and socialist-tending pacifist who grew up in Lancaster County near Amish and Mennonite people, Martin saw in their traditional culture and language impediments to social and political progress, and she found even their stereotyped virtues—cleanliness, honesty, thrift—to be repellent. She said, "I cannot idealize them because they are illiterate, they rationalize, they take things literally."[24] In a 1931 interview, she elaborated:

There really does seem to be a bovine dullness about the Pennsylvania Dutch equaled only (in my experience of the human family) by the rural inhabitants of some remote localities in England. It is their heavy, unceasing toil, the deadening sameness of their daily routine, the narrowness of their religious creeds, the absence among them of all lightness and frivolity, that makes them so dull. . . . Even in the matter of their meals they seem to have no imagination, very often serving the same dishes at breakfast that they had at supper the night before. . . . Their contentment in the monotony of their lives, their lack of all craving for diversion or excitement, has always seemed to me stupid rather than commendable. They are by nature conservative, unprogressive, stolid. Their idea of a woman's place in the economy of the universe is little better than a Chinaman's. They have no conception of her apart from her function of breeding and of making men comfortable in their homes.[25]

Significantly comparing the Pennsylvania German to the non-European "Chinaman," Martin captured the "dumb Dutch" stereotype of both plain and worldly speakers of Pennsylvania German at this time. In 1942, Earl Robacker noted that almost from their arrival, Swiss and German immigrants were misnamed "Dutch" (Deutsch) by English speakers in Pennsylvania and regarded with "differentness" mostly understood in terms of language, as remains true of the Amish today. He wrote, "At no time do they seem to be regarded simply as *people*, but always as a people apart and singled out for comment. Their use of a foreign language in itself would almost automatically create such a condition."[26] Amish plain dress and their refusal to adopt technology or embrace higher education only intensified this sense of "differentness" that came to mean "backwardness" in early twentieth-century imagination.

"Are they 'Dumb Dutch'?" This is one heading in Ammon Monroe Aurand's *Little Known Facts about The Amish and the Mennonites*, a pamphlet sold along the Pennsylvania Turnpike and at other tourist sites for several decades beginning in the 1930s. Despite the representations of chubby, juvenile Dutchmen and women on the booklet's cover, the author contended that these people are not ignorant: they *can* be taught to read and write, though they are not generally as educated as "we" are. For example, he reported that "there is a differ-

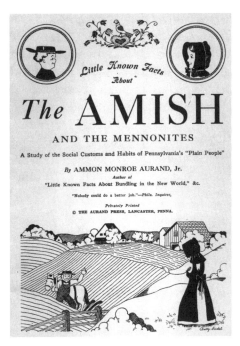

4.2 *Some Aurand publications are still available for purchase in Pennsylvania Dutch tourist regions.*

ence of opinion among some of these people as to the shape of the earth—whether it is round or flat," but he conceded, "conditions like this confronted even the most learned men up until the time of Columbus."[27]

In part of the pamphlet dealing with Yoder's home in the "back-sections" of Mifflin County titled, "Children Sometimes Backward," Aurand noted that "conditions among these people sometimes really require sympathy" because the shy youngsters scamper to hide behind corn-shocks at the sight of strange "English" visitors.[28] Yet, he stressed their European origins, noting that it is possible to communicate in "plain, simple, Pennsylvania 'Dutch'" with "German-born students, scholars and professors; Jews born in Germany, Romania, Latvia and elsewhere; Austrians, whether of the pre-war or post-war period."[29]

It is no accident that the Amish and Mennonites at this time were regarded as "backward" and the intellectual contemporaries of Christopher Columbus, creatures who were unevolved, uneducated, and possibly uneducable. In a survey of European society's perceptions of outsiders, cultural theorist Bernard McGrane has observed that nineteenth-century anthropologists regarded the difference of others as *historical* difference, then promptly transformed history into a narrative of progressive evolution.[30] Thus, non-Europeans were seen as living fossils from a previous point in the development of their European superiors. Although Amish people share a European heritage with their Anglo neighbors, their traditional, religious communities bluntly resisted all that was implied by American notions of progress during the early twentieth century: innovation, education, individuality as expressed in capitalism and the pursuit of one's "dream" and—paradoxically—cultural assimilation and conformity, as symbolized by the "melting pot."

At times, even Yoder could not refrain from considering the Amish "backward" in theology and culture, as he grew impatient waiting for them to embrace progress as he had. In a story still told in Big Valley, he appeared at an Amish farm during a particularly intense onslaught of army worms, pests that can strip the leaves from a field of cornstalks in a forenoon. Yoder, who corresponded with J. I. Rodale, founder of Rodale Press in Emmaus, Pennsylvania, about the virtues of organic farming, aimed to sell the farmer a sonic device that emitted inaudible waves to deter the worms. The Amish man laughed at the idea, and an exasperated Yoder is said to have muttered, "Let these Dutchmen eat army worms all winter if they're too stubborn to try something new!"[31]

Herein lies the conflict of the exceptional insider who encounters outsiders' negative representations of his own group. The images may, in fact, express some of the frustrations that he feels himself, but how can he admit this and also defend the group without becoming deeply divided? If Yoder were to have identified with the musical ambitions of Ezra, for instance, he would have had to make concessions to the libelous author of *Straw in the Wind*.

Similarly, if Elizabeth Horsch Bender were to have noticed the feminist intent in many local color novels—that the females portrayed in *Straw in the Wind* and Martin's books overcame the domination of patriarchs who cast them as either virtuous servants or harlot Jezebels—she may have had to divide her concern between writing about public representations of her own group and considering the position of its women. (Bender was both the daughter of the anti-modernist Mennonite patriarch John Horsch and wife of European-trained Mennonite scholar and churchman, H. S. Bender, whose interpretation of Anabaptist history constructed an American Mennonite identity during the 1940s.) By the time she encountered the local color novels, Bender had written a Master's thesis on portrayals of Anabaptists in German literature and an essay on Mennonite characters in a Swiss novel; her agenda was set.[32] Nevertheless, she, and certainly Yoder, must have felt considerable dissonance between a desire to protect the group and the need to clear a place for their own work and interests. In the all-or-nothing economy of community loyalty, however, it would have been difficult to imagine any other alternative.

Helen Martin sensed this ambivalence, and with no sympathy noted that her harshest critics were those Pennsylvania Germans who had risen above their humble backgrounds:

> My stories of the Pennsylvania Dutch have earned for me the bitterest resentment—not of the people of whom I write, for they do not read what I write; they do not read anything; but I have earned the resentment of those who had sufficient brains and forcefulness to have worked themselves free of the stultifying conditions of their farm life into a broader, fuller existence; and some of these people, full of loving sentiment for the home of their youth, for the quaint customs of their forbears, and even for the religions which they have discarded, are wounded by my perfectly accurate pictures.[33]

Rosanna as Resistance

Although he fit Martin's description in most regards, Yoder responded to her "accurate pictures" with more than criticism. "I resented that book deeply and determined then to carry out a long considered project—writing a book myself," he wrote concerning *Straw in the Wind*.[34] A great-niece recalled that Yoder also described *Tillie a Mennonite Maid* as a "slur on plain people" around this time, and cited it as the motivation for his writing.[35] During the late 1930s, Yoder wrote *Rosanna of the Amish* and hired the Mennonite Publishing House to print it through his own Yoder Publishing Company, whereby he assumed responsibility for editing and distribution, and also retained control of the book's copyright and profits. He managed this all despite a characteristically busy schedule. In 1936-37, he made 179 high school visits between November and March, and within two weeks during spring 1937 was the featured speaker at eleven high school commencement ceremonies scattered across Pennsylvania. Helen R. Martin died in June 1939, around the time that Yoder's book went to press.

Rosanna of the Amish is an example of "autoethnography," a term coined by Mary Louise Pratt to name those works of literature in which people present themselves in response to representations that others have made of them.[36] An Amish autoethnography is extraordinary because Amish people are unlikely to speak publicly on their own behalf, much less publish a work of literature for that purpose. Like his "Irish" that flared in self-defense when a schoolmate called him "Dutch" and pulled his hair, Yoder executed this project in a non-Amish spirit, informed by his "worldly" experience—education and early ethnographic work under the influence of M. G. Brumbaugh at Juniata College, affiliation with the learned men of the Teachers' Institutes, and previous experience publishing songsters. Yet, Yoder constantly claimed that his Amish background and his offense on behalf of that community had qualified and provoked him to write.

The title *Rosanna of the Amish* directly refers to Helen R. Martin's popular books, *Sabina a Story of the Amish* and *Maggie of Virginsburg*, and as if responding to challenges in a debate, Yoder countered the features of the local color novels point by point. To the strange dialects that Dobson and Martin concocted to represent the dialect's languages interface between German and English, Yoder responded by inserting into his informal but fluid English text, actual phrases of Pennsylvania German. Often, but not always, he supplied an English gloss in parentheses, but sometimes the English word appeared first, with Pennsylvania German serving as gloss. Such instances represented Yoder's two-language reality and both enact and bridge the gaps in meaning that always exist in cross-cultural writing. He thus signaled linguistic and cultural difference and stressed the significance of language in sustaining distinctiveness: there are names for some ideas or things that can not be translated.

By telling a story—the story of his mother's life and, within it the narrative of his own childhood—Yoder confronted and complicated the negative characters who populated local color novels and shaped common conceptions of plain people. At the same time, he expressed his and his mother's marginal positions in relation to the prohibitions and traditions of Amish culture. Among the Pennsylvania German types that Yoder addressed were those of the despotic male leader; the working drudge; and the "dumb Dutchman."

Like all conservative expressions of the Judeo-Christian tradition, Amish culture is patriarchal, and Yoder portrayed this clearly without turning the patriarchs into monsters. He was least sympathetic toward Rosanna's foster father, Bishop Shem, who represented the conservative side of church schism. Shem is remembered most for preventing Rosanna from becoming a teacher, a story that Yoder repeated at least six times in his memoirs. Although he acknowledged Shem's need to shore up his authority in the community, Yoder depicted the bishop as neither cruel nor deranged like Dobson's Bishop Moses Bontrager. When he learned of Rosanna's plans, Shem said only, "So?" and "feeling the full responsibility of the church on his shoulders," later explained to her foster mother that he could not preach against worldly wisdom and allow a member of his household to study to become a teacher.[37]

When she learned of this, Shem sensed Rosanna's disappointment and arranged for her to attend the traveling circus with her half-sister. Moreover, Little Crist, a preacher in the church, was a loving and considerate father and husband who "winked at" his sons' minor infractions of the *Ordnung*. Reflecting on a farmer who did not come promptly for dinner when his wife called him in from the fields, Crist said, "I saw then how wrong it is for men to treat their wives that way. I made up my mind then that I would never treat my wife that way, if I ever had one."[38]

Yoder rendered gender inequities in the community, pointing out that both Crist and Rosanna were strong singers, but because of her sex she was permitted to lead singing only at weddings; nor did she have a public voice in the community, whereas her husband was a preacher. Yet both Elizabeth and Rosanna were portrayed as valuable family members, capable managers of household affairs and small market enterprises, at times working in the fields beside the men, threshing and making hay.

Concerning the view that Amish people are overly driven to work, Yoder saw no need to counter the images of toil and thrift that have shaped perceptions of the Amish and Mennonites since their arrival in the New World. Benjamin Franklin regarded with disgust the frugal, German-speaking settlers that William Penn had invited to colonial Pennsylvania, who "under-live and are thereby enabled to under-work and under-sell the English."[39] Reflecting on his own childhood, Yoder wrote in *Rosanna of the Amish*, "The one great virtue in Amish training is learning to work."[40] Amish children may learn early to work and they work hard, Yoder stressed, but they are not mules; labor is respected and experienced as both joyful and creative, and idleness can only lead to evil. When a neighbor asked Rosanna if she ever found her life "awful hard work," she replied,

> And this is not hard work. With a new house and barn, a sober, industrious husband, new things in the house, beautiful horses to work and drive, and a chance to buy our farm when we wish, feeding chickens and pigs and making butter and cooking are not hard work,—it's fun and pleasure and enjoyment![41]

Amish people refuse to adopt labor-saving technologies because these devices devalue or eliminate the tasks that bind individuals in constructive relationships with family and community. The most menial labor is not despised, all who work efficiently and well are esteemed, and Yoder observed, "girls serving as housemaids were not looked down on in any way among the Amish, but were on the same level socially as the rest of the family."[42]

Addressing Amish resistance to higher education and the "dumb Dutch" type may have been Yoder's most difficult point, for although he believed that learning was inherently good and essential, he publicly supported Amish avoidance of higher education. Whereas he deeply resented the portrayal of the Amish Bishop Bontrager who "hates public education laws," Yoder defended Mifflin County Amish men who were fined and imprisoned for refusing to let their children attend public high school in 1950—and Yoder even visited the men and sang with them in the Mifflin County jail.

In a letter congratulating Walter Annenberg on his editorial, "Don't Persecute the Amish," published in the *Philadelphia Inquirer* at that time, Yoder wrote, "So long as they maintain their high quality of citizenship and support the government financially, would it not be reasonable for our legislature to grant them the right to maintain their peaceable way of life?"[43]

The same day, he sent a letter to Dr. Francis Haas, state superintendent of schools whom Yoder knew through his teacher institute work, articulating his ambivalence on the issue more fully and expressing his hope that the Amish would one day change:

> As you well know, Dr. Haas, I am not in full accord with their doctrine, but since they are otherwise quiet, law abiding, asking nothing from the government, not even accepting farm subsidies, I feel that probably the legislature, and the Educational Department could work out a plan which would allow them to live their religious way of life until such time that they can conscientiously espouse more fully the cause of education.[44]

In *Rosanna* it is evident that Yoder identified with his mother's desire to become a teacher, and her disappointment is portrayed with tenderness. When she learned that her older sister, Margaret, attended St. Mary's Academy for three years and worked as assistant librarian there, Rosanna told her brother, then visiting from Philadelphia, "'Momly and I planned that I would be a teacher, but later we thought best to change'. . . with a touch of pathos in her voice."[45] Likewise, Yoder chronicled his own complicated route to become a teacher, then earn an undergraduate degree after his thirtieth birthday, and his efforts to negotiate a relationship with the community after an Amish deacon had advised him against going to normal school.

Although he presented Amish characters who were "quick," shrewd, and full of practical knowledge, he also portrayed a world that forbade higher education, attributing this resistance to a biblically based avoidance of "worldly wisdom" and a desire to keep the community whole. Cultural assimilation is a great threat to a group that defines itself in opposition to dominant society, and so higher education is associated with danger and loss. Despite his best efforts to the contrary, Yoder's biography confirms the fear that Amish children who go away to school will not return and will be lost to the church of their parents.

TRUTHFUL AND TEXT WORTHY

It is doubtful that Yoder was conscious of the ways that he used the writing of *Rosanna of the Amish* to confront and negotiate between public perceptions of the Amish and his own ambivalent feelings. He described his task primarily as truth telling, an act of service to the community, rather than as a process of self-discovery or cultural production. As the emphasis below shows, his introduction to the book is riddled with claims pertaining to authenticity and accuracy—claims that are dubious in light of recent research into Rosanna's family history:

> The author begs to explain that he was prompted and inspired to write this present volume, ROSANNA OF THE AMISH, by the *fact* that several writers with seemingly *vivid imaginations* and apparently *little regard for the facts* have written books about the Amish and have missed almost entirely the cardinal virtues of this people. Some of them have *exaggerated* a certain characteristic out of all proportion and have made even a virtue look ridiculous. Their object seemed to be to write an *unusual story* rather than to adhere to the *truth*.
>
> Having been born of Amish parents and having grown to manhood as an Amish boy, the author knows the Amish people intimately, in *fact*, is one of them, and knows their customs and practices socially, economically, and religiously in minute detail.
>
> All the episodes in ROSANNA OF THE AMISH are *based on fact*. Every name in the book is the *real* name of the person mentioned, and the story is the *actual* life story of Rosanna. Instead of holding the Amish, a very devout people, up to ridicule as some writers apparently delight to do, the author desires *to tell the truth* about them, setting forth their virtues, and they have many, as well as their peculiarities. *The fact* is that what seems like a peculiarity to the outsider becomes a virtue when one's experience enables him to understand the underlying motives and principles.[46]

A review by a scholar without ties to Amish or Mennonite culture pursued this point, seeing a relationship between Yoder's literary work and the Amish reputation for honesty in business and every day life:

One of the tenets of the Amish religion is a wholesome regard for the truth, a characteristic so widely recognized in Pennsylvania that written . . . contracts among the Amish are all but unknown: an Amish man's word has been proved to be as good as his bond. Something of this quality of integrity is to be found in Yoder's book. . . . Better than any fictional work has done, the book gives an inside account of Amish life.[47]

If the Amish ethic of honesty eliminates the need for writing in business dealings, the expectation for truthfulness in published texts is all the greater. Andrea Fishman, in a contemporary study of literacy in this group, concluded that Amish culture always grants authority to texts, beginning with the biblical text, and expects that "a writer is responsible for the accuracy of and understanding derived from his text, so writers must and do tell only the truth as they know it."[48] If Yoder also brought this expectation to published texts, it would account for his outrage at the local color novels as well as his insensitivity to erroneous portrayals in the non-textual minstrel performances—beyond the obvious possibility that he may have been less sensitive to representations of minority people outside his own group.

The textworthy expectation assumes a responsible, sincere, and forthright relationship between writers and readers and a fundamentalist view of language. From its beginning, Anabaptism was predicated on literal readings of Scripture and simple confessions of faith. One of its founding doctrines was a refusal to take oaths of loyalty to the government because every word uttered by a believer must be true and binding. The great work of Mennonite literature, *Martyrs Mirror*, is always read as factual: "compiled from various authentic chronicles, memorials, and testimonies," its front dust jacket claims.

Until the latter half of the twentieth century, writings by Amish and Mennonite authors in Pennsylvania were largely historical or devotional; only rarely and recently has fiction appeared. So in 1902 when Helen R. Martin's "The Discipling of Mathias" appeared in *McClures Magazine*, she was visited by a Mennonite minister who intended to find the story's protagonist and restore him to right fellowship. When Martin explained that the character did not exist, that she had simply invented the story, the minister was puzzled and wondered why she would do such a thing. She told him that she got paid to write fiction, and the minister replied, "So, then, you write lies for lucre!"[49]

Yoder's commitment to truth-telling was noted by Goshen College professor John Umble, who also grew up in a Pennsylvania Amish home and who was one of the Elkhart Institute athletes under Yoder's charge in 1901. In a review published shortly after *Rosanna* appeared, Umble observed that the book is not fiction "in any commonly accepted definition of that term," but a hybrid of biography, history, and autobiography. He pointed out that despite its virtues, Yoder's method seemed to have a distinct disadvantage in that it "prevents the author from entire frankness in the presentation of unpleasant details."[50] Determined to rescue Amish people from ridicule but also committed to truthfulness, Yoder simply omitted unflattering aspects of the culture.

Umble failed to name the "unpleasant details" he found missing in Yoder's book, but it is significant that Yoder identified the only fictitious part of *Rosanna* in the preface: the name "Simeon Rhiel," a member of Crist and Rosanna's congregation who asked to be placed under the ban, or congregational discipline, for telling lies. Yoder's only invention deals with the practice of shunning, an aspect of the culture that is so important that it deserved mention, even in a work created to counter negative perceptions of the Amish.

As a corrective, Yoder's pastorale may have seemed as exaggerated in a positive sense as the local color novels were negative. His glowing representations were noticed and mocked by some, such as the reviewer in *The Sentinel*, a Lewistown newspaper published near Big Valley:

> A story of Never, Never Land situated in a Valley of Paradise, wherein the characters are either good angels or saints, never being provoked to anger or unwise words or acts; a novel without a villain, but with heroes and heroines galore; a Big Valley heaven without a Satan; a world wherein every human dream comes true and where self praise and laudation of one's neighbors goes on unceasingly—that is "Rosanna of the Amish" as envisaged by Rosanna's son Joseph. . . . Not much is missing from the book except the well-known villain. All the characters are sanctified beyond measure, even including Joseph who throws in some good words for himself—whole pages as a matter of fact.[51]

Despite what may now seem to be critical omissions or the overly sweet fruits of nostalgia, Yoder received numerous letters from individual readers, pointedly praising the accuracy of *Rosanna* in contrast to the

Dobson and Martin books. One Pennsylvania couple wrote, "We had both read the book *Tillie the Mennonite Maid* which we immediately stamped as an untrue picture of Amish life, customs, intelligence, and religion as we knew it in the Big Valley. . . . Therefore, we recognized in your book a true and authentic portrayal which we could accept completely." Another reader, referring to a current magazine article about Pennsylvania plain sects, wrote, "Your 'Rosanna' certainly makes that *Saturday Evening Post* author look silly. The unfortunate woman has the Amish, Quakers, and Mennonites confused." Closer to home, a Big Valley Amish man expressed the appreciation that some Amish and Mennonite readers felt for the truthfulness of Yoder's representation:

> I must say it is the only book about the Amish that gives the plain honest truth without any unjust criticism and without undue praise about the Amish that I have ever read. . . . You must have been a long time gathering up the facts and putting them in book form but it is surely taking well around here. . . . I have not found anything in all the book that is unfair to the Amish folks but feel that it should inspire us to adhere more closely to the plain honest faith of our Amish Fathers.[52]

The importance of truth-telling in this man's world is expressed by the repetition of the redundant phrases "plain honest truth" and "plain honest faith." A book, which for the first time represented the Amish in their own terms, touched both worldly and plain readers. One elderly Amish man who had migrated to a western state said with feeling, "It is all so true to life that it makes me homesick for Pennsylvania."[53]

In light of the popular but erroneous portrayals of the Amish people, *Rosanna of the Amish* was welcomed by many as long overdue, and the authenticity of the story was rarely questioned except by those who were very close to Crist and Rosanna. For them, the book was suspect because it did not meet their standards of accuracy and text-worthiness. Two individuals have said that Abraham S. Yoder, an Amish farmer, German school teacher and friend of Yoder's, said to him, "It's a pretty good book, but too bad you didn't write the truth!" The daughter of one of Crist and Rosanna's hired girls said her mother questioned many details in the book—especially Rosanna's zeal as a worker, and she is said to have asked, "You don't keep that book with our *good* books, do you?"

Rosanna of the Amish

and

Amische Lieder

THE YODER PUBLISHING CO.

HUNTINGDON, PENNA.

Nov. 2, 1950.

Dear John Andrew:
                    The very first printing of Amish Traditions
has just come off press and has just now arrived. Since I must
go to Bucks County to attend a funeral tomorrow, I am sending
the very first copy to go out to a REVIEWER.
     I want you first of all to review this book as a free
christian gentleman, and give me that opinion, and then if you do
not wish to have that opinion made public I will keep it secret,
but I want to know your candid opinion. I know I do not coincide everywhere with Mennonite doctrine, but I am not here to advocate, Mennonite, Amish, Dunkard or any other doctrine. I am
after the TRUTH in religion as set forth by Jesus and Paul, and
where they differ, and the DO differ somewhat, I accept the teaching of Jesus.
     I am positive that the Old Order Amish are building on the
wrong thing, Forms, Ordnung. I have no motive in view but to enlighten them. I know I shall be abused for writing this book. I
have already received a few abusive letters from Old Order Amish
Bishops, but I have a had a tremendous urge inwardly to write this
book, so after years of thought, Here's the book.
     This is a review copy, and there is no charge.
     Hoping you will have time soon to review it, and will send
me your review or reviews. If your opinion or review is such that
it will give my book a favorable comment, I will use it in papers
that might be concerned. And if any church refuses to sell or ad-
vertise this book, I think Gal. V. 1 - 6 will "put them on the spot!
     Thanking you for being interested in Traditions, I am,
                         Most cordially yours,
                            J. W. Yoder.

Ausbund

4.3 *J. W. Yoder's stationery decorated with Amish illustrations from his books,
1950.*

The authenticity of the book's "Amish-born" author remained even less certain—although in letters promoting it, Yoder repeatedly based claims of authority on his being Amish, "one of them," who "knows their customs and practices socially, economically, and religiously in minute detail." His personal stationery from the 1940s and 1950s was decorated with icon-like images derived from George Daubenspeck's illustrations for *Rosanna of the Amish*—figures of Rosanna and Crist—and a rendering of an old leather-bound edition of the *Ausbund*. Yet Yoder's claim of an Amish identity was dismissed by most Amish people. Levi J. Stutzman, in a letter to the *Budget*, the national Amish newspaper, confessed to having never read anything written by J. W. Yoder, but he expressed perplexity at Yoder's assertion of Amish identity:

> What I could not figure out was his picture in the *Budget* as author of the book he was advertising, and the next issue coming out with the statement that he was an Amishman, which did not make sense to me. For the simple reason that having your picture taken is against any sincere Amishman's religion, and much less would he have it put in a public paper.

Stutzman reminded his readers that they need not believe everything they read—challenging their expectations of print. Skirting the question of Yoder's authenticity, he pointed to a more trustworthy book: "if we are weak and inclined to believe all we read, we'd better stick to the one book which is the truth itself and that is the Bible."[54]

If being an authentic member of the community meant conforming to the norms of its *Ordnung* and carrying the marks of membership visibly on his body, Yoder had strayed far from his Amish roots. A Big Valley woman who remembered him well asked, "Why did he say he was Amish? He wasn't Amish. He didn't dress like us or live like us." Yet Yoder staked his claim of authenticity on the fact that he retained membership in what was called a "Church House Amish" group when he joined it at the age of sixteen.

More significantly, he carried memories of growing up in an Amish home, and he drew on a cultural heritage that for the rest of his life shaped his perceptions and sense of self—even though he had "gone to the world." The culture of his childhood was so deeply ingrained that it seemed impossible to stop being Amish, even as his life contained many other kinds of knowledge, drawn from experiences among other communities. Nevertheless, Amish culture is so communally constituted and linked to material customs and a commitment to embodying "the visible church in the world" that most Amish people could no longer count him as "one of them."

Amische Lieder

Around the time that *Rosanna of the Amish* was being printed in Scottdale, Yoder was considering a project that he had begun when he first studied music and learned the principles of composition at Juniata College. For nearly thirty years, he had felt torn between a belief that he could save the traditional slow tunes from gradual disintegration and his knowledge that the Amish would not accept musical notation. He knew very well that an endeavor to write and publish the tunes would consume time and money, and that such a book would probably only be of interest to a handful of people. In his words, "It looked like a pretty big job, and financially unsound. . . . I pondered wavering between duty and necessity on one hand and fear of losing both my work and my investment on the other hand. But I could not get rid of the urge to do this work, regardless."[55] Thus motivated, Yoder finally committed himself to the preservation of Amish tunes through musical notation.

He believed that variations in the performance of slow songs from community to community proved that the Amish tunes would be *lost* if the tools of pen and paper or printing press did not remove them from the world of human memory and fix them in note form on paper. For him, the gradual changes that are inevitable in oral tradition represented the erosion of a pure original, and he sought to make the tunes standard. Having survived for fourteen or fifteen generations, the songs suddenly seemed endangered, and he failed to see that the *means* of retaining tunes by rote was an essential part of the Amish musical tradition.

Perhaps his sense of urgency about the impending loss of the slow tunes was linked to a sense that the distinct Amish ethos was slipping away *for him*. Literacy caused him to perceive the impermanence of the oral text; for those who lived with the oral tradition, however, the hymns did not seem to be especially endangered. The Amish are one of many traditional cultures that recognize the value of keeping some information "by heart," even when writing is available. This belief was expressed by Plato when Socrates warned Phaedrus that those who rely on writing are bound to lose their memories. Assuming that they can always find the information in a book, he predicted, they will depend on "external signs instead of on their own internal resources."[56] Writing Amish tunes would eliminate the need for *Vorsingers* and therefore ensure that the tunes would become lost in their cultural context. Moreover, the Amish must have observed that among their Amish Mennonite neighbors the admission of musical notation, part-singing, and "fast" tunes eventually replaced the singing of melismatic "slow" songs altogether.

In 1939 Yoder decided to ask the *Vorsingers* whether they would co-operate with his project, wagering with fate: "If they agreed to sing for me, I was in for it; if they refused, I was free and my imagined duty and obligation was satisfied, and groundless."[57] When he approached Ben Byler, a progressive and gifted singer, he presented the problem in persuasive terms: the hymns would soon be lost if he did not agree to sing for him. Byler agreed to help with Yoder's project. Other song leaders in the church—John Y. Peachey, Jacob. E. Kanagey, Henry M. Zook, Joseph Sharp, Samuel H. Peachey, and Kore Peachey—also participated, and their names are recorded in *Amische Lieder* with the songs they lined out for Yoder to write. It took two years for Yoder to gather the tunes in the manner that he had previously worked with his father. With his retirement from Juniata in 1941, he devoted himself almost exclusively to working on *Amische Lieder* and promoting *Rosanna of the Amish*.

In addition to thirty-three slow tunes (*Langsame Weise*), he collected fifteen wedding songs (*Hochzeit Lieder*), of which four are traditionally sung during the marriage service and eleven are sung throughout the afternoon and into the evening of the wedding banquet. As well, he included sixteen fast tunes (*Bekannte Starke Weise*) that are sung mostly at Sunday evening services and after weddings; these are typically German hymns coupled with nineteenth-century gospel tunes such as "Jesus, Lover of My Soul" or "What a Friend We Have in Jesus" found in *das din Buchlei* (the thin book) or *Liedersammlung*. Finally, Yoder added some of his own innovations—adapting and linking German texts with thirty-three fast tunes that had never been used by the Amish. For instance, he coupled "Iris," the tune sung to the Christmas carol "Angels we Have Heard on High," with the German Text, "*Sieh! Wie Lieblich*." This seemed an exceptional blending of tradition and innovation, because the syllables "Glo-ri-a in-ex-cel-sis De-o" are sung in melismatic style in the chorus, as in traditional Amish singing.

Knowing that the Amish could not read notes, Yoder included a section titled *Rudamenten* with English instructions on reading musical notation, along with forty-eight singing exercises. The use of English in this German book suggests that of the two written languages—High German and English—English was the preferred means of conveying technical, abstract, and written information. This was probably as a consequence of public schooling. All the tunes were recorded in shaped notation, which Yoder believed the Amish could learn to read more easily. He found only one publishing company capable of printing both shaped notes and German text. But because both systems were approaching extinction in Pennsylvania by the 1940s, the bid for the job was exorbitant.

Yoder decided to try his hand as a music copyist. After some unsatisfactory attempts and with much practice plus some wasted engraving plates, he was able to prepare a set of scores by hand. These were converted into printing plates at the Mennonite Publishing House, where German type was set under the notes. Yoder's musical notation is remarkably precise; only very close inspection reveals that it is the work of a human hand. Pages dividing the four sections feature passages of hymn text and small illustrations depicting agrarian work or rural landscape. Bound in black with the title stamped in gold on the cover, the book is truly an object of beauty. According

4.4 *"Das Lobgesang" as it appeared in Amische Lieder.*

to his account in *Rosanna's Boys*, it took three years to produce *Amische Lieder*, and Yoder considered it his masterpiece, intended to preserve a musical tradition that he loved.[58]

When it was finally completed, the book bore the dedication, "In loving memory to my father, Preacher Christian Z. Yoder who was one of the recognized leaders of the Amish music and to my mother, Rosanna McGonegal Yoder who all her lifelong sang these hymns in loving devotion." Yoder wrote, "My father and mother loved this music; I was raised Old Order Amish and felt that I owed them any service I could render."[59] But it remained for him to convince Amish people to use the book. In the foreword, he explained the paradox of adopting a new technology to preserve an old tradition: "The writer wishes to state humbly that it is his great wish and desire to help all Amish churches who still sing these old hymns to sing them alike and as nearly as possible as they were sung in the olden times, by their Fathers."[60] But the Amish people saw no use for Yoder's songbooks, and they were not impressed with his effort. A former Amish person said, "It was a novelty to him, like an antique collector." For Yoder to include unfamiliar texts and tunes in a book called *Amische Lieder* struck others as false and presumptuous. One Big Valley plain-dressing book seller recently offered a copy for sale joking, "Sure it's in good shape. If you can find them, they're always in good shape—nobody ever used them!"

Yoder dismissed the musical notation taboo as Amish resistance to *eppes neues* (something new), and hoped that it would pass. But one thoughtful Amish person suggested in a 1947 letter that the prohibition against note-writing was not the issue. Rather, he pointed to the central contradiction in Yoder's project: although a songbook might have been accepted by the more progressive western Amish groups, they sang differently from the traditional Big Valley versions, or they had drifted from the "slow" forms altogether. Those who might be progressive enough to use a song book would also be progressive enough to sing fast songs. This writer also questioned Yoder's motives, directly addressing the arrogance of his having created something for people without asking them if they wanted it, particularly since he did not seem interested in observing their other traditions and cultural practices:

> I don't know if anyone told you it [singing by notes] being a sin or not. To the best of my knowledge I never told or thought anything like that. I have an old singing book that has some notes. I never learned them. Your books might of went in some of them

western churches. But they don't sing like we do, so they would have to change their tunes. Don't you think it would of been a wise plan to first ask the churches if they would except [*sic*] them. The reason I thought it was more for money. I thought if I were not interested in the Amish rules I wouldn't be in the singing either.[61]

Yoder described a conversation about his songbook he had with "one of the young bishops in the Valley." The young man said, "Joe, we examined your book, and we do not condemn it, but for the present we do not use it. We are afraid of what it might lead to."

"What might it lead to?" Yoder asked, then replied in thundering typography: "BETTER SINGING IN PREACHING" and "SOMETHING" for the young folks to "wean them away from the worldly things they are doing, going to Night Clubs, drinking, carousing, and violating the moral law." (He referred to reports from larger Amish communities in Lancaster County and Indiana where single, young people who had not yet joined church were "running around" indulging in worldly pleasures that he regarded as far more dangerous than his own defection to a country singing school.) He concluded that the consequence of musical literacy most feared by the bishops was part singing. By prohibiting this, they believed that the slow singing tradition would be preserved, but Yoder believed it could only be preserved through musical notation.[62]

Of course, Yoder had ignored the prohibition against musical notation from childhood. Drawing on textual authority rather than the authority of tradition, he claimed he could find no biblical basis to justify their beliefs: "If singing in parts is wrong, tell the young folks not to sing parts, then show the Scripture that condemns and forbids singing parts. And if you can show them the Scripture that forbids it I feel sure they will not do it. And neither will I." In one of his most impassioned passages, he continued,

> I have been hunting to find the words of Jesus or Paul where they say, "Do not sing bass; do not sing tenor; do not sing alto," but I can't find it and if Jesus did not forbid it, maybe it is not wrong. . . . Let's not be afraid, brethren, but let us 'Launch out into the deep,' as Christ said to Simon Peter as he sat in the boat on Lake Genesaret .[63]

4.5
*Promotional
pamphlets
from the late
1940s.*

Joseph W. Yoder
Singer - Lecturer - Entertainer
Author of
Rosanna of the Amish
and
Amische Lieder

Joseph W. Yoder
Author of
Rosanna of the Amish
and
Amische Lieder

Years later, it is said that Yoder attended an Amish service after he had published *Amische Lieder*. As often happened, the Amish people honored his vocal talent by asking him to lead the "*Lobgesang,*" but that time he refused, saying he had brought his own book—implying that if they also had copies of his book they would not need *him* to lead singing. This story was told to John A. Hostetler by a member of the Amish community as an indictment of Yoder's prideful spirit. Yet perhaps more plainly it expresses the painful tension between a communal, oral culture and literacy, which eliminates the need for a human medium and even human relationships. As Yoder wrote, "Now, what are notes and what are they for? When one understands notes, he can sing a new tune without hearing someone else sing it first or sing it for him."[64]

Yoder's book also gave outsiders access to sacred communal texts that previously had been inscribed only on Amish hearts. Socrates recognized this dangerous consequence of literacy: "once a thing is committed to writing, it circulates equally among those who understand the subject and those who have no business with it; a writing cannot distinguish between suitable and unsuitable readers."[65] Yet Yoder understood the paradox of literacy—sometimes to save a thing, it must be given away or removed from its context—so he occasionally brought Amish men from Big Valley to sing for Juniata College chapel programs, while he lectured on the traditional slow tunes.

In 1938, Alan Lomax, assistant in charge of the archives of American Folk Song at the Library of Congress, made recordings of some Amish hymns near Goshen, Indiana. Based on this recording, John Umble printed the first few bars of the *"Lobgesang"* in his 1939 article for the *Journal of American Folklore*.[66] But unlike these efforts, and unlike *Rosanna of the Amish*, which was intended for outsider readers, Yoder insisted that his project was primarily intended for insiders. The hymn texts were written in German, and tunes were painstakingly recorded in simplified shaped notation for Amish singers. Nonetheless, *Amische Lieder* was most enthusiastically received by ethnomusicologists who studied the old tunes as if they were fossils. The publication of Yoder's project, concluded George Pullen Jackson, proved "that there is an astounding absence of dependence, in the matter of tune persistence, on printer's ink—oral song enduring as oral speech endures."[67]

Embedded within the tunes, Jackson discovered the skeletal melodies of medieval European folk songs, long presumed to have disappeared. (The titles of the old melodies are printed in the *Ausbund* under the hymn titles.) The *"Lobgesang,"* for instance, is sung to the tune that accompanied "There Went a Maiden with a Jug." One scholar has suggested that the Anabaptists set their sacred texts to secular tunes to hide them from their persecutors.[68] From Renaissance times, however, there thrived a tradition of appropriating features of popular music into sacred songs, even fashioning entire "parody masses" around bawdy, tavern tunes. But unlike Martin Luther's hymn, "A Mighty Fortress Is Our God," set to a dance tune of his time that is still recognizable today, the melodies are no longer easily discernible in Amish hymn tunes. Through the years, they accumulated melismatic variations which Jackson hulled away to find the melody indicated in the *Ausbund* titles. He speculated that the tunes' elaboration or "orniment" was not deliberate on the part of such a plain people, but that in the practice of singing very slowly, slight shifts in tone entered the tunes.

Yoder favored a theory that the hymns were derived from Gregorian chant, a notion he formed one day while shopping for men's wear in Huntingdon. As was his usual custom, the store's proprietor, Morris Dollinger, asked Yoder to sing a song while he examined the new garments. Having just returned from Big Valley, where he had been writing hymn tunes, Yoder decided to sing the first two lines of the *"Lobgesang,"* wondering if the unusual Amish music might have Hebrew origins that the Jewish merchant would recognize. When he finished, a young boy whom Yoder had not noticed emerged from the clothing racks and said that the tune reminded him of the songs priests chanted on Good Friday. To test this theory, Yoder later sang for a Franciscan instructor of Gregorian chant at St. Francis College in Loretto, Pennsylvania. The Brother guessed that Amish singing, though not exactly Gregorian, might be related.[69]

This constituted sufficient evidence for Yoder and no doubt satisfied his desire to create connections between the Amish and Irish Catholic parts of himself. In the introduction of *Amische Lieder*, he mistakenly attributed the origins of the slow songs to the sixth-century project of Pope Gregory, adding that all churches originating with the Reformation must have sung Gregorian chants at one time.

CHAPTER FIVE

FROM SCRIBE TO PROPHET: *ROSANNA'S BOYS* (1949) AND *AMISH TRADITIONS* (1950)

And may I prophesy that when the Amish preachers of our Valley become better enlightened through honest education, our eight Amish churches will go together again, and form one strong evangelical brotherhood that will stress Christian fellowship and Brotherly love instead of the outward forms that now divide us. —J. W. Yoder

With the 1940 creation of the Yoder Publishing Company and the subsequent printing and sale of *Rosanna of the Amish*, Yoder became publicly recognized as an author, and he personally gained a greater sense of authority. A typed entry in his personal "Record of Bank Deposits" notebook reveals his own surprise at the book's success:

> Accounts pertaining to Rosanna of the Amish, 1940.
> 2000 copies were contracted for about July 25 with considerable misgiving, but by beginning sales about Nov. 5, the entire 2000 copies were sold by Dec. 15 and a second edition of 3000 copies ordered. The book has met with favor far beyond our fondest expectation.[1]

Created primarily for readers outside the community, *Rosanna* challenged inaccurate and demeaning representations of Amish people and recorded traditional folkways such as powwowing and bundling that had begun to slip from practice in some communities. *Amische Lieder*, with standard tunes for *Ausbund* songs and new German translations of English hymns, was published to conserve and enrich the musical tradition. Introductions to both projects state Yoder's intent to serve and preserve. To his mind, this literary and musical work earned him the right to comment on other aspects of Amish life. "I believe I have a right to write about another interest I have in the Amish people everywhere," he wrote, "and that is my interest in their religious practices."[2]

J. W. Yoder, the Reformer

During the 1940s, he began saving carbon copies of his personal correspondence, often typing several long letters a day to promote his books or explore issues in Amish communities in Pennsylvania, Ohio, or Indiana.[3] Although *Rosanna of the Amish* publicly identified Yoder with the Amish people, they rejected *Amische Lieder* two years later; and some in the local community believe that the loss of time and money, as well as his disappointment in the failure of his song book, accounted for Yoder's increasingly meddlesome and critical attitude. He may have been responding to critics who found *Rosanna of the Amish* idyllic and unrealistic, or the changes in his attitude may have stemmed from greater involvement with the Amish community.

After his retirement in 1941, just before gas rationing and the war, Yoder spent more time in Big Valley visiting Amish friends and family members to gather information for *Rosanna's Boys*. Moreover, he become personally involved with individuals who were experiencing "church trouble" with the Old Order congregation of his childhood, and he could no longer hide his frustration with their theology and cultural practices. Thus, his attempts at fixing tradition began to shift from merely recording the community's customs to reforming them.

A comparative reading of *Rosanna of the Amish* and its sequel, *Rosanna's Boys* reveals his shift in perspective. Aside from the most obvious features—the first book is a continuous narrative, whereas the sequel is a collection of essays, poems, and autobiographical and biographical reflections—the most striking difference between the two is that Yoder shifted from referring to himself in the third person, "he," in *Rosanna of the Amish* to the first person, "I," in the later work. The writer became an actor in his life, rather than an observer of it, a move that was especially meaningful in light of Amish understandings of pride and humility. Rather than name or promote oneself, a humble and obedient member of the Amish community typically prefers to let another person name or praise him in public because drawing attention to oneself is considered shameful. One Amish recipient of a letter from J. W. Yoder circled Yoder's use of the word *I* thirty-two times throughout the document and returned it to him as evidence and accusation of *Hochmut*, the sin of pride, the primary criticism that Amish and Mennonite people launch against Yoder even today.[4]

With his use of the first person in *Rosanna's Boys* came a subtle but more challenging attitude toward some aspects of Amish culture. As a sequel to *Rosanna of the Amish*, *Rosanna's Boys* aimed for an audience of outsiders, so criticism of Amish life was carefully balanced with praise of Amish industry, honesty, and religious devotion. Yoder also explored local Amish history in some depth. Nevertheless, *Rosanna's Boys* exposed sharper feelings, as Yoder revisited old hurts with new authority and freedom to disclose his personal views. This shift is evident in a comparison between accounts of Rosanna's disappointment in being forbidden to become a schoolteacher. In the first book, the heroine bravely dried her tears and endured her disappointment in silence:

> "Oh Momly, how can I ever give up being a teacher? I had my whole heart set on that work." Rosanna wept bitterly, but when she saw tears in Momly's eyes, she felt that she was not bearing this disappointment alone. That, together with her great love for Momly, her unlimited confidence in her and the firm purpose never to hurt her in any way, somehow gave her the strength to dry her tears; and all that the others ever knew of this great struggle was that the Irish lilt in Rosanna's laugh was missing for several days.[5]

In the second account, an older Rosanna, learning of her son Levi's desire to become a schoolteacher, reflected on her thwarted ambitions and confessed to having suffered three days of bitter weeping—in contrast to a temporary loss of her "Irish lilt":

> Mother pondered a bit and then said, "You know, Levi, that's what Momly planned for me to be, but when she married Bishop Shem, he told her that he could not have a schoolteacher in his

house because the church was opposed to Education, and if I was a schoolteacher and lived with them, it would rob him of his authority as a Bishop, so he asked Momly to stop me. . . . When I fully realized that I could not be a schoolteacher, I wept for three days so bitterly that I could scarcely help Momly with the work. "If you think you'd like to be a teacher, go ahead. I know you can do it. You're a man and times have changed a bit, and they can't stop you, because you don't belong to Church, so go ahead: I'll help you all I can."[6]

With the phrase *rob him of his authority*, the Rosanna/Yoder of the second book overtly criticized church authority and its rules. Female subjugation is mentioned, if somewhat obliquely, and Rosanna was determined to help her son in defying the community's conventions.

In 1948, the Mennonite Publishing House agreed to print 3,000 copies of *Rosanna's Boys* for the Yoder Publishing Company for a fee of $3,000. Yoder was so eager to get the book on the market that he eventually hired the Evangelical Press in Harrisburg, which matched the Mennonite bid and promised to deliver the books sooner. In a letter to Ralph Hernley, press manager for the Mennonite publisher, Yoder explained his decision to take the job elsewhere and also hinted at a forthcoming book, promising that the Mennonites could have that job if they could muster the "intestinal fortitude" to print "a technical treatise on Amish religion, touching lightly on a few Mennonite traditions, too."[7] If Yoder tempered his criticisms of the community in *Rosanna's Boys*, he saved them for this next book, intended for Amish readers.

As he had anticipated, the Mennonites at Scottdale chose not to print *Amish Traditions* for the Yoder Publishing Company and refused to help promote it, because they thought it unfairly represented Amish culture and wrongly challenged Mennonite practices and doctrine. Yoder responded to their decision, "I'm not looking for ecclesiastical favors: I'm looking for the Truth, and I'm 'Cutting to the line' and 'letting the chips fall where they will.'"[8]

Containing none of the nostalgia or discretion of the more public *Rosanna* works, *Amish Traditions* became notorious among Amish people and troubled many Mennonites. Aside from those who fondly remember a charismatic "Singer Joe," there are many in Mifflin County who recall the contentious author of this era. One former member of the Renno church described Yoder's behavior from an Amish perspective:

"About that time Joseph W. Yoder, an old man who had been raised in the Old Order church and went to college, married a Presbyterian woman and lived in Huntingdon, PA. He tried his best to get the Amish to see the error of their ways, but they paid very little attention to him for he could do nothing but rant and rave."[9]

By the end of the 1940s, the scribe of *Rosanna of the Amish* and *Amische Lieder* had become a ranting prophet whose chief goal had shifted from preservation and defense of the community to agitation for change and reform. His primary concerns were schism among the Mifflin County Anabaptist groups and their methods of excommunication or shunning. These matters are related, because disagreements about excommunication practices were often a source of congregational division among Anabaptists, and because both shunning and schism involve the painful severing of relationships due to disputes concerning right practice. In Anabaptist communities, division is sometimes the only means of peaceably resolving a conflict in a way that allows each group to retain its integrity because the departing members are not subject to excommunication by those members who remain.

Shunning and schism are almost unavoidable when numerous details of everyday life are read as outward signs of membership in the "visible church," a notion central to many Anabaptist groups. Some other Protestants consider the church invisible at times, existing primarily in the spirit, and known only to God. For them, beliefs articulated in language or held in the heart rather than material expressions of faith matter most.

From his earliest days at Brethren Normal School, Yoder felt liberated by pietist spirituality; and his later experiences among Reformed, Methodist and Lutheran churches only confirmed his commitment to fostering a spirit of Christian ecumenicity rather than sectarian difference. In fact, following more Protestant beliefs, he regarded outward signs of faith as "carnal" rather than spiritual, because, "there is something far deeper in the Christian religion than obeying outward rules and ordinances."[10]

Moreover, Yoder harbored a distaste for Amish and Mennonite "church trouble"—although he increasingly found himself at its center—having been born in the wake of a church schism that divided his family, having witnessed congregational splits among Big Valley Amish and Amish Mennonites during his young adult life, and having been peripheral to such tensions at the Elkhart Institute. Yoder recounted the history of Big Valley's congregational divisions in *Rosanna's Boys*, and when John A. Hostetler questioned the source of this information, he cited his own memory and family's experience:

> I remember all the splits in the Amish churches except the one in which Abram Peachey's church suddenly split into three branches, Church house Amish, Peacheys and Old School. This all took place about 1848, but all the others occurred in my time. . . . All the other splits but maybe the last one was talked over in our family, so [sic] was perfectly conversant on them.[11]

Elsewhere in the letter, Yoder wrote that he knew of no written accounts of the Amish divisions in Big Valley existing before his own survey.[12] Yoder's father and foster grandfather were involved in church leadership through several generations of schism, and he considered the emotional and psychological consequences of these splits to be "burdens" that placed unnecessary "limits on fellowship" among the Amish people.

By the mid-1940s, Yoder had become so troubled by the schismatic nature of the community that he reminded everyone who would listen to him—and many who would not—that one Amish settlement in Big Valley had fragmented into eight distinct groups. In both *Amish Traditions* and in a 1950 letter sent to 702 Amish persons in the United States, Yoder pointed out that non-Amish congregations in the Valley—Presbyterians, Lutherans, and Methodists—had not divided once during that time.[13] Yoder stressed the shameful contradiction inherent in so many divisions within a community that professed nonresistance and nonviolence, wondering what kind of "witness" such contentious behavior made to outsiders.

Concerns about excommunication and avoidance (*Bann und Meidung*) are as old as the Amish people and are recognized to be the source of the schism that divided the Amish from the Swiss Brethren in the 1690s. As expressed in the Schleitheim Articles of 1527, the Swiss Brethren held to "the ban," which follows the gospel policy of rebuking a sinful member twice privately and, if he remains unrepentant, a third time in public, before excluding him from communion. The 1632 Dordrecht Confession of Faith, drafted by Mennonites in the Netherlands, added to excommunication the practice of shunning, described as the social avoidance of an erring member, except in cases where he is in great need or affliction. Menno Simons, the dynamic leader of the Dutch Mennonites, made a strong case for shunning in several of his writings, and admittedly it was a more peaceable method of dealing with dissent than the torture and execution employed by Catholic and Protestant churches of his day. In later correspondence, however, Menno wondered whether his position had been too harsh.

Swiss-born Jacob Amman, a leader of the Swiss Brethren who had migrated to Alsace, also favored shunning. According to some analyses, he faced especially hostile military and civil pressures in Alsace and thus felt a greater need to draw firm boundaries around his group. In addition to shunning, the institution of twice-yearly communion and conservative patterns of dress finally distinguished followers of Amman—the Amish—from their Swiss Brethren precursors, who belong to the Mennonite branch of Anabaptism.[14]

About two hundred years after the Amish division in Europe, the practice of excommunication and shunning caused a division in the Peachey Church that involved Yoder's father. The conflict occurred when a Lancaster County Amish group of lay people who opposed *streng Meidung*—the strict avoidance of members who have joined another church—appealed to preachers in the Peachey Church in Big Valley for leadership.

At first it seemed that all of the Big Valley ministers agreed to help the new group. And because strict shunning had not been part of their practice, it is assumed that most of the people in the Peachey congregation approved this help as well. Then Bishop David C. Peachey refused to help the Lancaster group, while the senior Bishop John P. Zook, and Preachers Christian D. Peachey and Samuel W. Peachey chose to help them. A schism between a minority who favored adoption of *streng Meidung* and a majority who opposed it occurred in 1911. The group that did not adopt the strict shunning was called the Zook Church after their Bishop, John P. Zook.

As a consequence of this schism, the practice of *streng Meidung* entered Big Valley through a split in the Peachey Church. Katie B. (Yoder) Yoder recalled that her mother, who had joined the Peachey Church as a young person, amicably left the church of her parents to join the Locust Grove Church House Amish group early in the century. Only a few years later, however, when Katie's younger aunt followed her sister, she had to endure a shunning because in the meantime the church had adopted the *streng Meidung*. Yoder maintained that his father opposed strict shunning, although Little Crist remained on the preacher's bench of the Peachey Church after the division. In 1919, the practice was tested when two members of the Peachey church were placed under the ban, and the congregation was told to *meid* or avoid them. This caused such conflict that two preachers and a deacon withdrew from the congregation, taking forty members with them to join the Zook church, the group that had earlier pulled away when *streng Meidung* was first introduced.[15]

Although he must have gathered impressions of these schisms through conversations with friends and relatives in both the Zook and Peachey churches, it was not until the 1940s that Yoder became actively involved in shunning controversies himself, and not until 1950 that he revealed his full thinking on the subject in *Amish Traditions*. In this book Yoder traced the origin of Big Valley's *streng Meidung* to a 1809 document drafted in the German language by four Lancaster County bishops: Benjamin Byler, aged seventy-nine; John King, seventy-eight; Solomon Stultzfus, seventy-seven; and Jacob Fisher, seventy-six.[16] In his mid-seventies himself, Yoder mentioned the bishops' ages because he surmised that they were all born in the early 1730s, probably in Germany or Switzerland, where educational opportunities were limited due to religious persecution. Around this time, he added, an Amish bishop is said to have arrived in America unable to even write his own name.

Thus Yoder branded the *Meidung* doctrine erroneous because the old, poorly educated bishops could not possibly have been able to interpret Scripture. This idea—that a lack of education and misunderstanding of the Bible are sources of schism and incorrect practice—was the dominant theme in *Amish Traditions*. Yoder's presumptuous use of the first person plural (we/our) in his critique must have only added insult to injury: "Our trouble is not a lack of sincerity or devotion or earnestness, but our trouble comes in not being able to think clearly," he wrote, and "another great cause of our trouble is a lack of education among our preachers. . . ."[17]

The style of Yoder's critique of "our" Amish traditions differed significantly from that of another son of the Amish who would attain great prominence as analyst and defender of Amish traditions.

JOHN A. HOSTETLER

Several years before Yoder launched his campaign to reform the strict shunning practices of the Renno Church, a much younger person had already questioned the custom: John Andrew Hostetler, who would later become the distinguished Temple University professor and interpreter of Amish and Hutterite culture. The story of his career and relationship with the Amish people offers an illuminating contrast to Yoder's. When he was eleven years old, Hostetler's father was excommunicated from the Peachey Church (later Renno) in Big Valley. A successful farmer, the elder Hostetler had committed such progressive moves as registering a herd of purebred cows, installing a generator in a gristmill to supply electricity for the town, and building a stucco barn. An even greater offense, however, may have been his threat to bring a lawsuit against a relative who accused him of mishandling family funds.

After repeated attempts at reconciliation, Hostetler sold his farm and moved his family to Iowa, where he hoped to join a related Amish group. Although he continued to attend Amish services for the rest of his life, he was forced to remain under the ban there, leaving before the meal after worship because he was forbidden to eat with the rest of the congregation. Believing that he had been the victim of envy and an ill-willed bishop, John's father discussed his shunning long after it occurred, and his son grew up in sympathy with his father.

When John Hostetler was old enough to join the Amish church, he wanted to retain ties with an Anabaptist-pacifist group and also harbored secret dreams of gaining advanced education. Thus he chose to affiliate with a Mennonite congregation. At twenty-one, he "came of age," and announced his intention to leave the family farm and enroll at Hesston College, a Mennonite school in Kansas. His education was interrupted by World War II, and for a portion of his Civilian Public Service (CPS) duty, he was stationed at a mental hospital in Marlboro, New Jersey. In a CPS library sponsored by the historic peace churches, he encountered Menno Simons's views on shunning in John Horsch's *Mennonite History in Europe*. Through study, Hostetler became convinced that the severe excommunication endured by his father and others in that community was not in keeping with Anabaptist doctrine.

In July 1944, he sent an eloquent, four-page, single-spaced, typed letter to several Amish leaders and to J. W. Yoder. In the letter he pleaded with Amish bishops and preachers to reconsider the strict *Meidung* practice in light of original Anabaptist intentions and New Testament teachings of love and forgiveness. The letter cited Menno Simons and Thieleman J. van Braght, editor of *Martyrs Mirror*, who wrote that shunning should be reserved as a last resort for one who has flagrantly transgressed the moral law, and that it should be practiced in a spirit of concern and compassion with the intent of restoring the fallen member to God and the community, not "as a weapon of force to use for holding church members." In fact, Hostetler observed, coercion is entirely antithetical to the Anabaptist spirit, as described in 1561 by Heinrich Bullinger: "The true church of Christ has the characteristic that it suffers or endures persecution but does not inflict persecution on any one." In addition to lengthy references to Anabaptist writings, Hostetler alluded to passages from the Bible, quoting the words of Jesus concerning believers who did not follow his disciples, "Forbid them not," and citing many passages about the importance of brotherly love.[18]

In an interview, Hostetler could not recall to whom he sent the letter. Likely among the recipients was John B. Renno, who had become bishop of the Peachey church in 1942 following the death of Noah Yoder, the man who had shunned Hostetler's father. Hostetler did remember sending a copy to an older member of the Big Valley Amish community whom he described as a "faithful friend." More than fifty years later, Hostetler recalled feeling "ashamed to try to shake him up or to bring up the topic with him," revealing how deeply felt is the taboo against disturbing relationships in the community and upsetting its traditions—a taboo which Yoder frequently violated.

When Hostetler later visited the Valley as a Penn State graduate student, he sometimes slept in that man's barn and ate breakfast with his family the next morning, hoping that the topic of his letter might surface. It never did. Hostetler said that his letter got "an Amish burial"—it was simply ignored, although he believed the farmer would have forgiven him if the topic had come up. He got "the Amish treatment," he explained, because "you just don't bring up something that would make strong feelings or argumentation," adding, "there was no way I could argue with that old man." Later, Hostetler advised his father to stop talking and arguing about his shunning, because it was so personally upsetting, and it was clear that he could not change the situation.[19]

With the war's end, Hostetler completed an undergraduate degree at Goshen College and continued graduate study at Pennsylvania State

University, which he had chosen partly because the school is located near his ancestral home. At Penn State for the first time he encountered anthropology, the discipline which enabled him to understand shunning as a gesture of community boundary maintenance and to regard it in relation to the self-defining practices of other ethnic groups.

In this way, he came to conceptualize his father's fate in terms of *culture*, although his interpretation of the famous shunning case of Moses Hartz in *Amish Society* betrays Hostetler's insight into the ways that Amish people who are prosperous and progressive, as his father was, may become the targets of envy and excommunication.[20] To regard his family's experience within the sociological categories of a "closed" or folk culture enabled Hostetler to study his relatives as academic subjects and to interpret "church trouble" in terms of social systems integral to maintaining a cohesive community. In this spirit, he made a career of defending and protecting the community that had shunned his father and limited his own early educational experiences.

Like Yoder, Hostetler became an author through an act of autoethnography aimed at correcting misrepresentations of the Amish. His first, slim book, *Amish Life*, was published in 1952 to provide an alternative to the demeaning Aurand pamphlets sold to tourists along the Pennsylvania Turnpike and elsewhere. As their public careers developed, however, the paths of Yoder and Hostetler parted. While Hostetler made elegant arguments for the protection of Amish culture, arguing that "faith communities in America function as mediating structures in the pluralistic makeup of our society,"[21] Yoder urged the Amish to conform to American Protestant conventions, selectively retaining some traditions while no longer granting to them spiritual authority.

Former Amishman John R. Renno later reflected on the paradox of this approach in an interview: "Joe urged them to keep traditions but don't trust in them; but if you don't trust them, you're not going to keep them. Joe didn't seem to see that." While Hostetler argued that the First Amendment should protect the Amish "right to be left alone,"[22] Yoder urged a member who was shunned to sue his church because Amish *Ordnung* violates the American ideal of religious freedom. When Hostetler was still at Goshen College, he wrote some entries for the *Mennonite Encyclopedia* under the direction of H. S. Bender, and Yoder complained that a "Christian Encyclopedia" would have been a better project, because sectarianism is not biblical. Whereas World War II made Hostetler more steadfast in his Anabaptist belief, so that during the war he donated books on pacifism to public libraries in Newark and New York City, the war caused Yoder to become increasingly patriotic and eventually to denounce the German language.

Informed by different understandings of culture and very different intentions, Yoder and Hostetler fostered a friendship and corresponded for nearly a decade, but a strain is sometimes evident in their letters. Although Yoder willingly supplied the historical information Hostetler sought, he could become antagonistic toward the young graduate student's methods. When Hostetler questioned the source of a direct quote Yoder had attributed to an early nineteenth-century Amish bishop in *Rosanna's Boys*, for instance, Yoder replied,

> Now, John Andrew Hostetler, A.B., A.M., Ph.D., if you knew the Amish as I know them you would realize that they have never kept records of anything they did, so far as I know. . . . Then, again, if you knew the Amish as I do, you would know that the statement referred to is just about what any Amish Bishop would say when he was somewhat perturbed . . . nobody but a meticulous College Professor would ever even question the statement, since no consequence comes of it.[23]

For Yoder, trained in the nineteenth-century methods of historian and educator M. G. Brumbaugh, oral tradition and common sense served as sufficient evidence to make a worthy point, and he was perturbed that his authority was called into question by a young academic. Later in a brief note, Hostetler addressed Yoder's arrogant tone by greeting him as "Bishop Yoder," and he mentioned a collection of three hundred slides he had taken to preserve images of Amish art work, needle work, artifacts, farmsteads, houses and people, adding, "You wouldn't want to see them because you know everything about the Amish!"[24]

In 1950, when Yoder published *Amish Traditions*, he requested that Hostetler write a scholarly review of his book, sincerely seeking the opinion of an educated person who understood the culture. Hostetler's response, delayed by work on a 280-page master's thesis, was careful but negative. He conceded "emotional and intellectual agreement" on some points, admitting that Yoder "stated the case against the strict *Meidung* beautifully." Moreover, Hostetler mentioned that he was asked by someone at the Mennonite Publishing House in Scottdale to "take [Yoder] to task" concerning his views on the prayer veil, but he refused to do so, warning "they better keep hands off!" He declined to write the review, however, because he knew that siding with Yoder would jeopardize relationships with Amish people essential to continuing his scholarly research: "Frankly, Joe, the thing is too hot for me at this stage of the game. Until I get my Ph.D. and the data I want from Amish homes, I must keep my mouth shut."[25]

Throughout his career, Hostetler continued to treat the Amish community with respect, often serving as an authoritative if somewhat paternalistic spokesman on their behalf. *Amish Society*, which set a standard for sociological studies of religious communities when it was published, sold almost 100,000 copies through its third edition, and is now in a fourth. As a scholar and advocate, Hostetler has been far more effective than Yoder in altering the ways Amish people are regarded by other Americans and the ways some Amish and formerly Amish people understand themselves.

When Yoder received a copy of Hostetler's 1944 letter addressing Mifflin County shunning practices, he replied that he shared Hostetler's concern about "this bad practice of 'shunning,'" and that he had already sent letters to Bishop John B. Renno and deacon Joseph E. Peachey about the use of avoidance and the *Ordnung* in the Renno Church. As Yoder explained,

> I think they and all Amish are entirely wrong on both these points. Avoiding a member who has gone wrong and simple attire have their place, but when carried to extreme as they do, then I think they are definitely wrong. I was thinking of doing the same as you are doing—sending out a mimeographed letter to about 600 Bishops, preachers and deacons, and try to show them by Scripture where they are carrying some of these things to extremes, and are missing the whole point of Christ's teaching, which is LOVE. [26]

John D. Yoder

Three years later, on January 9, 1947, Yoder sent a four-page, single spaced, typed letter to sixty heads of household in the Renno Amish Church. Names and addresses of the letter's recipients were provided by

John D. Yoder, a disgruntled member of the community who was under the discipline of the Renno Church at the time. In this letter, and later in *Amish Traditions*, Yoder claimed authority to intervene in Amish affairs by asserting his own authenticity—that he is "a member of the Amish church"—and by reminding Amish readers of his literary and musical efforts on their behalf:

> When I say that I am very much interested in the welfare of all Amish people I think you can believe me, especially when I tell you that books were written about the Amish people that made fun of them, then I wrote *Rosanna* to set the Amish people in the right light before the public. The Bible says, "Let your light shine" and some of these books put our light under a bushel. I also wrote *Amische Lieder* so your singing would not be lost, and to make it possible for you to have better singing than you have ever had.[27]

Yoder's letter preached love, focusing primarily on the *Meidung* practice as it pertained to the case of John D. Yoder, who had been put under the ban about four years earlier. John Yoder's emotional volatility, marital problems, and disputes with neighbors were well known, so the community's incisive lexicon of Pennsylvania German nicknames dubbed him *Gedichtich Johnnie* (excessive, intense or extreme) for all of his adult life. After his death in 1996, a friend described the man who may have suffered from an undiagnosed manic disorder, "John was very charismatic, and jumped pretty high but had trouble walking straight when he hit the ground." In about 1946, Joseph Yoder met John D. Yoder on the street in Belleville and sympathetically listened to the story of his shunning, which became the unstable centerpiece of his argument against the Renno Church.

According to John, since he had fallen behind in his farm work because his wife was ill, he permitted a man with a tractor to plow his field instead of using horses. Bishop Noah Yoder insisted that he confess a fault for having his field plowed with a tractor, and John refused because he believed he had not committed a sin. "For that you excommunicated him like a low down fornicator, adulterer and drunkard," Yoder charged in his letter to the Renno church members, insisting that since there is no mention of tractors in the Bible, they were enforcing "man-made" rules. In asking John to "confess a fault," Yoder wrote, they were making him tell a lie. John Yoder eventually did confess a fault, but when he was not received back into church fellowship, he abandoned his family and moved to a settlement of Big Valley Amish in Stuart's Draft, Virginia. Because his wife would not consent to the sale of the farm in Pennsylvania, he returned for a brief time, but finally sold the farm and moved with his children to Lawrence County, Pennsylvania.

For several years after their initial meeting, John Yoder secretly corresponded with Joseph Yoder, once asking him to send letters in unmarked envelopes. On John's behalf, Yoder wrote and spoke with Bishop Renno and, in 1947, urged John to consider suing the Amish Church as a former Amishman named Andrew Yoder had done in Ohio. In his letter to members of the Renno church, Yoder compared John Yoder's fate to the biblical story in which Jesus saved a woman caught in adultery from public stoning: "If any one of you is without sin, let him cast the first stone. . . . Neither do I condemn you" (John 8). Wrote Yoder, "What difference between the treatment the woman got and the treatment Johnnie received? How slow we are to learn the Jesus way." Further, Yoder charged the Amish church with metaphorically stoning John by advising his wife "to oppose him."[28]

What Yoder did not seem to know or failed to understand was that at times John Yoder was an abusive husband and father, as his nickname, *Gedichtich Johnnie*, may imply. Although physical discipline of children and the submission of wives to their husbands is expected in Amish culture, John Yoder was not a typical Amish husband, and some in the community knew that he excessively beat his wife and children. To this day, some believe that Yoder was responsible for the death of a son who fell off a tractor due to injuries that he had sustained at his father's hand, which caused him to lose his balance.

There is no textual evidence that abusive behavior played a part in John Yoder's shunning, but one member of the Renno church did refer to John's temper in a letter sent to Yoder, to whom it would have been inappropriate to disclose the details of such intimate family and church matters. Moreover, in a letter in which Yoder plotted John's defense, he warned, "They are talking around that you get so angry when you talk. Be as careful as you can on that point, so they cannot get anything on you."[29] Whether the shunning was punishment for John's brutality or for his failure to repent for the plowing incident, it did provide temporary protection for his wife Mary, since a shunned member may not have sexual intercourse with a spouse who is still a church member nor eat at the same table with any other church members.

As a consequence of the shunning, Yoder moved away from his family, and there is evidence that leaders of the Renno Church urged his wife to "oppose him," at least in matters concerning the sale of the family farm. When John Yoder relocated with his children to a farm in Lawrence County, Mary remained behind for some time.[30]

That Yoder would view John D. Yoder only as a victim of legalistic bishops suggests his distance from the local community, and his defense of John Yoder greatly discredited his efforts among the Amish. Such a seemingly trivial shunning fitted well into Yoder's perception of legalistic, loveless, ignorant, tradition-bound, and divisive Amish leaders. Unlike the letter sent by John Hostetler, Yoder's letter did not stress a more faithful following of historic Anabaptist practice but instead appealed to a progressive ethic of love and grace as articulated in the Gospels and writings of Paul. He wrote,

> Why in heaven's name enforce the Dortrecht Confession of 1632? That was a time of great persecution, and every church persecuted its members if they did not obey that particular church, Catholics for example. They had not learned the Love that Jesus and Paul teach all the way thru [sic]. They put their faith in Doctring [sic] instead of in Jesus.[31]

Finding the Renno Church's practice of shunning antithetical to these teachings, Yoder reasoned that since this issue caused the 1911 division of the Peachey Church, the groups should simply mend that schism and regroup by dissolving *streng Meidung* in response to enlightened scriptural understandings. The letter concluded with an invitation to individual conversations: "To keep from embarrassing you I shall not speak of this letter to you, but if you should like to speak to me about it, I shall be very glad to talk it over with any of you or a number of you at any time you wish."[32]

Unlike Hostetler's, Yoder's letter did not get "an Amish burial." In *Amish Traditions* Yoder reported that he received twenty responses to the sixty letters he sent. He replied to every letter—reiterating his themes with lengthy arguments that sometimes bordered on personal insult.[33] An author of one response expressed the opinions of many: meddling in Amish affairs was "one of the most foolish things you ever done in your life," he wrote, and the letters had "done more to ruin your reputation among the orthodox Amish than anything else." To neglect their own traditions and longstanding teachings on "the advice of a high school professor surely would be the height of folly even though he may be full of worldly wisdom, as the wisdom of this world is foolishness with God," the author continued. Another unsigned reply was scrawled on the back of a returned letter, "Joe you don't talk very nice of us Amish, do you?" On the lower margin of another returned letter, the writer cited Acts 5, which recounts the story of Ananias and Sapphira, struck dead for saying that they contributed all of their profits to the community when, in fact, they had reserved a portion for themselves.

A reference to this story suggests that the author believed Yoder told only part of the John D. Yoder story:

> I will send this letter back to the spirit it was sent from. Making about Johnnie Yoder, which I can plain see just got one side of the matters which is unscriptural . . . where I believe you fall short [is] to take one side and just certain parts. in script. read *apostel geschicht* [Acts] 5 chapter.

Another letter summarized several conversations, relating an array of views held by "the Renno people:" one man said, "if it was the way J. W. says we would not have a Cross to carry," alluding to the belief that the faithful follow in the footsteps of a suffering savior. Another accused Yoder of "judging" them, counter to biblical teaching: "Judge not so you shall not be judged." A third said, "You broke the first commandment, didn't obey your parents, so now you don't feel right so you try and get others to think as you do." Another called Yoder *Fer-feurer*, probably meaning *Verfuehrer*, a tempter or seducer who leads others astray.

One thoughtful response, handwritten in graceful script on the back of three pages of Yoder's letter, alternated between English and German, incorporating paraphrased and direct citations of Scripture. In it, the author pointed to the irony of a departed member claiming concern for the community, and clearly expressed values central to the culture: living a quiet, righteous life in separation from the world, sacrifice, and submission of one's "own way" to the authority of God and community leaders:

> I think if you are interested in the Amish people, you would better take another way as I fear if the people would all do as you

have done there would be no Amish people any more and I think
you could have the same chance as I or anyone else if you would
have chosen it. . . .

    I can find very little Spiritual gain in the reading of this letter
so I will send it back as when we think of Spiritual gain we think
of the cross and giving up our will for God's will, and Jesus said
Love not the world or worldly things whosoever loveth this world
the Love of the Father is not in him . . . and about Johnnie Yoder
I believe I know as much about it as you do and Johnnie did not
have to do anything that would have hurt him or anyone else a bit
if he would just have been willing to give up his own way. . . . Now
if you think our forefathers made a great mistake when they tried
to obey their God and their fathers what do you think will become of us if we do not want to obey our fathers that we have seen
or if we cannot love and obey our fathers which we have seen how
do you suppose we may get a start to obey God whom we cannot
see and his commandments are so much more Just and Holy. . . .
Now Joe if we read the books of the Bible through we can often
see that we are not what we should be or would like to be but if we
try to do our best we are still behind and I believe if the preachers
try to obey their forefathers and the Lord there is no use that we
try to think that we can do much better and we have no right to
disobey them either.

In this letter, obedience to God, the preachers, and the community
is almost indistinguishable from obedience to one's parents. Borrowing
an argument from Jesus, the writer asked, How can you obey an invisible God if you cannot even obey your own father? (In the biblical passage this author alluded to, Jesus poses this question about *himself*, believed to be the human manifestation of the invisible God.) The analogy
between church discipline of a wayward member and discipline of a
willful child is clear: in both cases the intent is to bring the erring one
back into fellowship with a unified, religious family.

    Thus it is understandable that Yoder, an elderly man who was re-
garded as a disobedient child, would be dismissed by many in the Amish
community. Although he engaged in public exhibitions of filial piety—
dedicating *Rosanna of the Amish* to his mother and *Rosanna's Boys* and
Amische Lieder to both of his parents, long dead—everyone knew that he
had refused to inherit his father's farm or join his parents' church. Yoder

was marked by these refusals and reminded of them even in old age. How could a disobedient person be trusted to interpret what it means to obey God?

One member of the Renno church bluntly accused Yoder of corrupting young people in the community through his *Meidung* letter, which the writer admitted was "handed around quite a bit." He wrote, "You don't have any children. I think how would you like it if you had children, would try to raise them the way you thought was right, and some one would encourage them not to Obey. You know what the first Commandment is. Exodus 20:12." In reality, of course, "Honor thy father and thy mother: that your days may be long in the land which the Lord thy God give thee" (KJV) is the fifth commandment, although it has been called the first commandment in which a reward is promised. While still a child, Yoder listened fearfully as the bishop, in the presence of their tearful father, pleaded with Levi to join his parents' church, charging that he was in violation of this commandment. To obey one's parents and follow in their ways is the first commandment for Amish people, and obedience ensures the security of membership in the community and often the inheritance of farmland, as the biblical commandment promises.

Not only had Yoder violated the commandment himself, but he was a seditious, public figure who represented a challenge to the patterns of obedience to family and church. In *Amish Traditions*, he accused the Amish of "ancestor worship," pointing out that Jesus frequently questioned the authority of familial and social structures, as in Matthew 10:37: "He that loveth father or mother more than me is not worthy of me."[34] By the 1950s, Yoder was held up by many Amish people as a cautionary example of what a young person could turn into if he left his family and farm in pursuit of education. He posed a threat to Old Order teachings at a time when they were being questioned, and although he was clearly not solely responsible for change and stress in the Big Valley community, he certainly acted as a catalyst—as in the case of John R. Renno.

JOHN R. RENNO

Namesake and favored son of the bishop of the Renno Church, this young man joined his father's church at the age of eighteen. In an interview, he described his father, John B. Renno, as a strong leader, "a man who had physiological power to cause people to do things he wanted them to do." Bishop Renno used to say, "We believe in the one visible Church of God on earth, and we hope we are it. If we are not, it is somewhere." But by his early twenties, young John began to have "questions," not unlike the questions that Yoder had been raising concerning the history of schism. Renno wondered:

> Why is there one God, we all belong to him, we're all going to heaven, but why can't we get along? And one thing that impressed me so much was when Seth Yoder had sale. He lived on the Sammy Swarey farm and they couldn't make it go, so they were going to quit farming and move to Juniata County. We were there, my mother had two sisters—one was in the Zook church, one went to Locust Grove—and we went back there to help Seth Yoder get ready for his sale, and we all were like one big family there, no matter what church you belonged to, all differences were forgotten, we sat down and ate dinner together and had a good time. Sunday came, the lines were drawn, everyone went to his own, we wouldn't touch the other. I said to my dad, "Why is that so? I don't understand that. We're all one family on Saturday, and Sunday comes and we're all separate." He said, "You have some deep thoughts." [35]

Around this time, Renno recalled that "Joe [Yoder] was warning us of—he didn't say apostasy—but that's what he meant; we're on the wrong road, and the unreasonableness of our stance." Despite his own "questions," Renno argued with Yoder in a series of letters. "I was very strong," he recalled, "just like the apostle Paul, with great zeal for my religion." [36]

A year or more passed, and one day as Renno was walking along the road, a Mennonite friend offered to give him a ride in his truck. As they drove along, the two began to argue about the doctrine of assurance of salvation—whether or not a Christian can be certain of his soul's destiny in the afterlife. The Mennonite believed one could. Renno upheld the Amish position that one could not, and that to claim such a thing betrayed the sin of pride.

At that time, Amish preachers were actively resisting the teaching of assurance that had become popular among Big Valley's Amish-derived

Mennonites, calling it "doctrine of devils." Explained Renno, "The Scripture says that in the last days men shall come with 'doctrine of devils.' *This is it*, they said!" Nevertheless, Renno believed that his friend had won the argument: "It sounded logical; he had Scripture for what he said, and I didn't."

So Renno began studying the Bible in the German language. He described his conversion to the new doctrine:

> One time it just struck me like a bolt of lightening in Ephesians 2:8-9: "For by grace are ye saved through faith and that not of yourself, it is the gift of God: not of works lest any man should boast, for we are his workmanship created in Christ Jesus unto good works"—not *because* of good works—and that was the turning point.[37]

To have arrived at this conclusion was very troubling for Renno because it presented only two options: either he follow "the Scripture" and abandon his family or he deny the teachings of Scripture as he understood them and remain true to the Amish church. He recalled:

> Now the war began. I was devoted to the Amish church, and God revealed himself to me. Now what am I going to do? Will I follow the Scripture or will I follow my church? It was extremely difficult. I would gladly have faced a firing squad in comparison to what I had to face, because my father and I were friends, and my siblings, we all loved each other, we all got along good—and for me to leave them, every year we had our reunions, our get-togethers, and I would be excluded. It was like jumping off of a cliff.[38]

By this time, Renno had married Salina Peachey and bought the family farm from his father; he enjoyed working with horses, and postwar prosperity touched even Amish farms. He subscribed to magazines and read a great deal, always seeking more information. As well, he carried a New Testament out to the fields, and whenever he gave the horses a rest, he read. This caused others, including his father, to regard him with suspicion and finally to warn him that people who read the Bible so much can lose their minds and go crazy. Later Rennno wrote in his autobiography that his father "had seen by experience that folks who make very much of the Bible do not stay Amish."[39] He had resolved to "behave" and try to live quietly with his new convictions.

He could not resist talking with others, however, and many were beginning to notice the strange views of the bishop's son. Some were interested and eager to discuss what he had been learning, but most were afraid, as he recalled, "I was looked upon as a heretic who must be dealt with, for my doctrine was leaven and would corrupt the whole group." [40]

Around this time, Renno wrote a letter to J. W. Yoder apologizing for earlier arguments and revealing his new convictions. Yoder was elated. Recalled Renno, "Oh, he thought he had a convert now. He started writing letters: we got to do this, we got to do that, we got to get in there and change the Amish around!" But Renno replied, "Oh, Joe, don't get excited now. You handle this like you handle a hot potato. You don't go at it with both hands. You get a fork and pick around at it." Meanwhile, Bishop Renno was becoming alarmed. He knew that his son had corresponded with J. W. Yoder; a letter intended for the son had ended up in the bishop's hands, because Yoder had addressed it with the wrong initial. Fearing that his son had been infected with Yoder's ideas, he asked to read copies of other letters. The younger Renno had destroyed them, so the bishop wrote directly to Yoder requesting copies. Yoder then wrote to Renno to tell him that he had saved copies of their correspondence, but thought his father should not read the letters. He replied, "Send them, I have nothing to hide." They were sent, and Renno's convictions were finally known to his father. [41]

A series of meetings with the preachers during the early 1950s could not dissuade John and Salina Renno and another couple from their beliefs. Early one Sunday morning in March 1953, the bishop visited his son, while he was still milking in the barn and begged him to request to be put under the ban, so that all the charges against him would not be made public, and that upon proper restitution he could be restored to fellowship. Feeling he had done no wrong, the son refused. After church that morning, John R. Renno's shunning hearing was held, using evidence from letters he had written to J. W. Yoder. He was not permitted to attend the service.

Throughout the summer, Renno was *meided* or avoided by the congregation while church leaders attempted to restore him to fellowship. Salina was also instructed to avoid him. Because church members could not accept help from Renno, he refused their assistance in making hay or cutting and shocking wheat and oats—although they could help him according to the church rules—and he had to hire labor to complete the summer's work. For eighteen weeks, he met periodically with the ministers, but remained unwilling to change his beliefs and was finally "put out of church" in an excommunication service. In a February 1953 letter to Yoder, Renno wrote, "Yes, the Amish think I'm a Joe Yoder No. 2, and I'm serving the Devil and forsaking God, but the god I'm forsaking is the Amish god, and not the God of heaven."[42]

When Renno was expelled from the church, Salina was pregnant with their third child, and it was difficult to find someone to help them after the birth. Recalled Salina in an interview, "Oh, it was terrible hard, terrible hard, your parents come crying and your brothers and sisters, telling you how they wish you'd come back to church." When she visited her father, he fell to his knees and wept saying, "Oh God, God, help Salina." Because she refused to avoid her husband, Salina was eventually expelled as well, and all church members were instructed to avoid them. Some family members practiced avoidance more strictly than others; when a fourth child died at birth, one of Salina's brothers came to visit, but sat in silence, unable to utter his condolences.[43]

Finally, in 1957, Renno decided to buy a farm in Luzerne County, Pennsylvania, because he reasoned that the Valley belonged to the Amish:

> Since the valley was becoming full of people and the mountains held them in on every side, I looked around in preparation to leave the valley. I always believed that people with automobiles could easily go over the mountains and should leave the farms in the valley for the Amish.[44]

When he was put under the ban, Renno's uncle said that the worst shame of it was that someone under the ban should have the Renno home farm. In an interview Renno recalled, "I felt this isn't right for me to live centrally located on the home farm and all my brothers and sisters would drive by with long faces. Oh, it was so sad." Before moving, he sold the home place to a brother through a third party, because he could have no business dealings with a shunned member.[45] Since then, John R. Renno has been affiliated with several Mennonite-related congregations and worked as a long distance truck driver until his retirement. Although only educated through the eighth grade in the one-room, rural schoolhouse, he has written several books, including a short history of the Amish churches in Big Valley and a memoir, and he continues to write an occasional column for the weekly *County Observer* which currently serves Big Valley.

LAW AND GRACE

J. W. Yoder's 1947 *Meidung* letter and correspondence with members of the Renno Church, his intervention in the John D. Yoder case, and his private conversations with John R. Renno all occurred while he was drafting *Amish Traditions*. His personal involvement in these local controversies clarified his views and emboldened his voice. Published in 1950, when Yoder was 78 years old, *Amish Traditions* is the culmination of nearly a decade of conversation with Old Order Amish people of Mifflin County, particularly with members of what had been his parents' church. Whereas previous books were dedicated to his parents' memory, the title page of this book proclaims that it is "Dedicated to the welfare of THE AMISH PEOPLE everywhere to lighten their burdens and to all people searching for the TRUTH."

5.1 *"J. W. Yoder on the old homestead..." began the caption of this photograph posed at the old-style barn door to illustrate a 1948 article published in* Mennonite Community. *Despite such symbolic claims to authenticity, Yoder's interventions in Big Valley increasingly distanced him from the Amish community during this period.*

Through rhetorical and logical argument, occasionally appealing to academic biblical interpretation, Yoder attempted to correct doctrinal errors and change Amish beliefs. Each chapter argues against a distinctive religious practice or folkway, including selection of leaders by lot, church division, the use of the *Ordnung*, the ban, restrictions on education and singing, the ethic of separatism, the photography taboo, and use of the German language.

Yoder's arguments rest largely on the law/grace dichotomy as he understood it to be articulated in the writings of the apostle Paul. An abiding tension in Christian thought, this dichotomy is deeply rooted in the Reformation, when Martin Luther insisted that salvation comes not by law or works (outward demonstrations of belief through good deeds or the purchasing of indulgences from Rome), but by the grace of God (experienced as an inward emotional belief). This binary opposes concrete, context-bound visible gestures against abstract, content-based, invisible concepts or feelings, a pairing that may be analogous to the contrast between ways of making meaning that are grounded in action and tradition as opposed to those that are informed by literacy and reflection.[46]

The dichotomy also informed a fundamentalist stream of Protestant thinking earlier in the twentieth century, when the two elements were not seen as complementary or even opposed aspects of Christian belief, but as developmental stages—distinct dispensations corresponding with historical periods. Charles Finney, a nineteenth-century Reformed preacher of Holiness, taught that the Old Testament represented the dispensation of the law and the New Testament the dispensation of the Holy Spirit, beginning at Pentecost. Some went even farther with the dispensations. C. I. Scofield, who popularized J. N. Darby's dispensational approach to the Bible, divided history into seven Dispensations. The fifth, Israel under "Law," covered the time from the giving of the Ten Commandments to the death of Jesus (or from "the exodus to the cross"), and the sixth, the dispensation of "Grace" extends from the crucifixion of Jesus until the second coming of Christ.[47]

As nineteenth-century scientists viewed non-Europeans as chronologically "backward" and contrived evolutionary categories to express a narrative of progress, early twentieth-century churchmen developed similar schemes for theology. In keeping with them, Yoder considered the Amish analogous to Hebrews of the biblical age who lived under the Law of Moses. The New Testament he placed in opposition to the Old Testament, writing that "Scripture definitely teaches that the Old dispensation and the New dispensation cannot be mixed."[48] In *Amish Traditions*, Yoder posed many oppositions along the lines of this binary, which reflects tensions between tradition and the progressive modes he had adopted. (Numbers indicate page locations in *Amish Traditions*.)

LAW	GRACE
Old Dispensation	New Dispensation (24)
Salvation through Mosaic law	Salvation through Grace (24)

"Do this and be saved."	"Believe, thou shalt be saved." (24)
The Jews preached Law.	Paul preached grace. (28)
Outward, material practice	Inward, or spiritual condition (30)
Mosaic law	Liberty, which Paul preached (31)
World/Jews	Believers/Christians (32)
Piety in the "letter"	Piety in the heart and spirit (38)
Beards and bonnets	Mind and spirit (39)
Jewish circumcision	Faith that worketh by love (41)
Outward	Inward (42)
Strife, church splits (53)	"Brotherhood of Man, Fatherhood of God" (161)
Bondage of Bishop's rules	Liberty through Christ (57)
Force of domineering men	Seduction of Truth and Reason (58)
The way people dress	A transformed mind (67)
Bondage of fear and ignorance	Life, more abundantly (95)
Amish ways, German language	American ways, English (96)
European religious persecution	American religious liberty (96)
Old World educational deprivation	United States public education (96)
Old Testament	New Testament:
Works and punishment	Faith and charity (145-6)
Oldness of letter	Newness of spirit (161)
Jacob Amman, ritual	Modern evangelist, grace (173)

From the time of America's settlement by European religious dissenters—Amish immigrants among them—the ideal of democratic freedom has been entangled with Christian belief. The Declaration of Independence appeals to a divine mandate for human rights and liberties. Following the Civil War and Emancipation, evangelical revivalists preached of "bondage" to the law in opposition to "freedom" in the spirit, employing political terminology for spiritual conditions.[49] This language struck Yoder with great force when he encountered it at Brethren Normal School during the 1890s, when he was all too eager to exchange Amish "law" for Brethren "liberty." At that time, he joined the late nineteenth-century progressivists's project of building a Christian civilization shaped by the ideals of education and temperance, individual freedom and national democracy, and physical health and spiritual renewal.

Bondage, Liberty, and Lucy Hochstetler

In 1948, while working on *Amish Traditions*, Yoder became engaged in a literal manifestation of "bondage." Lucy Hochstetler, forty-one, a mentally ill Amish woman from near Goshen, Indiana, was found after being chained to her bed by her father, Bishop Samuel Hochstetler. Her story, relayed in the captions of two dramatic photographs that appear to have been posed, was syndicated in newspapers in January 1948, and published as far away as South America, Asia, and Europe.

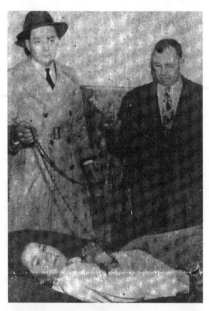

5.2 *"Sheriff Luther Yoder, right, and Chief Deputy Levi Bontrager, of Elkhart county, hold the chains which bound Lucy Hochstetler to her bed in her father's home near Goshen, Ind. This picture was made before the woman was released."* (The News-Democrat, *South Bend, Indiana, Jan. 23, 1948.*)

5.3 *"Samuel Hochstetler, 75-year-old Amish bishop, clutched a Bible in one hand as he submitted the other for fingerprinting in the Elkhart country jail in Goshen, Ind., today. He was sentenced to six months at the State penal farm on a charge of assault and battery after officers discovered his 41-year old daughter chained to her bed Thursday. Taking fingerprints is Chief Deputy Sheriff Levi Bontrager."* (The News-Democrat, *South Bend, Indiana, Jan. 23, 1948.*)

One photo showed an attractive young woman in bed, her hands folded together. A metal ring or tightly fitting bracelet on her wrist was connected to a long chain held by trench-coated Sheriff Luther Yoder and his deputy, Levi Bontrager, both Amish-derived family names. The caption claimed that the picture was taken before the woman's release. The second photograph showed her stern, white-bearded, seventy-five-year-old father clutching a Bible in one hand while Deputy Bontrager made fingerprints from the other. The caption reported that Bishop Hochstetler had been arrested on charges of assault and battery and sentenced to six months labor at the state penal farm.

On seeing the photographs in his local newspaper, J. W. Yoder immediately wrote a letter to Sheriff Yoder in Goshen. In an unusual and telling instance of clarity about his own church affiliation, Yoder introduced himself as having been raised Old Order Amish and currently belonging to the Amish Mennonite church. He explained that he usually attended his wife's Presbyterian church and had been asked by the men's Sunday school class there to interpret the Hochstetler case the following week. He demanded more details: Did the bishop chain his daughter to the bed because she wanted to join another church, or was she crazy before that? "If he tied her to keep her at home, and to prevent her from joining another church," he stressed, "then it should be thoroughly publicized." Yoder then described his own project of sending letters to heads of families in the Renno church concerning John D. Yoder's excommunication. In conclusion, he insisted that "the Law" should be interested in knowing if the bishop's punishment caused his daughter to "lose her mind."[50]

The sheriff replied that the newspapers had "greatly exaggerated" the conditions under which the woman was confined. Her late mother had secured five-foot calf chains to her daughter's wrists more than a year before, because she frequently ran away, and the family feared bodily harm from her. About ten years prior, the family had taken her for treatment to a hospital in Chicago, which lasted eleven weeks. The sheriff concluded that "the cause of her condition is not definitely ascertained," although police had a signed statement from a witness saying that she had wanted to leave the Amish community when she was eighteen years old. The family attested that "when she first showed signs of being abnormal she attended church regular and didn't voice any desire of leaving the Amish Church."[51]

Although he was deeply interested in public representations of the Amish, J. W. Yoder did not seem to see that the widely syndicated report of Lucy Hochstetler's unfortunate case may have said more about America than it said about the Amish. With Yoder, a nation in the grip of a cold-war reveled in the supremacy of its own democratic freedoms over against the repressions of alien, un-American cultures. The Hochstetler case provided another example of punishment for a traditional, anti-democratic enemy, a German-speaking group that had not contributed to the war against fascism in Europe. Having been criticized all of his life for leaving the Amish church—and sometimes denying that fact—Yoder focused on the possibility that Lucy must have gone mad because her father had tried to stop her from leaving an Old Order group. Meanwhile, Mennonite professors from Goshen College, John Umble and Guy F. Hershberger, believing that the bishop was the victim of cultural misunderstanding and anti-Amish sentiment, rallied the support of American Mennonites and petitioned the governor of Indiana for the bishop's pardon. He was paroled in April 1948, after serving less than half of his sentence at the county penal farm.

Recent research that sheds new light on the Hochstetler case suggests that Yoder's intuitive sense of the situation may have been nearly correct.[52] Of interest to this study is Yoder's immediate interest in Lucy as an individual, in contrast to the Mennonite professors who saw the case in social and political terms and therefore assisted the Hochstetler family in gaining the bishop's release. While Yoder suggested that "the Law" should determine whether the confines of Amish community caused Lucy to lose her mind, Umble and Hershberger rushed to protect the bishop—and by association themselves and all Anabaptist groups—from the American legal system, bias, and public disgrace.

At the age of seventy-five, Yoder had reached a place where he felt more sympathy for the liberty of an individual than for the rights of a separatist, traditional religious community. Yoder believed that Amish insistence on obedience to religious and family traditions made them enemies of a Christian nation devoted to liberty and preserving individual rights. Indeed, by 1950, he believed that "Christian America" had been achieved and reigned as normative, and so he argued against the ethic of separation on principle, claiming that ninety-eight percent of Americans were Christian.[53] In a chapter of *Amish Traditions* titled "The Unequal Yoke," he criticized the Amish practice of refraining from entering into business ventures with non-Amish people or using electricity from public lines, in obedience to the biblical teaching, "be ye not unequally yoked with unbelievers." If nearly all Americans are Christian, why fear being unequally yoked? He wrote, "I would rather err on the side of being too lenient and charitable toward those whom I do not know, than to look askance at everybody except the few in my own little church."[54]

The two-percent of Americans who did not belong to the Christian nation, according to Yoder, were Jews and Communists. In a surprising move, he compared traditional Amish people to both groups. The Amish resemble Jews because both comply with the "Old Dispensation" and live under the "Law," and Yoder concocted interesting linguistic blends to capture this parallel; for instance, Hebrew dietary laws became "the Jewish *Ordnung*."[55] An implicit reference to the Amish refusal to accept assurance of salvation is evident in Yoder's criticism of "the corrupt Jewish mind that was never sanctified by being born again for it depended on works."[56] He wrote, "I doubt that there are any real out-spoken unbelievers in the United States outside of the Jewish people."[57] Mention of Jews, the opponents of Christianity, is quickly followed by mention of Communists, the opponents of democracy: "All Communists who try to destroy the government of the United States and bring in Communist Russia, are unbelievers. The Communists are a godless, unbelieving, treacherouus [*sic*] lot."[58] The Amish resemble Communists because their leaders use coercion to advance an ideology:

> When you compel a man to do something against his will and wish, then you are using force. When the Communists take a country over and the people do not want to accept Communism, the Communists in power, use force: they kill the people. Which is the worse, to kill a man physically or to try to kill him spiritually?[59]

Individual liberty and a liberal, democratic society depend on public education, because learning makes possible independent thought and participation in the electoral process. With the zeal of his twenty years of working as a student recruiter for Juniata College, Yoder advocated education throughout *Amish Traditions*, repeatedly insisting that poor teaching and learning among the Amish preachers were the source of their schismatic spirit, primitive understandings of Scripture, and stubborn separation from the world. Following M. G. Brumbaugh's old formulation, Yoder attributed Amish resistance to historic and social conditions. Leaders of the Anabaptist movement were educated men, but they were quickly killed by the state and state church. Then, Yoder reasoned, the Mennonites decided, "Let us not educate ourselves until the persecutions are over." The persecutions lasted more than one hundred years, including the time of the Amish division, and the Amish have preserved a resistance to education ever since. "Had Jacob Amman been an educated man," Yoder speculated, "I candidly believe he would never have separated himself and his followers from the Mennonite church."[60]

Furthermore, Yoder believed that the prohibition against "worldly wisdom," based on 1 Corinthians 3:19, came from a failure to comprehend fully the language of High German Scriptures by a people who spoke mostly Pennsylvania German but learned to read and write English in country schools. The preachers were poorly educated in English and even less in High German, Yoder argued, so although they can read the words well enough, they did not always understand their meaning.

He then challenged his Amish readers to translate into English a German prayer they recite every Sunday to see if they fully understood it. Amish children at that time learned English in public school and German in private lessons, but Yoder pointed out that the German classes were generally taught by farmers who could read the language, but could not interpret it very well. Yoder recalled being superintendent of the Sunday school at Belleville when they still used German for worship, but when he went away to Brethren Normal School and studied under a professor educated in Germany, he realized how little he actually knew of the language. How then, he wondered, can Amish preachers understand the involved writings of Paul where he "goes deeply into the plan of salvation?"[61] For Yoder, clarity of abstract concepts was more important than tradition or the aesthetic sense expressed by some in his community who believed that German was "more religious," and closer to God.

Beyond questions of biblical interpretation, he had political reasons for urging the Amish to abandon German: "since we live in America, and since the language in America is English, we should adopt the English language." Although he had published poems in dialect early in the twentieth century, his views had shifted by 1950. Whereas the use of

Pennsylvania German once signaled a resistance to the dominance of Anglo culture and history, Yoder now believed that speaking dialect after two world wars betrayed a loyalty to Germany. Many non-Amish speakers of Pennsylvania German had abandoned the language during World War II, and Yoder feared that the Amish would appear backward or even evil if they persisted. "Avoid the appearance of evil," he quoted from the apostle Paul, explaining that Germany "has changed from a Christian nation to an almost atheistic nation under Hitler." Yoder characterized fascist Germany as "idolatrous"—and admonished the Amish to "Be not unequally yoked together with unbelievers" in this regard. Further, he urged the Amish to speak English as a sign of their gratitude for "protection" and religious liberty in the United States:

> But America has shielded us from persecution, gave us a home when there was much persecution in Germany and Switzerland, and America now gives us protection and all the liberties of a free government, and when America does that for us, should we not be loyal to America and speak the language spoken in America? [62]

Yoder's relentlessness during this period was dismissed by many as the obnoxious and pitiful behavior of a distinguished but disappointed old man. Driven by religious conviction, unable to respect cultural relativity or see that his own values would never be persuasive within an Old Order world, he expended diminishing time and funds to publish books, distribute mimeographed letters, and meet with individual members of the community to argue the errors of their ways. When John A. Hostetler asked why he had "gone off half cocked" in writing the *Meidung* letter, for instance, Yoder replied that the apostle Paul did not hesitate to write to the early Christian churches.[63] That most people ignored his messages only seemed to prove to himself that he spoke with the voice of a true prophet.

But his journey from scribe to prophet was fraught with many contradictions. Amish tradition and culture remained the deep source of his creative work, which had begun by facing a worldly audience and ended up facing his own community. The authoritarian and sexist stereotypes that offended him when he encountered them in the character of Moses Bontrager in *Straw in the Wind* were precisely the elements of Amish life that he attacked in his last book. But even as he argued for individual rights against the force of tradition and urged Amish people to adopt some aspects of contemporary culture, Yoder also hoped for increased Amish solidarity and sovereignty, never wishing that they lose their distinct culture and become absorbed into the American stream. Perhaps his distress about shunning, schism, disintegration, and the failure of relationship in the Big Valley congregations stemmed from a sense of his own dissenting impulses. His plea for the various groups to overcome the "forms that divide us" may well have been spoken to the various, contradictory parts of himself.

CHAPTER SIX

A FINAL PLEA FOR LIBERTY: *THE PRAYER VEIL ANALYZED* (1954)

If the preachers of the Plain churches would let the women decide for themselves whether they would wear caps and bonnets, or not, caps and bonnets would disappear from those churches like mist before a morning sun. "Where the spirit of the Lord is, there is liberty. . ." (2 Cor. 3:17).
—*J. W. Yoder*

"I am retired but not 'tired' by a long ways, 75 years old and always having been interested in health, I am sound as a dollar and strong as ever," Yoder wrote to J. I. Rodale, publisher and champion of organic gardening.[1] A few years later, in a letter to L. Ron Hubbard, he wrote "I might say that I am just about 82 years old, but by practicing Physical Culture and care in selecting the right food, I am in quite good health, and I have a passion to help other people be well."[2] As had been his pleasure since the 1890s, Yoder in old age continued to pursue alternative and experimental approaches to personal health, fitness, and farming—along with spiritual renewal and religious reform.

Joseph and Emily Yoder were both vegetarians, and their Huntingdon neighbors remember herbs creeping from overcrowded beds into the lawn of their home on Mifflin Street. When that lot proved too small, they cultivated vegetables in garden plots along Moore Street on the Juniata campus. Yoder's files from the '40s and '50s contain letters ordering various gadgets to sustain their dietary needs—a home flour mill, automatic sunflower seed huller, vegetable juicer—as well as nursery plants, including asparagus, sweet potato vines, berry bushes, and fig trees. Summers, they took in lectures on religion and health at the ecumenical Victorian institute for arts and religion at Chautauqua Lake in New York State.

HEALTHFUL VISIONARY

In addition to his public speaking and writing projects, Yoder energetically advocated healthful living. "Be careful what you eat, get plenty of rest, sufficient exercise, and breathe all the fresh air you can," a 1942 *Belleville Times* profile article quoted his advice. It reported that he "sleeps out of doors every night the whole year round. His bed sets on top of a flat porch roof, exposed on all sides and he sleeps there, even in stormy weather. He recommends horseback riding as the best exercise."[3]

In keeping with the critical tone of the rest of the book, the final chapter of *Amish Traditions*, reversed Yoder's earlier defense of the Amish ethics of work and thrift. "I strongly urge Amish men and women to shorten their hours before a breakdown comes, for when a severe breakdown comes, good health rarely returns," he wrote. "I urge especially shorter hours for expectant mothers." He attributed low birth weights and the small stature of the Big Valley Amish and Mennonite people to overwork and poor nutrition: selling milk rather than feeding it to their children and diets dependant on "the three great foods . . . white bread, meat, and potatoes," rather than unpeeled fruits and vegetables. He wondered whether "Ennui, sameness, lonesomeness, and lack of relaxation" accounted for the high incidence of mental illness in their community, comparing Amish people to the Benedictine farmer monks, whose motto "Ora et Labora" (Work and Pray), reflects a sprit of medieval asceticism.[4]

In 1952, he also inquired of "Simmy" Levi Yoder about purchasing an acre of land next to the Mennonite school in Big Valley, where he believed he could "quietly try to start some improvement in Amish churches." He imagined building a cottage in an organic Eden so that he could live among the Amish and "mingle with the people in the least offensive way." He wrote, "Besides this, I would also like to plant a small orchard and have a small truck patch where I would like to try out the

Organic Gardening method, so as to grow fruit free from blight without poisonous sprays and vegetables without poisonous powders and sprays and thus have healthier foods for all of us who wish good health and joyous living."[5] People in Big Valley recall Yoder's strange ideas and diet, remembering that he claimed he would live to be one hundred years old, but few regarded his advice as more than a curiosity.

In Huntingdon, Yoder conducted experiments with Dr. A. L. Laney, a local figure who is said to have treated Emily with telepathy. Yoder and Laney bought X-Ray tubes from Sylvania Electric and conducted research into "radiation therapy." Although he described their investigation mostly in terms of health and healing, in 1948 Yoder sent a letter to the War Department's Division of Bacterial Warfare describing their efforts to create a radiant mechanism that could detect germ assaults. He urged them to send a scientist from Washington to observe their device:

> From our findings we are morally certain that we as a nation are being subjected to Bacterial warfare right now, and something should be done about it. We are willing to serve in the defense of this apparent attack, but we cannot serve if we are ignored by those whose duty it is to give us the green light and stand by us.[6]

There is no evidence that Yoder ever received a response to this invitation, and it may be that his experiments with radiation contributed to the stomach cancer that eventually caused his death in 1956.

In many of his endeavors, Yoder was both behind and ahead of his time, and boldly so. His commitment to wholistic health and spirituality would not have seemed so strange in the 1890s—or even the 1990s—but in the 1950s, most Amish and Mennonite people regarded him as an eccentric at best. Nor does his concern for the threat of a biological threat in the United States seem outlandish in the twentieth-first century. It was common during the progressive movements of the early twentieth century for concern for individual health and well-being to involve a commitment to global peace, but Yoder held this belief during the Cold War era. An outline for a speech that he apparently presented in Chicago, Detroit, and Harrisburg sometime during 1947 suggests that he was deeply concerned with the advent of the Atomic Age. He warned his audiences of the "Frankenstein" potential of American science to "wipe out a nation in a few hours" and "ruin civilization." "We must make war impossible," he declared and argued that atomic energy should not be developed even for industrial use. In conclusion, he referred to the text from Deuteronomy 30:[7]

> See, I have set before thee this day life and good, and death and evil; In that I command thee this day to love the Lord they God, to walk in his ways, and to keep his commandments and his statutes and his judgments, that thou mayest live and multiply: and the Lord thy God shall bless thee in the land whither thou goest to posses it. . . . I call heaven and earth to record this day against you, that I have set before you life and death, blessing and cursing: therefore choose life, that both thou and thy seed may live (KJV, 15, 16, 19).

6.1 Striking a well-known pose of Crazy Horse, Yoder described this view of himself overlooking Big Valley, probably taken in 1948, as "Crazy Horse Yoder points to Jack's Mountain." The famous warrior was captured at Little Big Horn five years after Yoder's birth, and the Indian Wars were only some of the conflicts that marked Yoder's childhood.

THE PRAYER VEIL

Yoder's final project, a booklet on the prayer veiling, only offered further proof that he was not quite in tune with the spirit of his day. "Since I was never called to fill any high church office or position, I did not feel called upon to defend the church but was free to proclaim the Truth as it was revealed to me," he explained in a letter describing his project to Bishop A. J. Metzler, Mennonite Publishing House publishing agent.[8] In particular, Yoder believed that his unorthodox views on the prayer veil were divinely inspired. "After years of study I had what was next thing to a revelation on that chapter, and I wrote true to the revelation," he said in a letter to J. C. Wenger, another prominent Mennonite leader.[9]

The prayer veil, also called "head covering" or "devotional covering," is a white, bowl-like cap made of a stiff, thin fabric such as tulle, worn on the back of a woman's head. Although it first may have served primarily as a symbol of Mennonite separatism along with other articles of plain dress, the veil has come to signify male domination.[10] It is interpreted as a reminder of male "headship" or the gendered hierarchy supposedly justified by 1 Corinthians 11: "But I would have you know, that the head of every man is Christ; and the head of the woman is the man; and the head of Christ is God."

During the eighteenth century and the first half of the nineteenth century, some form of head covering was commonly worn by women in many American churches, but the custom began to disappear in most denominations after the Civil War. As early as the 1880s, mention of the head covering began appearing in *The Herald of Truth*, and John F. Funk called for a public discussion of the topic in 1904—indicating that the custom may have been falling out of practice among Mennonites as well.[11] S. F. Coffman published a series of articles in favor of the veil that year, but in 1906, preacher Amos Bauman anticipated one of J. W. Yoder's arguments against it, pointing out that the so-called "head covering" of the biblical era concealed a woman's entire body and served to protect her from the lustful male gaze. In light of this information, he argued, the small, white cap promoted by Mennonite leaders was meaningless, and should be abandoned. A corrective reply by David Burkholder followed Bauman's piece.[12]

By the beginning of the twentieth century, the prayer veil—previously sustained among Mennonites through tradition and nonverbal ritual—gained the status of an ecclesiastical ordinance, justified with rational and scriptural explanations.[13] Daniel Kauffman's 272-page *Manual of Bible Doctrine*, published by John F. Funk at Elkhart in 1898, lists the woman's prayer veil among the seven ordinances of the Mennonite church (along with baptism, communion, the rite of foot-washing, the holy kiss, anointing with oil for healing, and marriage). Inclusion in this book gave the prayer veil great weight because Kauffman was the most powerful man in the North American Mennonite community in his day. His *Bible Doctrines*, a 1914 revision of *Manual of Bible Doctrine*—combining evangelical religious doctrine with a commitment to "non-

6.2 (above) For a photograph taken to illustrate an article for the Chicago Chronicle, *these women dressed to illustrate Mennonite plain clothing— prayer veil and floor length or cape dresses—worn by members of the Prairie Street Mennonite Church, Elkhart, Indiana, 1903. Notice Lavona Berkey, standing back left and Anna Holdeman, front right.*

6.3 (below)*This is how the women of the class of 1901 actually dressed for their graduation portrait at the Elkhart Institute, when J. W. Yoder was on the faculty. Note Lavona Berkey, second row, far left; and Anna Holdeman, second row, second from right.*

conformity" or Mennonite distinctive dress and belief—was the seminal articulation of Mennonite practice in the early twentieth century and was known by some as "the Mennonite Bible."[14]

From 1908 until 1944, Kauffman also edited *Gospel Herald* at Scottdale, the successor of Funk's *Herald of Truth*. He replaced exchanges of readers' ideas with the "Question Drawer," wherein Kauffman responded to questions he fabricated himself as well as actual queries from readers. This monologic practice is emblematic of an authoritarianism that was common between 1898 and 1944, a period that Mennonite historian Leonard Gross has named "The Doctrinal Era," isolating it as an unfortunate and anomalous period in American Mennonite experience.[15]

During the first half of the twentieth century, the head covering and other manifestations of distinctive dress were the topic of official scrutiny and moral persuasion by the General Conference of the Mennonite Church, its national governing body. James Juhnke described how regulated dress, particularly the prayer veil, replaced the German language and social isolation as visible means of separating "old" Mennonites from American society and other Mennonite groups.[16] With Juhnke, Donald Kraybill believes that the veil became an "ethnic symbol of resistance" to urbanization, industrialization, and assaults on traditional community life made by public education and Christian fundamentalism. As such, it signified the group's obedience to a distinct biblical mandate and the wearer's conformity and commitment to the group, community boundaries, and sex role stratification.[17] Although they tried, church leaders never realized full uniformity of dress among Mennonites, but Pennsylvanians conformed to the dress codes more consistently than those in the West, and women complied more fully than men.[18]

During the Doctrinal Era, the head covering encountered ongoing resistance in J. W. Yoder's congregation at Belleville. Sometimes called "the Hollywood Church" by its critics, Maple Grove attracted those Amish Mennonites who would not submit to the rules of other more conservative churches, counting among its members some college-trained men and women, industrialists like Yoder's older brother Levi, bankers, professionals, and men active in local politics—those who had traveled beyond the rural, one-room schoolhouse and family farm. In 1925, Elmer Hess began progressive leadership of the congregation, introducing such innovations as a written church constitution drafted by a committee of its members, a ladies chorus that performed in worship services, and a name change from Belleville Amish Mennonite Church to Maple Grove Mennonite Church. By 1930, Maple Grove was known to be the most liberal congregation in Mifflin County, and in 1933, the bishops encouraged the congregation to respond to tensions in the church by engaging a more moderate minister, Aaron Mast.[19]

An elderly member of that congregation recalled this time and spoke of the reluctance of her mother and herself to wear the prayer veil. She recalled being told to wear either a net head covering or black bonnet in lieu of a mortar board at her public high school baccalaureate in 1928. So that she would be permitted to attend the ceremony, she finally agreed to wear a borrowed bonnet, because she owned none herself. "I didn't want to be plain," she stated in an interview. "I never was a plain Mennonite, and I am not now." It is significant that the church required her to display a sign of Mennonite identity and female submission at a school function, thereby setting her apart from her classmates and marking her allegiance to the religious community in a ceremony that afforded public recognition of her academic achievement in a secular institution. One Sunday morning during the 1930s, this young woman and a friend agreed to walk bareheaded into church, although they knew that stunt would reap a tongue-lashing from the bishop.

This rebellious act foreshadowed a much later Sunday morning, probably during the late 1960s or early 1970s, when she and three other women were the first to stop wearing head coverings to worship services. Around that time she found an article written by Mary Nissley in *Gospel Herald* arguing against the headcovering on biblical grounds; she clipped the piece and pasted it inside the cover of her Bible. She has always believed that the head covering was inextricably bound to gender inequity, recalling one episode during the 1950s when the bishop forbade her to stand before the congregation to lead a performance of a chorus that she had directed.[20]

This woman also recalled the support that Joseph Yoder gave to both mother's and daughter's resistance to the head covering. A loyal student of Yoder's singing schools, she remembered hearing her mother and Yoder denounce the head covering as "unbiblical" in heated conversations during Sunday dinners when she was still a girl. She regarded him as an articulate champion for women like herself and her mother who did not want to be "plain." She said, "He was just too much for the bishops. He knew how to argue it." It is probably not surprising that the Doctrinal Era was accompanied by the emergence of powerful bishops in the Mennonite church. Concern about the modern world and cultural assimilation created a climate of uncertainty wherein the Mennonite community was willing to grant authority to a few conservative and powerful individuals who could regulate change. Perhaps not incidentally, this era also saw the rise of powerful nation states and totalitarian leaders in the Western world.

Nowhere did Yoder hint at personal factors that may have shaped his own views on authority and the head covering. Some speculated that he was influenced by his worldly, Presbyterian wife, yet even before he met Emily, Yoder was well aware of women's issues. This perspective was probably shaped by the progressive views he encountered at Brethren Normal School, Elkhart Institute, and at Northwestern during the 1890s. At Elkhart, he shared the frustrations of female colleagues who were criticized for wearing conventional "worldly" attire for dress and athletics. During the years that he lived with the Hooleys, he watched their daughters grow into young womanhood, and he was active in the Women's Christian Temperance Union, an organization that from its inception at the Chautauqua Institute in 1874 followed president Frances E. Willard's support of suffrage and other liberating measures for women.

Throughout the *Rosanna* books, Yoder strongly identified with his mother and respected her physical and intellectual abilities. Especially sympathetic are his portrayals of the loyalty between female friends: Rosanna's foster mother, Elizabeth, and Bridget, Rosanna's birth mother; Elizabeth and Rosanna; Rosanna and Mary Carson, who loved her Amish mistress so much that she trudged across the snow banks so she could die in the Yoder home; and Rosanna and the non-Amish village girls who appeared unexpectedly, weeping at her funeral. The *Rosanna* books acknowledge the importance of women's work in the Amish community, while exposing inequities. In the depiction of Rosanna's baptism, the description of plain dress for new female church members is twice as long as the description of plain dress for men. On her way to the ceremony, Rosanna unselfconsciously unties her covering strings, which dance in the summer breeze. This gesture is more than vaguely symbolic, for by mid-century when Yoder published the

6.4 The Howard Hammer Evangelistic Crusade at Belleville in 1954. Joseph (in bow tie) and Emily (in black hat) Yoder s are in roughly tenth row on the left, seats 4 and 5, among members of the community who wear plainer dress.

Rosanna books, a common maxim referring to laxity in dress for Mennonite women warned, "When the strings go, everything goes!"

During and after World War II, as Mennonite pacifism and separatism collided with a spirit of unified patriotism in the nation, church leaders sought to buttress the nonconformed identity for both sexes. Mennonite archives contain numerous pamphlets and short booklets printed during the 1950s to disseminate official doctrine concerning the prayer veil. Artifacts of a bitter struggle, these little books represent a direct response or general backlash to cultural assimilation, increased education, and the changing roles of women in American society. The most substantial attempt was J. C. Wenger's 1951 volume, *Separated Unto God*, subtitled "A Plea for Christian Simplicity in Life and for a scriptural Nonconformity to the World." Written by a well-respected Goshen College and Seminary professor of Bible and philosophy, this book presented scholarly, theological and historical justifications for conforming to the beliefs and symbolic dress codes of the group.[21]

When *Amish Traditions* appeared in 1950, baptized Mennonite women in Mifflin County were required to wear the covering because it was scriptural and as a sign of subservient relationship to men in the church. Any memory of a time when the prayer veil was not part of official doctrine seems to have vanished. The issue became inflamed during the mid-1950s when tent preachers came to the Valley promoting spiritual renewal; during this time some people began to wear plain dress daily, not just for worship. In 1955 Don Augsburger and Clarence J. Ramer conducted a series of meetings focused on non-comformity.[22] Thus Yoder's increasingly pointed argument against the prayer veil represented a timely confrontation to clerical authority and contemporary practice. On one hand, it questioned gender roles symbolized by a head covering, upsetting the "order" of authority in the Mennonite home and religious community during an era when such roles were beginning to be destablized in mainstream American society. On the other, it challenged the emphasis on nonconformity for both sexes. In such a cultural and political climate, Yoder's views could not stand without censure.

Paul Erb

In 1951, editor and minister Paul Erb denounced *Amish Traditions* in a book review printed in both *Gospel Herald*, the official Mennonite news magazine, and in *The Budget*, a nationally distributed newspaper that prints reports from Amish settlements across the United States and Canada. In private correspondence with Yoder, Erb explained that he hesitated to give the book any notice at all until some wondered whether it had been printed at the Mennonite Publishing House, as *Rosanna* had been.

Erb started his review by observing that although Yoder had presented an unrealistically positive view of the Amish in his earlier *Rosanna* books, "the defending attorney has gone over to the prosecution." He expressed "embarrassment in reading the book, such as he would have felt in listening to a family quarrel." Especially unsettling was the chapter on the "Prayer Veil," in which Yoder argued that the apostle Paul, influenced by the misogyny of his historical and cultural setting, failed to follow Jesus' revolutionary example of honoring women. In consultation with scholarly commentaries, Yoder deviated from a literalist reading of 1 Corinthians 11, concluding that Paul's views were not divinely inspired and were not intended to be teachings for all time. To this, Erb responded forcefully:

> To the serious Bible student the doctrine of the devotional covering looks none the worse for this word-twisting. The expositor must know that the church in which he says he holds his membership cannot and will not follow him in his strange interpretation. Nor does any exegete of recognized ability.

The review's concluding paragraph unequivocally condemned Yoder's book with a call for Anabaptists to avoid it and a reiteration of the familiar fear that "outsiders" would think ill of the plain people because of it: "The Amish will not buy this book. It is not recommended to Mennonites. We can only hope that it will not mislead the general public who are trying to understand the underlying spirit of the Amish-Mennonite tradition."[23]

Although he had anticipated widespread resistance to *Amish Traditions*, such strong criticism from an educated church leader disturbed Yoder. Before publishing a rebuttal, he wrote a personal letter to Erb describing his own background and explaining the twenty-year "inward urge" that motivated him to write *Amish Traditions*. He then asked Erb to describe *his* experience with the Amish: had he been raised in an Old Order Amish community, how often had he attended an Amish preaching service, and did he speak the Pennsylvania German language? In a gesture reminiscent of undergraduate days and as he had occasionally done with the Amish bishops in Mifflin County, Yoder challenged Erb to a public debate. He closed the letter, "Hoping I may hear from you and that we may come to some understanding and thus promote the kingdom of God, instead of hindering it."[24]

In a letter that was more conciliatory than his review, Erb, the son of a Kansas Mennonite leader, replied that he did not share Yoder's knowledge of the culture and language of the Old Order Amish people. Nevertheless, he shared a concern for their spiritual welfare, hoping that their religious beliefs would gradually take more Protestant forms. He claimed to have had "some part in changing Amishmen into Mennonites" through a Sunday school in Kansas that evolved into an entire congregation composed of formerly Amish people. Further, he mentioned a lecture in which he had heard John A. Hostetler "give evidences of the breaking down of the Amish culture." He continued, "It will be a long, rather slow process, but I think gradually and slowly the change will come. . . . the ideas of the truly scriptural church will be coming to them." As evidence, he noted such evangelical touchstones as a growing interest in mission work among some Amish communities, but warned that Yoder would not help the cause by attacking them with argument. "What I chiefly question and what I question in my review is your method," he wrote.[25]

Concerning Mennonite beliefs on the covering, however, Erb was adamant: "Of course on the doctrine of the devotional covering I must be absolutely against your position. I cannot accept your major premise that Paul was not inspired, nor can I agree with your exposition." Erb admitted that some contemporary religious leaders found it difficult to persuade the "modern woman" to wear a head covering, but that should not concern the literal-minded faithful of his own group: "For us Mennonites it is not a question as to whether we can get people to wear it or not; if God teaches it, then we teach it." He concluded that a public debate would probably not be profitable, since neither of them seemed likely to change his mind.[26]

Yoder waited a month and a half before responding to Erb's letter, although he wrote that he thought of it "almost day and night." In a three-page, single-spaced, typed response, he emphasized his own concern for the Amish people and called his book "the most earnest endeavor to help the Amish ever made." Unable to accept Erb's resistance, Yoder imagined that Erb was "forced" by "uncharitable . . . ritualistic brethren" to discredit the book. He desperately begged him to read *Amish Traditions* again, "prayerfully and devoutly, then write a Christian review of the book and ask every Amish man and woman to read it." Yoder was most distressed by the "harm" that Erb had done by reaching beyond the Mennonite community to publish his review in *The Budget*, which he described as "THE Amish paper."

He added that their "difference of opinion" should not be "a contest for supremacy, nor a mere defense of a questionable church doctrine," but a genuine quest for "TRUTH." Yoder's TRUTH was expressed in his dismissal of traditional, "outward" or material forms, what he called "clothing religion" and in the recitation of two New Testament teachings: "Christ and Him crucified" and "Thou shalt love thy neighbor as thyself." In closing, he urged Erb to correct the "evil effect" of his book review.[27]

After this private exchange with Erb, Yoder sent a rebuttal to *Gospel Herald* printed as a letter to the editor. Almost twice as long as Erb's initial review, Yoder's piece charged that Erb had less personal knowledge of the Amish than he and stressed that he was "*for* the Amish people." He cited specific, negative words Erb used to discredit his arguments and exposed his strategy: "It's an old rhetorical trick to turn the minds of the Amish and the Mennonites against me, so that when he comes to the great issue, the veil, he can finish me with one stroke." Alluding to his own college education, Yoder seemed especially offended that Erb would question his ability to interpret Scripture and biblical commentary on "the great issue."[28] This offense to his training and intelligence seems to have helped motivate Yoder to study the matter for several years and eventually draft his last published work, *The Prayer Veil Analyzed*.

As the rebuttal continued, Yoder urged Mennonite and Amish readers to use their literacy to *defy* authority as some had done during Reformation times—to ignore official ecclesiastical teachings and to interpret his book critically for themselves. Referring to Erb, he wrote,

> Does he mean to insinuate that the Mennonites are not able to read a book and decide for themselves what is truth and what is falsehood? Does he try to take you back to the Dark Ages when only the priests were allowed to interpret Scripture? . . . Why not buy the book, study it honestly and judge for yourself whether it

is truth or falsehood? Why let an editor do your thinking? Editors rarely dare think for themselves. They are under orders.[29]

In conversation with Erb, Yoder often mentioned Erb's official status as Mennonite editor and minister, implying that whatever personal views Erb may have held were bound to conform with institutional policies in public. According to his own mythology, Yoder refused to conform in dress or thought to anything that compromised his individual conscience, beginning with his first taste of "liberty" as a student at Brethren Normal School—and perhaps well before, given the "Irish liberty" in his Amish home. As a young man, he rejected external symbols that marked Amish and Mennonite separation from the world, although he recognized the value of wearing a *muthze* or Amish coat to honor his parents when he attended their church. In his first letter to Erb, Yoder had introduced himself as an individual situated outside church institutions, and claimed that this is largely due to dress:

> In 1898-01 as I taught at The Elkhart Institute, forerunner of Goshen College, I said to them as I left to continue my education, "When I am thru college, if you need me, I'll come back and teach for whatever salary you can pay,—for board and room if you cannot pay more." But they never called me. I suppose because I could never bring myself to wear a straight collar coat and to go without a necktie. The Mennonite church never used me, even debated at the Allensville Conference about ten years ago, whether they could let me lead a hymn because I did not have a regulation coat. This has left me entirely free. I could do my duty as I saw it, without danger of losing my position. I am quite sure that there are other men who feel the same as I do in *Traditions*, but who would not say it or write it—they might lose their jobs or favor with the bishops. I had nothing to lose either financially or ecclesiastically.[30]

Yoder regretted never having been called to teach at Goshen College, yet he recognized that his refusal to wear the "regulation coat"—a dark, Nehru-style suit jacket that served as a sign of nonconformity for Mennonite men—afforded him freedom to speak and publish his own convictions. Central to Yoder's experience and to his argument against the prayer veil for women was the idea that confines on the body—through regulated dress—imposed confines on the mind and spirit.

This argument continued to resound in Yoder's local community and congregation.

JAMES PAYNE

In late summer 1951, around the time that Yoder published his response to Erb's review in *Gospel Herald*, he printed an even stronger and more lengthy rebuttal in *The Belleville Times*, the local Big Valley newspaper. He reiterated his concern for the Amish churches in Big Valley— "the lack of Christian fellowship, Sunday schools, Bible instruction, and the bearing of useless burdens"—claiming that this concern led him to write *Amish Traditions*, although he knew he would be "persecuted" by churchmen like Erb. In addition to the arguments put forth in the *Gospel Herald* letter, this piece accused Erb of bearing "false witness" when he wrote that "no exegete of recognized ability" disagrees with the wearing of the veil. Erb's review was incited, Yoder wrote, by a fear that Mennonites would become "enlightened on the veil" and recognize with Yoder that "Jesus never subordinated woman . . . and wearing a veil to subordinate woman to man is an oriental custom that has no rightful place in Christianity."[31]

Although many Mennonites and Amish people in the local community were annoyed by Yoder's public criticism of Amish and Mennonite traditions, only young James Payne challenged Yoder in writing. A marginal member of the community, marked by a non-Mennonite name, Payne's story and his engagement with Yoder trace the contours of the debate about the head covering in Big Valley as well as later changes in the covering's role as an emblem of belief and cultural identity.

Payne's father had grown up in the Methodist church on the Eastern Shore of Maryland and refused to enlist in World War I because of personal religious convictions, unaware of Quakers, Mennonites and other historic peace churches. At Camp Meade, he first met Mennonite pacifists. After the war, he moved to another Maryland community where Mennonites from Mifflin County had settled, and through those people, visited Big Valley and met and married James's mother. The couple returned to Maryland, but she became so homesick that during the Depression he sold his farm on the Eastern Shore and moved to the Valley to work as a day laborer. Health problems made it difficult for him to keep a steady job, and he was never accepted into that community.

Payne recalled growing up with a feeling that he did not belong either, partly because—like Yoder—he had a parent from outside. "When I grew up, I had two goals," he recalled. "One was to get a steady job, the other was to be accepted in this Valley."[32]

Publishing a letter that expressed popular sentiment against J. W. Yoder was one way to gain community acceptance. Previously, Payne had published a letter in the newspaper suggesting that the county agent cooperate with local farmers to remedy a rat infestation. He urged everyone to set poison at the same time, and had ridden his bicycle around the community to make sure that even Amish farmers got the message and complied with the plan, which was successful. Discrediting Yoder would be easier than ridding a Valley of rats, he thought, so Payne composed the letter. In retrospect, he guessed he felt compelled to defend Paul Erb and the church. "I was a young guy then—nineteen or twenty years old. I was pious and conscientious. After I asked more questions and so forth, I changed [later in life]," he recalled in an interview.[33]

Payne's argument addressed Yoder's interpretation of 1 Corinthians as well as asking the questions that were on many lips and minds concerning J. W. Yoder: If he is so concerned about the Amish, why is he offering this book for sale to everyone and thereby shaming them in public? Why did he live a "double life"—calling himself Amish yet refusing to act or believe as an Amish person?[34]

When the letter was published, Payne became a local hero. Even Presbyterians praised him. However, Payne also felt uncomfortable with approval "coming from outsiders" who didn't wear the prayer veil themselves and only objected to J. W. Yoder's critical approach. He recalled, "Everybody said somebody should do it, but no one would do it. People were glad I did it. Nobody, even outside the Mennonites, criticized me, although I got some postcards that said something about packing up and going someplace else, but I don't know where they came from."[35] In Yoder's correspondence, a letter from a supporter included the following passage, which is probably what James received as an anonymous postcard:

> Now here is what happened to the Allensville boy who tried to come back at you: Dear Jim—Your recent article published in the public press had qualified you for immediate service in Korea— kindly get your Bibles and all needed material ready and possibly if your [sic] so almighty you can end the conflict and bring peace

to the world. Yours for a better world to live in P.S. hope you will live to be as old as bro. Yoder now is. You will know more. Signed a Mifflin Co. Tax Payer.[36]

Yoder inquired about the identity of the young letter writer at local stores, but he never met him. His rebuttal to the "young man, Payne" in *The Belleville Times* called Payne's letter "a heterogeneous conglomeration of irrelevant generalities which says exactly nothing," and Yoder wondered whether "when he gets older he may learn how to write." The piece referred to numerous Scripture verses while reiterating the main points of *Amish Traditions*. Yoder then offered good wishes for his friends in the Valley and good will toward his "enemies," reminding them of his experience and assuring them once more of his intent:

> I am older than most of you, I have traveled more than most of you, I have worked with many different Christians. I think I have learned something and I am just trying to pass what I have learned on to you. To find fault with you? No. To condemn you? No. But to help you and to start you to thinking, and not just blindly, follow a leadership which has left us unscripturally divided, lacking in the charity that thinkest no evil, and in the unity that makes us one in Christ Jesus.[37]

The exchange with James Payne prompted letters to *The Belleville Times* from a Harvard theology student named Paul H. Bennett, a Catholic-born Mennonite convert from New Jersey who was familiar with the Big Valley community. Bennett lamented the "critical frame of mind that so many 'educated' folks get into" when they leave their home communities, and criticized Yoder's approach as well as his views on the prayer veil, citing biblical references.[38] In a published response, Yoder accused Bennett of trying to curry favor with the Mennonite bishops.[39] Bennett replied with lengthy but evenhanded responses to each of Yoder's major criticisms of the Amish, defending their customs through readings of Scripture.[40]

Meanwhile, Payne enrolled for one year at Eastern Mennonite College, the Virginia school created in 1917 as a conservative alternative to Goshen. He then returned to the Valley to teach at Belleville Mennonite School and married Marian Yoder, a fellow schoolteacher and Big Valley native, whose father was a friend of J. W. Yoder from their childhood days in the Peachey Amish church. A pupil of Yoder's singing schools,

Marian would later lead the Belleville Mennonite Chorus, which sang hymns at J. W. Yoder's funeral. Finally accepted into the community, Payne was later ordained for mission work and called to pastor a Mennonite congregation in Martinsburg, Pennsylvania, while also teaching public school. There, in 1965, he again encountered the prayer veil question, but this time from a quite different position.

The trouble began when a young woman returned to the congregation from studies at Moody Bible Institute and refused to wear a head covering to church. She explained her position to Payne, who accepted it. Significantly, her father supported his daughter's decision and opposed the church council on her behalf, threatening that the entire family would go to another congregation if the covering became a test of his daughter's membership. Payne sought to resolve the conflict by writing to Mennonite church conferences countrywide to discern their perspectives. He was surprised to find that a great amount of discussion and research was underway—but none of it was being published.

It became clear to Payne that leaders were amid a discreet and thorough examination of the prayer veil. "But I wouldn't have known this if I hadn't written to people all over the church," he recalled, "and I couldn't use any of that [information] because the bishops wouldn't let me." He aimed to write a discussion paper to distribute to his local church members, but the bishops also forbade him to do that. A written text, able to travel beyond the immediate congregational conversation, could have invited broader conflict and possibly impeded the leaders' secret proceedings. Finally, though oral discourse, Payne persuaded the church council unanimously to accept a statement in favor of individual interpretation of tradition and Scripture: the church condoned wearing of the prayer veil, but individual women could decide for themselves.[41]

A retired minister in the congregation "lost sleep over that," in Payne's words, and appealed to another older member of the congregation who was active in church-wide organizations. This man said, "You can't do this," and he went to the bishop who said, "You can't do this," Payne recalls. The question came back to the church council through the executive committee of Allegheny Conference, a regional oversight body. Eventually, the conference decided that although they strongly upheld the covering, conference regulations could not stop a local congregation from taking its own position on the issue. By that time, Payne resigned from the pastorate after a deacon of the church requested that he be "silenced," or formally forbidden to preach or function as a minister. Payne gave a year's notice and continued to serve the congregation while a replacement was found. Within a few years, the head covering was no longer required as a test of membership for women in the Allegheny Conference of the Mennonite Church.[42]

The father of five children, Payne left the ministry altogether and completed a doctoral degree in education at Pennsylvania State University, funded by a government scholarship program. He then taught teacher education at Shippensburg State University for twenty years before retiring. Marian also holds an advanced degree in education and worked in the Shippensburg public schools as a supervisor of reading instruction. Their story highlights tensions between an authoritarian, localized, and literalist, traditional community and the forces that gradually caused it to change.

Emblematic of that change was the disappearance of the head covering, which served the dual purpose of symbolizing rigid hierarchies that ordered families, gender and ecclesiastical authority, and signifying communal solidarity and separation. It may be significant that Payne and his wife both become educators in public institutions. Particularly for him, it is apparent that values obtained through his own education—textual research, critical thinking, writing, and an emphasis on individual interpretation of texts and circumstances—contributed to his demise as a Mennonite pastor. In this way, his story is not unlike J. W. Yoder's, but unlike Yoder, Payne drifted into a profession in mainstream society rather than returning to convert his home community.

In retrospect, Payne believes that although J. W. Yoder appeared to be meddlesome and arrogant at the end of his life, he acted out of concern, and that "he was much more sincere than we ever gave him credit for." In his training and work in Pennsylvania public education, Payne occasionally heard people speak of J. W. Yoder as an esteemed member of the educators' community. Yoder was more respected outside the Valley than within, believes Payne, because the very things that "got him ahead" in his career—an aggressive, self-promoting, outspoken personality—caused consternation in the Valley. "You're not supposed to get ahead, just to get accepted," Payne reflected. He now thinks that Yoder "desperately wanted to be accepted in the place where he grew up. At the same time, he could no longer accept what they believed."[43]

"In the Dog House"

The public scandal around Yoder's views of the prayer veil, as it played out during summer 1951 in reviews and published letters to *Gospel Herald* and *The Belleville Times*, had immediate consequences in Yoder's own congregation. Some members of Maple Grove still remember a heated argument between Yoder and Bishop Aaron Mast that took place in the aisle after worship one Sunday morning shortly after *Amish Traditions* was reviewed in *Gospel Herald*. Those who witnessed the episode confirm that it concerned the prayer veil.

A letter from Yoder to Mast written a week after the altercation indicates that the bishop had raised questions as to whether Yoder should share in "communion" or the ceremony of the Lord's Supper, due to his views on the veil. In response, Yoder first stated his principled objection to the church's policy of "closed" communion, which permits only those who are members of the local congregation—and perceived to be in accord with the community's interpretation of biblical teachings—to participate in the rite. Valuing personal interpretation, individual belief, and ecumenicity, Yoder held that "closed" communion turns small issues like the prayer veil into a test of membership, and argued that all who "feel that they have peace with God" should be permitted to partake of the Lord's Supper—a view that is counter to more communitarian Anabaptist understandings. As a compromise with the bishop, he agreed to absent himself from church on the Sunday that the Lord's Supper was observed to "avoid strife, contention and maybe division."[44]

Further, Yoder stated in the letter that as the oldest living member of the Maple Grove Church, he did not relish the idea of a "bishop coming in from outside" and pushing him out. He was referring to the fact that Mast had been installed at Maple Grove about twenty years before to replace the liberal Elmer Hess, who eventually left to pastor a congregation of "new" or General Conference Mennonites in Lancaster County. At that time, some supporters of the progressive Pastor Hess also transferred their membership to the General Conference church at Richfield in Juniata County, some distance from Big Valley. When the prayer veil controversy began to heat up, Yoder explored the possibility of transferring his own membership to the General Conference—following a jump that had been made thirty years before by old Mennonites at Goshen College who were beleaguered by anti-modernist bishops from the East. A 1951 letter from General Conference historian Cornelius

Krahn indicates that Yoder had written him a letter expressing an "inclination to join a General Conference Mennonite congregation." Krahn welcomed the possibility but also expressed his feeling that the General Conference had "fallen into another extreme, ignoring the values of a true spiritual nonconformity to the world," and that J. W. Yoder had overlooked this "factor" in *Amish Traditions*.[45]

Already anticipating "church trouble" the previous year, Yoder had written a letter to Paul Witmer, his 1898 student from the Elkhart Institute who later served as a dean at Goshen College. Yoder asked Witmer why Noah Byers, the bright, young president of Goshen College, had left the old Mennonite church and joined the General Conference, along with former Goshen dean and historian C. Henry Smith, and Witmer himself. Although he may not have known the details of their difficulties at the time, Yoder remembered that this first generation of graduate school-trained Mennonites encountered conservative pressure that eventually closed Goshen College. Nearly thirty years later, he reached out to faculty members of "the old Goshen," linking his predicament to theirs—a connection that was not so far-fetched. In a letter to C. J. Stahly, a former Mennonite from Curryville, Missouri, who had written to Paul Erb in support of Yoder's *Amish Traditions*, Erb himself implied that Yoder's approach to the prayer veil had been influenced by "modernist interpreters." Yoder explained to Witmer, "I suppose I will be in the Dog House soon, so maybe I will have to look for a place to go."[46]

Witmer replied that while he was dean of Goshen, he had been destroyed by Mennonite traditionalists concerned with female attire:

> The old brethren were constantly nagging us about the way the girls dressed. Some of these girls were members of the churches served by our worst critics. They demanded us to do what they were unable to do. After standing this for eight years my endurance was exhausted.[47]

Unable to control their daughters and maintain "order" at home, the leaders asked the larger religious institution to enforce the dress code. Thus, the issues of obedience and control in the family were entangled with authority patterns in the community. When these patterns intersected with the educational agenda, tensions mounted with constituents, on whom the school depended for financial support.

J. E. HARTZLER

Byers and Smith, arguably the most gifted Mennonite scholars of their day, also suffered at the hands of traditionalists and fundamentalists during the Doctrinal Era and eventually sought academic and ecclesiastical freedom at Bluffton College, affiliated with General Conference Mennonites. In a letter to Yoder, J. E. Hartzler, the flamboyant former president of Goshen College, explained the position of many early Elkhart Institute graduates who later joined the General Conference: "We did not 'leave' the Old Church. We were, in fact, eliminated. Conditions were such in the leadership of the Old Church that an intelligent man could not remain there and maintain his personal self-respect."[48]

J. E. Hartzler resigned from the presidency of Goshen College in 1918. According to an official college history, he had been a popular preacher as a young man, but Hartzler's training at Union Theological Seminary in New York City raised questions about his ideological purity among conservatives during the Doctrinal Era. More significantly, perhaps, his expansive vision for Goshen College contributed to a substantial deficit, and fund-raising efforts that included appeals to non-Mennonite donors neither dissolved the debt nor assuaged charges of "liberalism" from Mennonite board members.

Hartzler was replaced by a series of successors partly chosen in hopes of regaining the support of a Mennonite constituency.[49] Hartzler believed that he was forced to resign because of his Union Theological Seminary education: "[Bishop Aaron] Loucks told me definitely that the problem at Goshen College was not financial, but the fact that I was a Union graduate and that my students were following my advice rather than the advice of the older leadership."[50] His final break with the "old" Mennonite Church came in 1920 when he was denied communion in the Lord's Supper at a Kansas Mennonite congregation, by a bishop responding to anti-modernist pressure from Hartzler's former bishop in Indiana. The Kansas bishop who refused to let him take part in the Lord's Supper was T. M. Erb—father of Paul Erb, who had taken Yoder to task for his views on the prayer veil.[51] In 1926, Hartzler published *Education Among the Mennonites of America*, which launched an argument similar to the complaint in J. W. Yoder's books: that restrictive bishops were responsible for educational limits and theological difficulties.

Yoder found a kindred soul in J. E. Hartzler, who was also raised in an Old Order Amish home, but whose education carried him far from the beliefs of his background, although he moved back to live in the Mennonite community at Goshen during his final years.[52] During the 1950s, Yoder was bolstered by at least one visit to Hartzler's home in Goshen and by many supportive and entertaining letters that greeted him as "My dear Professor." These letters often contained optimistic, pithy slogans expressing progressive Christian sentiments reminiscent of a previous era. Selections from these letters include the following affirmations of forward-looking men of faith, which both perceived themselves to be:

> Christianity is not a religion that makes everybody think alike. It is the one religion that makes people love each other when they do not think alike.[53]

> Somebody must go "too fast" in every generation if people of the next generation are to go at all.[54]

> Time is always on the side of the progressives; never on the side of the conservatives. . . . Only the things shot through with eternity will remain.[55]

Yoder also sought Hartzler's advice on transferring his church membership, possibly to a non-Mennonite denomination, six months *before* Erb's printed reprimand or the altercation with Bishop Aaron Mast. In response, Hartzler traced his own troubles with the Mennonite church but suggested coercive tactics of the bishops had softened since the 1920s. He found it "unfortunate at [Yoder's] age," and in light of his contributions to Amish and Mennonite culture, that he should seek "refuge" in another denomination. But, he conceded, "this often happens to men who think and have ideas and convictions."[56]

Naturally, Hartzler praised *Amish Traditions*, which Yoder had sent for his review, seeking especially his response to the chapter on the prayer veil. Hartzler replied that if "our people" were to follow the Bible literally, the bishops should wear bonnets, not the women! (As evidence, he referred to verses in Exodus, Ezekiel, and Isaiah commanding men to cover their heads.) Besides, he observed, the contemporary Mennonite woman bears no resemblance to her draperied oriental counterpart, but looks more like a "battleship with a postage stamp pasted on it." He concluded, "all of this only shows what absurdities people get into when they take the literalistic view of the Scriptures."[57]

The Prayer Veil Analyzed

From 1951 until 1954, Yoder worked diligently on his final project, *The Prayer Veil Analyzed.* The introduction to this fifty-five-page, staple-bound booklet situates it in conversation with spoken and written texts: "The writer of this pamphlet would like to say that he was so severely criticized for his chapter on the Prayer Veil in his book *Amish Traditions,* that he thought he might be wrong." Ostensibly self-doubt compelled him to study popular novels such as *The Robe* as well as scholarly Bible commentaries and *The Interpreters Bible.* J. E. Hartzler, who taught and studied in Beruit and Israel, also provided insight into Middle Eastern custom; in the book Yoder acknowledged this "friend" who "does not wish his name mentioned."[58] As well, Yoder's files include correspondence with biblical scholars and cribbed translations of Greek texts.

The project represents something of a departure, for Yoder drew heavily on research from beyond his own memory and conversation. No longer concerned with representing the Amish to the world through popular literature, or even representing the Amish to themselves in hopes of changing their customs, the work seriously engages a theological debate focused on the meaning of 1 Corinthians 11: 2-16. *The Prayer Veil Analyzed* is a quirky text nonetheless, because Yoder's pet themes and characteristically rambunctious diction flavor his arguments.

In general, he vigorously reiterated the law/grace dualism established in *Amish Traditions* and blamed the prayer veil doctrine on uneducated churchmen who failed to distinguish between a hollow tradition and a meaningful ordinance. The head covering, or "veil of subordination," he claimed, is a vestige of an ancient, barbaric, ignorant, sexist, and legalistic age, and therefore it belongs to the Old Dispensation of the Law. Under the New Dispensation of Grace, women were liberated through the teachings and example of Jesus Christ, and any attempt to dominate women is regressive and sinful.

Yoder drew an analogy between ritual male circumcision, another controversy during Paul's day, and the veil, because both are ancient and irrelevant "outward forms" of religion. By retaining the veil for women, he wrote, the Plain churches have "fallen from grace," emphasizing material rather than spiritual values and relying on works rather than grace for salvation. In his words, "Judaism stands for authority: Carnal man enjoys it. Christianity stands for Liberty . . . carnal man resents it." In the class of "carnal" men, Yoder included "Bishops and preachers who enjoy their authority which has been derived from compelling women to wear the veil."[59]

Yoder also blamed church schism on the carnal desire to dominate others, and elsewhere he observed that power struggles between preachers prove that they do not like to be subordinate themselves, and he guessed that neither would they like to wear "an emblem of defeat" on their heads as women must.[60] The will to dominate women and others is neither Christian nor democratic, and Yoder blended spiritual language and political rhetoric, linking church and state in a way that may have bewildered most sectarian Mennonites. "America stands for freedom and liberty: the veil stands for subordination and subordination forbids both liberty and freedom. To compel women and girls to wear veils is not only unchristian but it is un-American. Let any legalist deny that."[61]

Moreover, Yoder called the veil "backward." Because it functioned to protect women from sexual libertines in antiquity, the head covering should shame contemporary Christian men who presumably have developed the ability to control their passions. At the same time, he wrote, Christian education has advanced women beyond the status of slaves and made it unnecessary for them to keep silent and submissive, as instructed by the apostle Paul. Concerning Paul, Yoder indulged in some speculation about the source of his "ungracious attitude toward women," noting that he was educated in the university at Tarsus, where Greek philosophers regarded marriage only as a necessary evil. Yoder speculated that Paul, a bachelor, was probably also unattractive to the opposite sex. (Yoder's only evidence for this is Paul's "thorn in the flesh," cryptically mentioned in 2 Cor. 12:7.) In any case, he argued that Paul's writing on the matter was not inspired by an "inner" or divine guidance, but shaped by exterior, cultural forces.

In contrast to misogynistic Paul, Jesus loved women and was loved by them. In fact, Yoder believed that Jesus was "the first man in the world to exalt woman."[62] He sketched several biblical narratives in which Jesus values women in defiance of cultural norms of his time: the woman caught in adultery, the Samaritan woman at the well, Mary Magdalene, Jesus' mother, Mary, and the sisters Martha and Mary. Yoder imaginatively reconstructed these stories, so that Jesus lounges with Martha's sister, Mary, discussing "the sorrowful plight of woman" and promising her that he will "begin a civilization and a culture in which woman would be exalted and some day be as free and as highly honored as man."[63] Yoder even revised the story of Eve, so the blame for the Fall is shared equally by Adam, who, if he had been "any kind of man," would have said, "No, dear, I cannot let you eat that fruit. It is 'forbidden' and I will not eat of it. We must not sin in the sight of God." Instead, Adam eagerly tastes the fruit and "doubtless" demands to be served another by his female partner: "Can you get me some more?"[64]

The consequences of the erroneous prayer veil doctrine, according to Yoder, range from a blight on fashion to the impoverishment of a community that does not benefit from the talents of half of its population. The prayer veil has "worked untold hardships on beauty loving women of the Plain churches," he wrote.[65] Arguing as an artist on behalf of a Divine Creator, he insisted that a love of the beautiful and ornamental is "God-given" in both men and women: "Men love well groomed horses: why not treat our women as well as we treat our horses? . . . God has beautified almost everything in the world, flowers, animals, skies, rainbows and sunsets: why discourage and forbid beauty in women?"[66] The females who are subordinated and denied an education, as his mother Rosanna was, never develop their musical, literary, or oratorical talents. This loss is greater than an individual one, for many others are then denied the benefit of these women's edifying productions and performances:

> There is no question about it, the Veil has done untold harm to our fine Christian girls. Many girls with fine voices could have become beautiful singers, and inspired thousands, but the subordination veil forbid training. How many might have become writers of inspiring books and articles, but they were subordinated and were not allowed education. Some with fluency of speech could have become fine Readers, and given inspiration to thousands, but the subordination veil closed every opportunity for training.[67]

Even when education is possible for some females, the prayer veil works its sinister intent psychologically. According to Yoder, it signifies that the woman is not entirely free, and therefore the veil constrains both her mind and imagination by diminishing her self-esteem and confidence:

> Besides being a sacrifice that does no one any good, wearing a cap humiliates and depresses many women, so that their God-given

talents are smothered by the thought of their being subordinated to man by the cap. No one can do his best spiritually or materially if he feels . . . bound and hindered by another person or persons.[68]

Bondage as a metaphor for both sin and tradition was familiar to Yoder's readers and central to much of his thinking concerning Amish and Mennonite customs. He often cited another of Paul's letters to the Galatians (5:1): "Stand fast therefore in the liberty wherewith Christ has made us free, and be not entangled again in the yoke of bondage." A Big Valley preacher from the Spicher Amish church (now Valley View Amish Men-

6.5 J. W. Yoder and his "prideful bow tie," c. 1954.

nonite) recalled that Yoder visited their service one morning and listened to his sermon. Afterward, Yoder complimented the preacher on his surprisingly sound treatment of the biblical passage, but challenged, "Now, can you shave your beard?" When the man replied in the negative, Yoder announced, "Well, then you're still in bondage!"

Defying both church teaching and common practice, *The Prayer Veil Analyzed* got little public notice after its release in 1954, and apparently it was largely ignored by Amish and Mennonite readers. Yoder's correspondence contains a few letters of support from his friends and some rebukes from plain people. One man, for instance, scolded him for his flamboyant demeanor, "prideful bow tie," and for publishing the "deceptive booklet":

> "You are the first and only so-called Mennonite that I ever heard of with such kind of wild tasteless expression. What else is it, but false teaching from false brethren? . . . Now, here are plain facts, that Paul is writing just what he received from the Lord. He did not suck it out of his own thumb [like you did].[69]

During his final years, the Yoders spent much time in the Amish and Amish-Mennonite hamlet of Pine Craft, on the outskirts of Sarasota, Florida. There he continued speaking and occasionally arguing with members of the plain churches who were vacationing from their homes in Pennsylvania, Ohio and Indiana. By winter 1955, he showed some signs of sickness, but he was ill for only a few months before his death from cancer in the hospital at Huntingdon on November 13, 1956.

His funeral reflected a restored relationship with the Mennonite community at Belleville, from which Yoder never transferred his membership. About five years after his memorable altercation with Bishop Aaron Mast, Mast took part in the service, although by then he had retired and was living in Lancaster County. He was joined by Jacob Weirich, the Maple Grove pastor at that time, J. Raymond Powell, of Emily's Presbyterian Church in Huntingdon, and Bishop A. J. Metzler of the Mennonite Publishing House at Scottdale, who preached the sermon. The choir from the Belleville Mennonite school sang Yoder's favorite songs from the church balcony during the service, including the German hymn "*Ich Weiss Einen Strom*," and the casket was borne by his Big Valley nephews.

6.6 Gravestone for Joseph W. Yoder in Locust Grove Cemetery, Belleville, Pennsylvania.

Yoder was buried in the Amish Mennonite cemetery at Locust Grove. A modest headstone above a single grave there announces, "Joseph W. Yoder / Author of Rosanna of the Amish." He is not identified by the relationships that often identify individuals in such places—husband, father, son—but known only by his chosen identity.

After his death, Emily Yoder tried unsuccessfully to find a publisher who would keep all of Yoder's books in print. In 1961 Herald Press at the Mennonite Publishing House negotiated to assume publishing rights for *Rosanna of the Amish* and *Amische Lieder* only, and Emily arranged for royalties to be sent to her own heirs. Herald Press bought for resale the remaining six hundred copies of *Amische Lieder* at ninety cents a piece, but never reprinted it, and published a paperback edition of *Rosanna of the Amish*, which remains among the company's best-selling titles. During the 1970s, pocket paperback editions of *Rosanna of the Amish* and *Rosanna's Boys* were published and distributed by Choice Publications, a division of the Mennonite Board of Missions. Sold in racks in restaurants and other public places, these books are designed to appeal to the curious outsider and tourist, as Yoder intended.

In 1995 Herald Press also reissued a new, quality paperback edition of *Rosanna of the Amish* to mark the centennial of Rosanna's death. This version includes new maps, bibliographical information, and a foreword by Yoder's great-neice. Unfortunately, this edition was so heavily edited that a comparison between it and the 1940 edition reveals substantial changes not only in Yoder's diction and syntax but also in historical content. It is as if the editor-bishops at Scottdale had finally managed to domesticate Yoder's quirky language, correct his unproven oral sources, and, finally, dress the willful author in a plain coat.

EPILOGUE

FIELD WORK
AND FOLK TALK

Isn't storytelling always a way of searching for one's origin, speaking one's conflicts with the Law, entering into the dialectic of tenderness and hatred. —Roland Barthes, The Pleasure of the Text

Although I was unaware of it at the time, this project began in 1992 when I published *Sleeping Preacher*, a collection of poems partly based on family stories from Mifflin County, Pennsylvania, where I was born. As the book was about to be released, I experienced a conflicting array of emotions—satisfaction, even pride, shame, fear, guilt, and an inescapable sense that I had betrayed my family and community. Although I recognized that the poems express some attempt to preserve and usefully interpret a traditional culture and landscape that my parents had begun to leave before I was born, my deepest feeling was an ill-defined sense of transgression. Publication had transformed me into an author in the eyes of my family and community, albeit one who had bartered communal stories for personal success. Although I had been thinking of myself as a writer for many years, this new sense of authority came with great awkwardness. There was the awkwardness of others' esteem that seemed out of proportion to my own sense of self and the pain of strained relationships that had little hope for conversation; I did not know how to respond to either.

The appearance of my book may have been unusual from the perspective of the Mennonite community, but it easily found a place on the long shelf of multicultural poetry published during the latter part of the twentieth century, and within the growing genre and academic discourse of minority and regional literatures. The "ethnic author"—her struggles with authenticity and her sense of dislocation and disconnection that come from publishing texts related to oral tradition—had become a familiar figure in the writings of literary critics who worked to enlarge the American literary canon and to develop a deeper understanding of the relationship between written and oral discourse.

Seeking my place in this conversation, I found the work of Trinh T. Minh-ha to be especially useful, for although she has dealt with the writing of Third World women and women of color, she meaningfully captured several tensions that resonated with my own experience. Chief among these was the author's complex sense of guilt: for straying beyond the norms of the community, for calling its norms into question, and for exposing its knowledge to a broader world. Trinh recognized that a book like mine is bound to "breed fault and guilt," and in doing so, it becomes a "discourse of authority and arrogance."[1]

It was difficult for me to admit my own authority and arrogance, concepts which are diametrically opposed to the Anabaptist spirit of humility and the mild demeanor expected of Mennonite women. Consequently, I investigated those tensions in the most quiet way possible—as a graduate student at New York University. Far from the landscape described in my poems and the homes of its most worrisome readers, I read and wrote about the tension between oral and written discourse and about the construction of literary authority.

Eventually I realized that this distant, bookish approach would not suffice. I had to return to the one place and find the only stories that would help me to understand and perhaps atone for what I had done. Although nearly all of my literary influences and teachers previously had come from beyond the Mennonite subculture, I turned to my heritage to explore the tensions between communal and authorial voice. Like Alice Walker and many others whose work has drawn on family memory, I sought to recover predecessors from my own tradition and a method of understanding that tradition from *within* itself, to situate my literary work and the work of other writers like myself in relation to traditional sources and non-academic audiences.

Thus I was drawn to the life of Joseph W. Yoder. I believed that he could show me how it is possible to become an author and also remain part of traditional Mennonite culture. Because his life both preserved and transgressed the codes of his native community, it seemed that he denied once and for all the American myth that insists that a writer must leave home to become an author, and that once she has gone she cannot return. By maintaining conversations with Amish friends and family members in Mifflin County, Yoder seemed to have been able to defy that plot, fostering relationships with the folks back home while also making substantial literary and musical contributions. In the course of my research, I discovered that Yoder's relationships were far more awkward and strained than I had imagined. Although I did not discover exactly what I had hoped to find, I learned a great deal about him, his community, and myself.

In *Rosanna of the Amish,* for instance, I recognized my great-great grandfather Levi Hartzler—a neighbor of Rosanna and Little Crist—driving the wagon that transported the heroine's coffin near the end of the book. Throughout the English text, I found words and fragments of Pennsylvania German that had persisted in my English-speaking home—words that I had never seen written before, and certainly had never seen in print. Most important, I traced to their traditional sources some ideas and preferences of my parents, who appear otherwise to live culturally assimilated lives. For example, I heard an uncanny echo of my father's wish that the family visit a zoo rather than an art museum on one of my visits home, because he would "rather see what God made than what people made." In *Rosanna*, Yoder explained,

> It was not against the rules of the church for Amish people to go to a circus if there were animals on exhibition. . . . Of course, it was understood that if you paid to see the animals, there was no reason, since you were right there anyway, why you should not go in and see the rest of the performance. But the argument was that God made the animals and surely it could not be wrong to go to see them.[2]

More than sociological studies of Amish and Mennonite culture, Yoder's narratives illuminated specific aspects of a world that had influenced my early years. I also recognized in his work a familiar love of the land and family. Although Yoder left home in the course of becoming a musician and author, Big Valley and its people remained the source of his literary and musical efforts.

Finally, I returned to central Pennsylvania in June 1995 to do my fieldwork, seeking the sites of verbal and epistolary archives as well as the landscape and rituals that shaped and inspired Yoder's literary activity. When I arrived, the laurel was blooming on the mountains: hay season, strawberry season, peas just past and beans coming in, one of the busiest times of the year for farm families. Yet my aunt, Sharon (Peachey) Spicher, took time to meet me at the train stop in Huntingdon. As we drove into their farmyard, my uncle ran toward the pickup, his arms spread wide in welcome, shouting that one of the cows was in labor. We went first to the barn, and the birth of a calf on my first day of field work seemed a good sign. The next morning when my aunt dropped me off at Juniata College, the newborn bull was soberly caged in the back of the truck, bound for auction and the veal pen—an ambiguous omen, after all.

I spent a week at Juniata College, reading and photocopying about six hundred pages of correspondence between J. W. Yoder and members of the Amish and Mennonite communities. Gradually, the contours of his engagements and disputes with the community emerged. Sometimes I encountered familiar names in those stiff pages: great-aunts and great-uncles who in the 1940s and 1950s belonged to what was the Zook, then Spicher, Amish Church.

As I read the letters in chronological order, Yoder's voice became increasingly shrill in matters ranging from salvation to his own traffic violations. When the library closed each evening, I walked two blocks to the home of Jane (Eby) Crosby. A teenager in Lititz, Pennsylvania, during the 1930s, Jane was enticed to attend Juniata College by Yoder the charismatic high school recruiter, although her old Church of the Brethren family had traditionally attended Elizabethtown College. Jane later returned to teach and eventually married another Juniata faculty member. For many years, the Crosbys lived next door to J. W. and Emily on Mifflin Street, and in addition to her generous hospitality, Jane offered insights into Joe and Emily that could not have come from my Amish Mennonite relatives. When I left, she passed on to me a set of china bouillon cups and saucers hand-painted by the elegant Emily Yoder.

I then spent a week in Kishoquillas Valley, commonly called "Big Valley," my parents' home and the home of J. W. Yoder, returning alone for one of the first times since the childhood summers when I stayed there with relatives for several idyllic weeks at a time. Research began before Sunday services in the parking lot of the Locust Grove Conservative Conference Mennonite Church where I spotted Percy Yoder, a retired farmer, songleader, and amateur historian. "Hello! Do you know who I am?" I called to him across car roofs, framing my face with both hands. "I sure do," he cried. "I knew about Tom, and Tom, and Gideon, too!" naming my grandfather, great-grandfather, and great-great-grandfather. As he was saying this, I realized that if I looked just beyond his shoulder I could see the cemetery were all those men are buried. When I explained that I had come to learn about J. W. Yoder, Percy told me he'd been a pupil in Yoder's singing schools and that his sister, Minnie, lives in the house where Yoder grew up. He then made plans to escort me there the next day. Unable to believe that I could understand anything about a man if I had not visited the farms where he had lived and the fields where he had labored, Percy insisted, "You must get a feel for the lay of the land." I would remember Percy's counsel later, reading a letter in which J. W. Yoder explained the sources of historical information in *Rosanna's Boys*: what he had not experienced himself, he gathered with his "ear to the ground."[3]

The next morning we first stopped at the old Jack Armstrong homestead, an eighteenth-century stone house and barn that had been the home of J. W. Yoder's grandparents. There in the hay mow I saw numbered beams hewn from ancient trees, and realized this was the site of the scene in Yoder's memoir where he and his brothers rigged a trapeze after a trip to the circus. We wandered through the house nearby, built for Yoder's parents after they were married. Then we drove past the Maclay fields, where Yoder and his brothers worked as hired hands for ten years. Driving from place to place, Percy told me stories about my family. He'd grown up on the farm next to my great-grandfather Spicher, whom he characterized as "a fine Amish man," who unhitched his horses and let them cool down in the field before coming in for supper so they would not over-drink at the watering trough: anecdotal proof of an unnamed attribute.

By the end of that week, I had had formal conversations about J. W. Yoder in fifteen different settings, and I felt as if people had helped me tremendously through talk, through the emblematic and specific details of gossip, and through offerings of food. Even with strawberry stains on their hands, women greeted me graciously at doors when I appeared, sometimes unannounced. They would stop their work and begin "to visit," remarking how much I resembled my mother and the Peacheys, though I have those bright Spicher eyes. "You can't hide where you belong!" someone said. Each conversation or interview, tape-recorded or not, followed the same pattern. First we would establish who I was—which means who my parents are and how they are doing, and possibly also who my grandparents were. Then I would ask a few questions, and with the mention of each new name, we would establish whoever he or she was, in relation to family members I might know. The tracing of kinship became a constant refrain that enabled me to venture further with my inquiry, then retreat to safe territory. I was careful to always ask the question that prompts a recitation of kinship connection, "Now, how was that?" or "And how are they related?"

I wore long skirts and closed-toe shoes, removed my earrings, and tied back my hair. Although familial connections granted access to people's homes, I was constantly aware of the limits I had internalized as a child: how loudly or emphatically I dare speak, how far I could pursue a delicate line of questions, how much I should reveal about my own life and learning. Much of my mind as well as my body remained hidden from view. Although my knowledge of and sensitivity to the norms of that community may have granted me access to conversations, they also prevented me from asking the most demanding questions about J. W. Yoder, perhaps the most important ones. The self-consciousness with which I conducted myself and my conversations during those days left me exhausted each evening. After a hot, humid week of careful talk and rich food, I felt too heavy to absorb much more and finally headed out of the Valley along the road that follows Back Mountain, seeking traces of my own life inscribed on that landscape.

In a car borrowed from my uncle Tom, driving past the farm where my grandparents had lived during my childhood, I remembered Leon Zook, my father's first cousin, who had worked for grandpa after his youngest son left for college. When I was no more than four or five years old, Leon heard me cry gleefully, "Here comes a chariot!" as a horse and buggy appeared at the end of the lane one afternoon. Leon told that story to the grownups and teased me without mercy. Still vivid is the awful adult laughter and my shame for having used the wrong word. A word from a Bible story can not name something as ordinary as an

Amish buggy, but because I was growing up among cars, the only name I had for a horse drawn conveyance came from the story of Philip and the Ethiopian eunuch. Nevertheless, I loved Leon, who yodeled in the barn and invented lyrics about cows and my brother and me. On Sunday mornings, after he had been up all night catching chickens in dusty brooder houses, he would rouse us with songs accompanied by harmonica and guitar—which he played at the same time, like Bob Dylan. Suddenly, I realized that Leon is the son of Yost Zook, great-great nephew of J. W. Yoder: *That* is where all his mischief and music came from! Catching myself in the Valley's habit of genealogical and analogical thinking, I recognized the primary method of my inquiry—something I had learned as a child growing up on the margins of my parent's home community in Mifflin County.

In those days, I was attuned to the voices and stories of my great-aunts and grandparents, and this project is shaped by a sensibility schooled in their kitchens and vegetable patches. Following the most basic biblical hermeneutic—wherein believers seek comfort or guidance by finding parallels between their lives and the lives of biblical characters—storytellers read and name an individual through her resemblance to the lives that preceded her. In a community advanced through many generations of intermarriage, knowledge comes not so much from an appreciation of genetic principles as from the habit of tracing ancient shapes in the present. Time is not continuous; generational cycles repeat narrative fragments that recur as predictably as family names, so *now* always is understood by looking at *then*, and the distinction between past and present erodes beneath a steady stream of talk. This is how people remain meaningfully linked across time in a culture that had few photographs longer ago, and where—aside from diary entries and some community chronicles—little was ever written for posterity. Someone always recorded genealogy, though, as carefully as they traced the bloodlines of prize cattle and horses.

Working on this project, I came to appreciate and recognize an organic epistemology I had learned by listening to those conversations. What I once regarded as a rich source of language and stories, I came to see as a complex system of metaphorical and analogical meaning making. The recognition of resemblance and repetition was a major source of knowledge until the end of the sixteenth century, Michel Foucault has observed in his history of Western thought. From the play of sympathy and antipathy, distinct categories of resemblance emerged. Analogy provided limitless possibilities for constructing relationships and connections between different elements across time and space, always situating the human subject at the center. In such an epistemological system of sympathies or resemblances, antipathy checks the potential for things to lose their identity altogether.[4]

When I told people that I wanted to conduct an inquiry into the life of the Amish-born author J. W. Yoder, therefore, some immediately expressed a sense that I was "right" for this work. Although Yoder and I are not closely related, other resemblances are instantly evident. More than one person said that I am like Yoder—a writer, someone interested in local stories, yet living away—but then they quickly stressed that I am also unlike him—not so proud, not so loud. Perhaps circumstances of gender and history prevent me from becoming him, although I often felt points of identification and sympathy. For instance, I could not help but feel a sting of rebuke when one of my great-aunts characterized Yoder as "someone who liked to make money without working." When I asked what she meant, she explained, "Oh, he wrote books and gave lectures."

I could not have reconstructed J. W. Yoder's life or come to make any sense of his world without thinking through analogues, anecdotes, and resemblances—the habits of mind that foster good conversation, that kind of knowledge I learned from listening to people talk. When asked about Yoder, my informants offered stories that were profoundly rich in detail and meaning but almost devoid of abstract interpretation. Attempts at analysis always pointed me toward another story or person who was both like and unlike Yoder. I have included many of those emblematic stories in this book, trying to remain somewhat faithful to the community's narrative and analogic epistemology and also trying to impart some of its grace and brilliance. I now realize that my initial desire to compare my experience to Yoder's, analogically to bind my life to his, betrays the impulse that seeks to find meaning by recognizing resemblance.

In 2000, I moved to Bellefonte, Pennsylvania, within easy driving range and more or less equidistant between Belleville, Huntingdon, and Lock Haven, into a house that was built the year Yoder was born. Here, I took up his story again. Now I am less interested in what Yoder can teach me about Mennonite community and literary authority and more interested in filling in the gaps that existed in my earlier draft of his life. Removing myself and my own concerns from the story, I have been able to glimpse more of the Yoder. A little distance opened spaces to pursue his involvement in "muscular" Christianity and physical culture, for instance, and his status as a bachelor in his day. With new research and through the findings of S. Duane Kauffman concerning what I had been calling "the lost years," 1910-1930, I now see that Yoder's life was shaped by work and relationships with many communities, and that to construe his work only in terms of Amish and Mennonite culture would have been a great loss. Now I most appreciate Yoder's curiosity and passion, his lifelong pursuit of "the strenuous life" and his playful and emphatic voice, although he seemed heedless of his audience, and at times almost incapable of self-consciousness or thoughtful reflection.

*7.1 Gravestones for Little Crist, Rosanna, and Lizzie Yoder in the Locust
Grove Cemetery, Belleville, Pennsylvania.*

After a visit to the Amish and Mennonite cemetery at Locust Grove during my field work in Big Valley, I idly observed that the graveyard seemed smaller than I had remembered. "Yes!" my great-aunt immediately replied, "Yes, isn't that strange? It *is* small, yet somehow *everyone* is buried there." Everyone, she meant, who is related to us and has not left the Valley. Even the people who leave and live elsewhere for a while sometimes return to be buried there, as J. W. Yoder did.

"Why do you consult the dead on behalf of the living?" the prophet Isaiah asked Hebrew captives living in Babylonian exile (Isa. 8:19). Perhaps people have always turned to the past for comfort and answers, and the need to tell stories may be most keen among those who have left their home places and cannot return. During the course of this project, at least four of the people I interviewed in search of J. W. Yoder's story have died. Twice I returned to Mifflin County for funerals, often taking advantage of those gatherings to ask more questions. I cannot stop begging the aged for stories of a man who has been dead for nearly fifty years. They do not find this strange and respond to my questions as they are able, as if they understand that their answers matter very much, that they hold insights toward understanding a man's life, and—by analogy—many others.

When I began this project, I believed that there were few models for writerly authority in my background, but now I see that American Mennonite literary authority has been associated with the publication of written texts for more than one hundred years in this country. In the latter half of the nineteenth century, John F. Funk's *The Herald of Truth/Der Herold der Warheit* established at Elkhart, Indiana, a center of communal authority and truth in bilingual editions. The community's truth then moved to Scottdale, Pennsylvania, in 1908, where another kind of authority was situated in doctrine and disseminated in English through *Gospel Herald.*

Recognizing the link between authority and publication, Joseph W. Yoder formed the Yoder Publishing Company in 1940 to print his own truths, only hiring the Mennonite and Evangelical printing presses to produce his books. The awkwardness of authority in this community and others like it has less to do with writing, and much to do with knowledge and power—the makings of individual authority. For Yoder, a modern progressive, truth and the basis for authority could be found in the biblical text and an educated reading of it. For many of his opponents, truth resided in tradition and the community's faithful practice. And the conflict emerged with the questions: whose truth gets printed? Whose truth stands as the public representation of the entire group? Whose truth—or which secrets—will save the people from extinction?

I am reminded of the mystic stories from Polish Jewish folklore, wherein a person can make from mud a golem, a zombie-like humanoid who is brought to life when the Hebrew word *Emeth* (truth) is inscribed on his forehead. To kill the golem, who grows larger and stronger every day but cannot speak, one need only to erase the first letter, transforming his name to *Meth* (death). In communities that remember and sustain a sense of themselves as an endangered people, works of literature act like golems, created in the image of the group, incapable of dialogue, and fearfully dangerous. An author assumes the precarious position of rendering images of the group and thereby exposing it to the scrutiny of the dominant culture. Yoder's early *Rosanna* books were accepted because they represented the community in a constructive fashion, while *Amish Traditions* and *The Prayer Veil Analyzed* challenged the authority of the bishops, criticized the community's practices, made the sect vulnerable to criticism from outside, and lacked the appeal of story.

Thus, it might seem that Joseph Yoder finally emerged as a heroic author who refused to yield to the religious community of his birth and who was able to write his own life, defining himself and his truths in terms that were broader than his relationship to that community and its God. Like his industrialist brother, Levi, Yoder can be seen as a self-made American man who blazed a path for an Amish-Mennonite performer and author where there had been none before. In this version of his story, the *Rosanna* books are *Kunstroman* that recount Yoder's education as an artist. That is one American story. Following the patterns of immigration and westward migration, it maps a progression from identification with traditional family and sect to identification with the democratic, pluralistic nation, propelled by education and creativity.

But a life is never that orderly, and as many times as he left the Valley, Yoder returned, until at last he was buried there. When he resolved to study medicine in Philadelphia, he instead accepted J. S. Coffman's invitation to teach at the new Mennonite school in Elkhart; bound for journalism school at Harvard, he decided to go to Lancaster to teach the Mennonites how to sing harmony in four parts. He followed a ragged course, abruptly yanked between Amish austerity and Irish liberty, German and English, tradition and invention, piety and progress, rarely coming to rest in a comfortable synthesis.

And then there were almost twenty years when he lived with John Hooley and attended the Reformed church, apparently quite far from his home community. From youth, his passion for singing and what he called his "restless ambition" led him beyond the bounds of the sect—curious, resistant, and as bold in his success as he was in his failures. He was able to draw closer to his home community at the end of his life because of the skills that also distanced him from it: the ability to abstract from the details of immediate experience, to identify the culture's unifying principles, and to represent and question them in written form.

Working on this project, some days I wonder why I have spent so much time writing his story. Between paying a debt to the ancestors and raging at ancient constraints, what space is left to write my own life? Some days the space between loyalty and frustration pinches my imagination as painfully as it must have pinched Yoder's—as surely as those mountains pinch the fields in Big Valley. But as John R. Renno, the shunned bishop's son once observed, people who have cars can drive over the mountains. I once knew that a prayer covering stifles a woman's head and chose to wear one anyway. I was thirteen years old then. It was 1976, the year the United States celebrated the bicentennial of its great act of rebellion. I was clever. I believed I could wear a head covering for my own reasons. I believed I could have it both ways: identify with conservative female relatives and gain their approval while also keeping my own liberty. If I made my own meanings in private, it did not matter what the official version said. That was my way of writing a life within and against a greater story.

By the end of the last chapter of this project, I find myself joining Yoder in his denunciation of the head covering, although that feels like a betrayal of the women who wear them, the ones I love and longed to emulate even after my own mother stopped wearing hers. At thirteen I was able to imagine more ambiguity concerning the head covering than I can in my thirties. Although the prayer veil has vanished from many Mennonite congregations, the old prohibitions have not entirely passed from my mind or the minds of others. Some days I feel that I could become an ideological terrorist, too.

But whom would I terrorize? I could never disparage those strong women in plain dress whom I have watched command steaming kitchens during canning season and behead chickens without flinching. The beautiful women who, during their younger years labored beside husbands on successful, independent dairy farms, seemingly indomitable, entirely nonconformed to any American sense of frail femininity. Yoder's example is useful as I try to resist the extremes that come from choosing either the role of scribe or prophet—and now I see that it is quite possible to speak and live outside that opposition altogether.

It is a heavy privilege to be able to name a place of origin, to be bound to that place and people with such intensity that one will always have stories to write *from* or *against*. In memory, the voices that trace my body back to its sources, the words that name person and place, speak from between the ragged edges of tenderness and restraint. But I also recall the strong command to "let the dead bury the dead." Chosen to listen before I could choose anything else for myself, I continue to narrate, although now I see that there are many voices to attend to in this world, and many stories to tell.

NOTES

ABBREVIATIONS

YF—RG 13, Individual Collections, Yoder, Joseph W. (Box 5, Miscellaneous Papers; Box 6, Publishing Records, and Box 6a, Papers and Imprints.). Juniata College Archives, Huntingdon, Pennsylvania.

AMC—Archives of the Mennonite Church, Goshen, Indiana

Rosanna—*Rosanna of the Amish* (Huntingdon: Yoder Publishing, 1940).

Lieder—*Amische Lieder* (Huntingdon, Pa.: Yoder Publishing, 1942).

Boys—*Rosanna's Boys* (Huntingdon, Pa.: Yoder Publishing, 1948).

Traditions—*Amish Traditions* (Huntingdon, Pa.: Yoder Publishing, 1950).

Prayer Veil—*The Prayer Veil Analyzed* (Huntingdon, Pa: Yoder Publishing, 1954).

SERIES EDITOR'S FOREWORD

1. James W. Loewen, *Lies My Teacher Told Me: Everything Your American History Textbook Got Wrong* (New York: Simon & Schuster, 1995), 239.

INTRODUCTION

1. S. Duane Kauffman, *Mifflin County Amish and Mennonite Story, 1791-1991* (Belleville, Pa.: Mifflin County Mennonite Historical Society, 1991), 245-47, 252-55; John A. Hostetler, "Joseph W. Yoder (1872-1956)," *Mennonite Historical Bulletin* XVIII, no. 1 (January, 1957), 1-2.

2. Carl F. Bowman, Brethren Society: *The Cultural Transformation of a "Peculiar People."* (Baltimore: Johns Hopkins University Press, 1995), 251.

CHAPTER I

1. S. Duane Kauffman's ongoing research into U.S. Census records, tax lists and other public documents from central and eastern Pennsylvania has yielded little support for Yoder's account. In fact, several serious discrepancies between Yoder's story and the public records raise questions about whether Rosanna's parents were born in Ireland and whether the men reported to have been her brothers may have actually been uncles. Kauffman anticipates publication of his findings when his research is complete, and I appreciate his willingness to share his discoveries with me before publication.

2. *Rosanna*, 2.

3. *Rosanna*, 12.

4. *Rosanna*, 21.

5. S. Duane Kauffman, *Mifflin County Amish and Mennonite Story, 1791-1991.* (Belleville, Pa: Mifflin County Mennonite Historical Society, 1991), 86-87.

6. Kauffman, 62.

7. Kauffman, 138 and 369 from RG 13 Pennsylvania Archives, Harrisburg, Pa.

8. *Rosanna*, 208.

9. Several historical accounts of this division agree that it was the consequence of a protracted dispute between Bishops Abraham Peachey and Solomon Beiler concerning the proper mode of baptism. John A. Hostetler has described the events of this period in an article tracing the career of a Mifflin County Amish deacon and bishop: "The Life and Times of Samuel Yoder, 1824-1884," *Mennonite Quarterly Review* 22, no. 4 (October 1948): 226-41. Correspondence between Yoder and Hostetler from the 1940s suggests that Yoder served as a minor source of information for the article. Later, in his seminal study of Amish culture, Hostetler detailed the numerous divisions among the Mifflin County Amish in *Amish Society* (Baltimore: Johns Hopkins, 1993), 290-299. Theron F. Schlabach has portrayed similar tensions within the context of American Amish history in *Peace, Faith, Nation: Mennonites and Amish in Nineteenth-Century America*, The Mennonite Experience in America, vol. 2 (Scottdale, Pa: Herald Press, 1988), 201-299.

10. *Rosanna*, 210.

11. English translations of accounts of these meetings have recently been published by Paton Yoder and Steven R. Estes, eds., *Porceedings of the Amish Ministers' Meetings, 1862-1878* (Goshen, Ind.: Mennonite Historical Society, 1999).

12. Sandra Cronk, "Gelassenheit: The Rites of the Redemptive Process in Old Order Amish and Old Order Mennonite Communities," *Mennonite Quarterly Review* 55, no. 1 (January 1981): 5-44.

13. Cronk, 17.

14. *Rosanna*, 227.

15. *Rosanna*, 227.

16. Paton Yoder, *Tradition and Transition: Amish Mennonites and Old Order Amish, 1800-1900* (Scottdale, Pa.: Herald Press, 1991), 79-80.

17. Donald Kraybill, *The Riddle of Amish Culture* (Baltimore: Johns Hopkins University Press, 1989), 32-33.

18. "Little Crist" should not be confused with C. Z. Yoder (1845-1939) the prominent minister of the Oak Grove Amish Mennonite congregation in Ohio.

19. Kauffman, 370-371, compiled from accounts by A.F. Gibboney Miller for the November 5, 1879 and March 9, 1881 issues of *Lewistown Gazette*.

20. *Rosanna*, 254.

21. Kauffman, 215-217, quoted from *The Lewistown Gazette,* February 14, 1866.

22. *Rosanna*, 17.

23. *Rosanna*, 18.

24."We Notice That," n.a., *The Lewistown Sentinel*, December 18, 1940.

25. *Boys*, 229.

26. *Boys*, 148-49.

27. This discovery from S. Duane Kauffman's research was reported in an electronic mail letter to the author, 3 August 2001. It is possible that Rosanna was answering the census question in terms of her adoptive rather than her biological parents, but Kauffman's extensive research has found no evidence for Yoder's version of the story in the public records.

28. *Boys*, 223-4.

29. Oral tradition in the Harleysville, Pennsylvania, area, reported to the author by John Ruth.

30. *Rosanna*, 182.

31. *Boys*, 60.

32. Quoted in John A. Hostetler and Gertrude Enders Huntington, *Amish Children: Education in the Family, School, and Community* (Fort Worth, Tex.: Harcourt, Brace, Jovanovich, 1992), 66.

33. *Boys*, 198.

34. *Boys*, 157.

35. In Pennsylvania during this period there were never enough professionally trained teachers to fill positions in public schools, and rural districts generally employed teachers with the lowest qualifications. Teachers were recruited largely from the classroom, as was Levi, sometimes without further training. After the passage of the Normal School Act of 1857, a term's work at a summer normal school represented the minimum teacher preparation, followed by a spring session at a state normal school, or a summer session at a college or university. Given Levi's (and later Joseph's) experience, it appears that schools in Big Valley were not unlike other rural districts that hired teachers and principals with little supervision and only the most basic training. William S. Taylor, *The Development of the Professional Education of Teachers in Pennsylvania* (Philadelphia: J. B. Lippincott, 1929), 177, 192.

36. *Boys*, 91.

37. *Boys*, 102.

38. *Boys*, 211-212.

39. *Boys*, 212.

40. Buleah Stauffer Hostetler has explained that the nineteenth-century move by progressive Anabaptist and Pietist groups to build meetinghouses was not a meaningless adaptation. Worship in a meetinghouse symbolically removed religious life

from the everyday spheres of stable and hearth. To cease worshipping in houses or barns eliminated the annual event of preparing and opening one's home to the entire community. A meetinghouse also meant that the congregation could include more people than could be contained in a farmhouse, and under these circumstances, members would no longer know one another intimately. Thus, the meetinghouse had profound implications for human relationships in the community and changed the way religion interacted with everyday life. "The Formation of the Old Orders" *Mennonite Quarterly Review* 66, no. 1 (Jan 1992): 5-25.

41. Kauffman, 135-137.

42. *Boys*, 209.

43. John Samuel Noffsinger, *A Program for Higher Education in the Church of the Brethren with Special Reference to the Number and Distribution of Colleges* (New York: Teachers College, Columbia University, 1925), 4.

44. John Stoltzfus, "Short Account of the Life, Doctrine and Example of our Old Ministers," in Paton Yoder and Steven R. Estes, eds., *Proceedings of the Amish Ministers Meetings 1862-1878* (Goshen, Ind.: Mennonite Historical Society, 1999), 241.

45. *Rosanna*, 300.

46. *Boys*, 213-14.

47. *Boys*, 257.

48. *Rosanna*, 300.

49. *Boys*, 214.

50. Earl C. Kaylor Jr., *Truth Sets Free: A Centennial History of Juniata College, 1876-1976* (Huntingdon, Pa.: Juniata College, 1977), 158.

51. *Boys*, 12.

52. In addition to the temperance issue, Yoder mentioned conflict over the wearing of a mustache. When Bishop Abraham Zook ordered a young man to shave, Preacher Joseph H. Byler pointed out that there is no Scripture pertaining to that. After a protracted series of such disputes, Zook and 118 of his followers withdrew in 1897. A more reliable history lists among issues in the division: the use of buttons, haircuts, part-singing, folding buggy tops, meetinghouse renovations, adoption of the English language for worship, and probably Sunday school (Kauffman, 122).

53. Traditions, v.

54. Robert J. Higgs, *God in the Stadium* (Lexington, Ky.: The University Press of Kentucky, 1995), 89.

55. Kaylor, 112-13

56. A. B. Brumbaugh, *Juniata Echo*, vol.3, no.4 (February 1894), 1.

57. Thomas Wentworth Higginson, "Saints and Their Bodies," *Atlantic Monthly* 1 (March 1858), 586.

58. *Boys*, 276.

59. *Rosanna*, 301-304.

60. A.B. Brumbaugh, 2.

61. Earl C. Kaylor Jr., *Martin Grove Brumbaugh: A Pennsylvanian's Odyssey from Sainted Schoolman to Bedeviled World War I Governor, 1862-1930* (Cranbury, N.J.: Associated University Presses, Inc. 1996), 68.

62. *Boys*, 231.

63. *Boys*, 234.

64. *Rosanna*, 311.

65. *Boys*, 90.

66. *Boys*, 236.

67. Yoder to Hubbard, July 30, 1954, YF.

68. Yoder to J.S. Coffman, May 10, 1994, Hist. Mss. 1-19, J.S. Coffman 3/5 Correspondence. Elkhart Institute Faculty, 1895-1898, AMC.

69. C. Henry Smith, *Mennonite Country Boy* (Newton, Kan.: Faith and Life, 1962), 109-110.

70. Schlabach, 298.

71. *Boys*, 236.

72. All letters from J.W. Yoder to Coffman are collected in Hist. Mss. 1-19, J. S. Coffman 3/5 Correspondence. Elkhart Institute Faculty, 1895-1898, AMC. Concerning the closing of the July 22 letter, humble style has been noted in the correspondence of Amish and Mennonites of the late nineteenth century by both Paton Yoder and Joseph C. Leichty in his article "Humility: The Foundation of Mennonite Religious Outlook in the 1860s," *Mennonite Quarterly Review* 54, no. 1 (January1980): 5-31. Closings such as "Your insignificant (*geringer*) friend," used by the very accomplished Mifflin County Amishman Shem Zook were not uncommon, and individuals often confessed their spiritual poverty (Yoder 81). However, both historians note that in matters of business, the humble stance seemed to vanish.

73. *Rosanna*, 2.

Chapter 2

1. Clipping from *The Elkhart Truth*, July 16, 1894, in Scrap book, V-4-1, Elkhart Institute, box 2, AMC.

2. "The Elkhart Institute," (1897-98) pamphlet, GC/EI v-4-1, Box 2, Promotional Pamphlets folder, AMC.

3. Susan Fisher Miller, *Culture for Service: A History of Goshen College 1894-1994* (Goshen, Ind.: Goshen College, 1994), 5.

4. James Juhnke has noted the significance of Mennonite reactions to what John Funk called "the *world's* Fair." In Funk's 1883 piece in *The Herald of Truth* he discouraged Mennonites from attending: "the great Exposition at Chicago is really and exclusively the *'World's Fair.'* It is not for the Christian, but for the world." Juhnke regarded this event and responses to it as symbolic, marking "the watershed between a simpler, agrarian-commercial past and a complex, urban-industrial future. As Americans of all kinds responded to the event in Chicago, they revealed who they were and were becoming." Funk as well as J. S. Coffman eventually selected a few events to attend. James C. Juhnke, *Vision, Doctrine, War: Mennonite Identity and Organization in America, 1890-1930*. The Mennonite Experience in America, vol. 3 (Scottdale, Pa: Herald Press, 1985), 21-22.

5. Bender used the term in *Sunday School Centennial* (qtd. in Joseph C. Liechty, "Humility: The Foundation of Mennonite Religious Outlook in the 1860s," *Men-*

nonite Quarterly Review 54, no. 1 (January 1980): 7. Theron F. Schlabach has pointed out that "Great Awakening" is a partisan term that serves the interests of progressives who regarded traditionalists as being asleep in spirit. He has argued that an admiration for the late nineteenth-century flurry of activity in the Mennonite community overlooks the quiet value of the more traditional Mennonite ethos of the mid-1800s, which was marked by humility and nonresistance. *Peace, Faith, Nation,* 300-321.

6. *Boys*, 237-8.

7. First secretary Book of the Philharmonic Society (1897) Box V-4-1, Goshen College/Elkhart Institute Materials box 1, AMC.

8. Elkhart Institute Literary Society minutes (1897-98), Box V-4-1, Goshen College/Elkhart Institute Materials box 1, AMC.

9. Elkhart Institute Literary Society minutes (1897-98), Box V-4-1, Goshen College/Elkhart Institute Materials box 1, AMC.

10. *Boys*, 238.

11. Letter from Yoder to J.S. Coffman August 10, 1898, Hist. Mss. 1-19, J.S. Coffman 3/5, correspondence. Elkhart Institute Faculty (1895-1898), AMC.

12. Letter from Yoder to J.S. Coffman August 10, 1898, Hist. Mss. 1-19, J.S. Coffman 3/5, correspondence. Elkhart Institute Faculty (1895-1898) AMC.

13. Letter from Yoder to J.S. Coffman September 4, 1898, Hist. Mss. 1-19, J.S. Coffman 3/5, correspondence. Elkhart Institute Faculty (1895-1898), AMC.

14. *Boys*, 239.

15. William C. Ringenberg, *The Christian College: A History of Protestant Higher Education in America* (Grand Rapids, Mich.: Christian University Press, 1984), 148-150.

16. In Tony Ladd and James A. Mathisen, *Muscular Christianity: Evangelical Protestants and the Development of American Sport* (Grand Rapids, Mich.: Baker Books, 1999), 37.

17. The term *muscular Christianity* was first used by T. C. Sandars in an 1857 review of Charles Kingsley's novel, *Two Years Ago*: "His ideal is a man who fears God and can walk a thousand miles in a thousand hours. . . . " In his introduction to a collection of articles which employ current cultural and gender theories to explore the social, religious, and literary significance of muscular Christianity, Donald F. Hall notes that in this first instance, a "central, defining characteristic" of the movement was established—physical strength, religious certainty and the ability to shape the self and the world. Donald F. Hall, ed. *Muscular Christianity: Embodying the Victorian Age* (Cambridge University Press, 1994), 7.

18. "A Christian Club," *New York Times,* 18 July 1869, 5, qtd. in Tony Ladd and James A. Mathisen, *Muscular Christianity: Evangelical Protestants and the Development of American Sport* (Grand Rapids, Mich.: Baker Books, 1999), 24.

19. YF, February 18, 1950.

20. "The Oratorical Contest," *The Academian* 2, no 16 (June 13, 1899), 25.

21. "Class Day," *The Academian* 2, no 16 (June 13, 1899), 25.

22. *Boys*, 238.

23. *Boys*, 238-39.

24. *Boys*, 239.

25. Fisher Miller, 26-28.

26. Letter to John A. Hostetler (July 5, 1948), YF. Corroborating Yoder's view of the quarrel between church and school is Barbara Coffman who wrote that Funk was "trying to make up for lack of discipline in business by being overly strict and even harsh in church discipline." *His Name is John* (Scottdale, Pa.: Herald Press, 1964), 329.

27. Fisher Miller, 32.

28. *Boys*, 146-147.

29. I am helped in this distinction by Michel Foucault, who distinguishes between slavery (the appropriation of another's body), service (submission to the will of the master), vassalage (offering of labor and allegiance), monastic asceticism (mastery over one's own body), and the model of the Enlightenment era, when the body began to be seen as a machine that could be analyzed and perfected for the purposes of economic utility and political obedience. Alan Sheridan, trans., *Discipline and Punish* (Vintage: N.Y.: 1979), 137-138.

30. Elkhart Institute brochure (1897-98), 3 in GC/Elkhart Institute V-4-1, Box 2, Promotional Pamphlets Folder, AMC.

31. *Elkhart Institute Memorial* (Elkhart, Ind.: Elkhart Institute Alumni Association, n.d.), 52.

32. Harold H. Hartzler, "Joseph Warren Yoder," *Yoder Newsletter* 15 (April 1990), 3.

33. *Boys*, 240.

34. These figures come from the writings of physician and physical culture advocate, Dudley Allen Sargent, whose weight training system and pedagogy program at Harvard influenced raising awareness and concern for fitness in education as early as the 1880s. Robert Ernst, *Weakness is a Crime: The Life of Bernarr MacFadden* (Syracuse, N.Y.: Syracuse University Press, 1991), 37.

35. Ladd and Mathisen, 90.

36. *Juniata Echo* vol. XI, no. 8 (October 1902), 123.

37. Earl C. Kaylor, *Truth*, 159. The elders may have heard rumors that the urban YMCAs had become centers of homosexual social life, the history of which is explored in several studies by George Chauncey and John D. Wrathall that are gathered by Howard P. Chudacoff in *The Age of the Bachelor: Creating an American Subculture* (Princeton: Princeton University Press, 1999), 161-162.

38. *Boys*, 262-63. The Brumbaugh family of central Pennsylvania played a prominent role in the creation and early leadership of Juniata College. Of those mentioned in this study are founding figures professor Jacob H. Brumbaugh (1851-1934), who directed J.W. Yoder into the Normal English program, and his physician brother and physical culture advocate Dr. Andrew Boelus Brumbaugh (1836-1908). These men were uncles of Yoder's mentor, Juniata president and Pennsylvania Governor, Martin Grove Brumbaugh (1862-1930). Elder H. B. Brumbaugh, a cousin of Jacob and Andrew, served as the college's second president from 1888 until 1893, and was the father of I. Harvey Brumbaugh (1870-1937) who was a friend and peer of J. W. Yoder, and who served as acting president from 1899-1911 and became the

school's fourth president from 1911 to 1924.

39. Higgs, *God in the Stadium* (Lexington, Ky.: University of Kentucky Press, 1995), 37.

40. Kaylor, *Truth*, 161.

41. Vol. 12, no. 4 (April 03), 57-58.

42. *Boys*, 275.

43. *Rosanna*, 296-297.

44. Ernst, 37.

45. Ernst, 35.

46. Ernst, 31-33.

47. Theodore Roosevelt, *The Strenuous Life: Essays and Addresses* (New York: The Century Co., 1900); Bartleby.com1998. www.bartleby.com/58/. [March 16, 2001], para. 14.

48. Quoted in Ernst, 120.

49. *Boys*, 275.

50. Yoder, "A Thing Worth While," *Juniata Echo*12, no.10, 51,

51. Yoder, "A Thing Worth While," *Juniata Echo*12, no.10, 150-151.

52. Yoder, "College Life," *Juniata Echo* 12, no.5, 71.

53. Yoder, "College Life," *Juniata Echo* 12, no.5, 71.

54. *Juniata Echo* 12, no.2, 27.

55. *Boys*, 277-78.

56. Kaylor, *Truth*, 164.

57. Letter to John A. Hostetler, YF, March 21, 1947.

58. Kaylor, *Brumbaugh*, 117.

59. Kaylor, *Brumbaugh*, 113-115.

60. Yoder, "The Amish," *Juniata Echo* 13, no. 2, 19.

61. Yoder, "The Amish, 20.

62. *Boys*, 209.

63. Yoder, "The Amish," 20.

64. Earl F. Robacker, *Pennsylvania German Literature: Changing Trends from 1683 to 1942* (Philadelphia: University of Pennsylvania Press, 1943).

65. *Juniata.Echo* 13, no. 5.

66. Kauffman, 252.

67. "Do Something," reprinted in *Boys*, 329-330.

CHAPTER 3

1. *Boys*, 103.

2. Beulah Stauffer Hostetler, "The Formation of the Old Orders," *Mennonite Quarterly Review* 66, no. 1 (January 1992): 7-8.

3. John W. Jordan, LL.D., editorial supervisor, *A History of the Juniata Valley and Its People* vol. 1 (New York: Lewis Historical Publishing Co., 1913), 577.

4. *Boys*, 146.

5. *Boys*, 145.

6. The terms *self-made man* or *Masculine Achiever* and *Christian gentleman* come from Anthony Rotundo, "Learning about Manhood," in J.A. Mangan and James Walvin, eds., *Manliness and Morality: Middle-Class Morality in Britain and America, 1800-1940* (Manchester, UK: Manchester University Press, 1987), 35-48.

7. U. S. Bureau of the Census, *Fifteenth Census of the United States, 1930: Volume 2: General Report, Statistics by Subjects* (Washington, D.C.: Government Printing Office, 1933), 842 qtd. in Howard P. Chudacoff, *The Age of the Bachelor: Creating an American Subculture* (Princeton, N.J.: Princeton University Press, 1999), 247.

8. Kevin White, *The First Sexual Revolution: The Emergence of Male Heterosexuality in Modern America* (New York: NYU Press, 1993), 9-12.

9. Chudacoff, 224.

10. Chudacoff, 224.

11. *Boys*, 241.

12. *Boys*, 243.

13. *Boys*, 245.

14. William S. Taylor, *The Development of the Professional Education of Teachers in Pennsylvania* (Philadelphia: J.B. Lippincott, 1929), 289.

15. *Boys*, 343.

16. YF, May 26, 1905.

17. YF, June 5, 1905.

18. *Boys*, 328.

19. *Boys*, 341.

20. *Boys*, 342.

21. YF, May 26, 1905.

22. YF, May 5, 1905.

23. *Boys*, 342-43.

24. Beulah Stauffer Hostetler, "Old Orders," 17.

25. S. Duane Kauffman, *Mifflin County Amish and Mennonite Story, 1791-1991* (Belleville, Pa.: Mifflin County Mennonite Historical Society, 1991), 252.

26. *Herald of Truth* 35 (April 1989), 99, quoted in Theron F. Schlabach, *Peace, Faith, Nation: Mennonites and Amish in Nineteenth-Century America*, The Mennonite Experience in America, vol. 2 (Scottdale, Pa: Herald Press, 1988), 70.

27. The articles cited include COR. *Herald of Truth* 19 (April 1906), 137 and Pupil. *Gospel Witness* 17 (October 1906), 455.

28. *Herald of Truth* 35 (April 1,1898), 99.

29. *The Normal Bulletin (Central State Normal School)* (April. 1906), 37-38.

30. *The Normal Bulletin (Central State Normal School)* (June 1906), 26-27.

31. Pupil. *Gospel Witness* 17 (October 1906), 455.

32. YF, August 14, 1906.

33. Chudacoff, 225.

34. YF, letter to Paul Erb, June 22, 1951.

35. *The Normal Bulletin* (Central State Normal School) (November1906), 22.

36. Quoted in Stanley Sadie, *The New Grove Dictionary of Music and Musicians* 12 (London: Macmillan, 1980), 105.

37. *Boys*, 285.

38. *Boys*, 287.
39. *Boys*, 288.
40. Yoder described his negotiation with members of the community and his process of recording the tunes in several places, among them the introduction to *Amische Lieder* and 228-293 in *Rosanna's Boys*.
41. *Boys*, 143-44.
42. *Boys*, 227.
43. All quotes from "Minstrels Make A Multitude Merry on Opening Night," *Clinton Republican,* 24 February 1909, 2.
44. *Boys*, 241.
45. http://billysunday.org/sermons, May 22, 1901.
46. *Newtown Enterprise* (May 29, 1915).
47. S. Duane Kauffman interview with Hooley neighbor Muriel Briggs, secretary of the Addisville Reformed Church, e-mail to author, June 29, 2001.
48. Kauffman interview with Polly Scully, granddaughter of John and Myra Hooley, e-mail to author, June 29, 2001.
49. Memory of "an older man in the community" recollected by Hooley neighbor Muriel Briggs. Kauffman, e-mail to author, June 29, 2001.
50. Clyde Griffin: "Reconstructing Masculinity from the Evangelical Revival to the Waning of Progressivism: A Speculative Synthesis," in Mark C. Carnes and Clyde Griffen, eds., *Meanings for Manhood: Constructions of Masculinity in Victorian American* (Chicago: University of Chicago Press, 1990), 193.
51. *Newtown Enterprise* (January 17, 1913).
52. *Doylestown Daily Intelligencer* (July 25, 1929).
53. YF, June 4, 1946.
54. YF, letter to Mrs. Frazee, June 4, 1946.
55. Earl C. Kaylor, *Martin Grove Brumbaugh: A Pennsylvanian's Odyssey form Sainted School Mam to Bedeviled World War I Governor, 1862-1930* (Cranbury, N.J..: Association of University Presses, 1996), 256.
56. Carl F. Bowman, *Brethren Society: The Cultural Transformation of a "Peculiar People"* (Baltimore, Md.: Johns Hopkins University Press, 1995), 245-51. John Ruth, drawing on oral sources in south-eastern Pennsylvania, has written, "Regarding Brumbaugh, when he got worldly and became governor of Pa, the local Dunker verdict was that he 'hat die ganze Bruderschaft verschaemt'—he brought shame on the whole brotherhood." E-mail to author, 9 November 1995.
57. An unsigned notebook attributed to someone in the Irene L. Bishop family preserves a record of three singing schools, held January through May and July through October 1913 and April through July 1916; the book belongs to the collection of the Mennonite Historians of Eastern Pennsylvania at Harleysville, Pennsylvania. *Gospel Herald*, October 1913, p. 473 also notes that Yoder was leading singing at the Deep Run congregation. Tim Rice (see note 61) has noted that Walter Rush recalled that Yoder started classes at Deep Run in 1912. Walter D. Rush Collection, Hist. Mss. 1-4, Box 1, Folder 20, Mennonite Historians of Eastern Pennsylvania.
58. Unsigned notebook attributed to someone in the Irene L. Bishop family.
59. YF, Undated template letter.

60. Unsigned notebook attributed to someone in the Irene L. Bishop family.

61. Timothy Rice, *Deep Run Mennonite Church East: A 250 Year Pilgrimage, 1746-1996* (Perkasie, Pa.: Deep Run Mennonite Church East, 1996), 48-50.

62. *Doylestown Daily Intelligencer* (14 August 1919).

63. *Newtown Enterprise* (18 October 1919).

64. Alvin Detweiler in a Deep Run East storytelling session, November 19, 1995, quoted in Rice, 49.

65. Memory of Anna Detweiler, John Ruth, "Yoder Notes," e-mail to author, February 9, 2001.

66. John Ruth, "Yoder Notes," e-mail to author, February 9, 2001.

67. George Riley, "Deep Run Mennonites Had a Song Festival," *Doylestown Daily Intelligencer* (March 4, 1940). In 1952 Henry Gross tape-recorded J.W. Yoder leading singing at Deep Run, a copy of the tape is in the collection of Mennonite Historians of Eastern Pennsylvania.

68. Ruth, conversation with author, November 10,1996.

69. Pamphlet, YF.

70. Quoted in James C. Juhnke, *Vision, Doctrine, War: Mennonite Identity and Organization in America, 1890-1930*, The Mennonite Experience in America, vol. 3 (Scottdale, Pa.: Herald Press, 1989), 215.

71. The fire at Tabor College was never proven to be arson. See Juhnke, 218-241.

72. Quoted in Kauffman, 294.

73. Juhnke, 237.

74. Juniata College, I. Harvey Brumbaugh, Admin Corr. T-Z, February 7, 1917.

75. Juniata College, I. Harvey Brumbaugh, Admin Corr. T-Z, May 8, 1917.

76. Juniata College, I. Harvey Brumbaugh, Admin Corr. T-Z, October 18, 1918.

77. S. Duane Kauffman interview with Hooley neighbor Muriel Briggs, e-mail to author, June 29, 2001.

78.Bucks County Deeds Book 576, 273.

CHAPTER 4

1. Ruth Lininger Dobson, *Straw in the Wind* (New York: Dodd Meade, 1937), 32.

2. Dobson, 26.

3. Dobson, 69.

4. Dobson, 118–19.

5. Dobson, 31.

6. Dobson, 186.

7. Dobson, 211-12.

8. Dobson, 218.

9. Dobson, 222.

10. Dobson, 103.

11. Dobson, 103-4.

12. Dobson, 104.

13. Dobson, 105.

14. Dobson, 105.

15. Dobson, 106.

16. Dobson, 225-26.

17. Dobson, 106.

18. "Criticism of 'Straw in the Wind' with July 18, 1938 letter to Fred A. Walker, YF.

19. "Criticism of 'Straw in the Wind' with July 18, 1938 letter to Fred A. Walker, YF.

20. "Criticism of 'Straw in the Wind' with July 18, 1938 letter to Fred A. Walker, YF.

21. Elizabeth Horsch Bender. 'Three Amish Novels," Review. of *Sabina a Story of the Amish* by Helen R. Martin, *Straw in the Wind* by Ruth Lininger Dobson, and *Rosanna of the Amish* By J.W. Yoder, *Mennonite Quarterly Review* 10, no. 3 (October 1945): 273-284.

22. Conversation with Carol Burkhart Spicher, Mountville, Pennsylvania, July 14, 1995.

23. Robacker, 124.

24. Interview with Helen R. Martin, Lillian L. Thompson, "A Critical Biography of Mrs. Helen R. Martin," Master's thesis (Pennsylvania State University, 1935), 10.

25. Helen R. Martin. "The Pennsylvania Dutch," *Bookman* 38 (November 1913), quoted in Lillian L. Thompson, "A Critical Biography of Mrs. Helen R. Martin," Master's thesis (Pennsylvania State University, 1935), 45-47.

26. Earl F. Robacker, *Pennsylvania German Literature: Changing Trends from 1683 to 1942.* (Philadelphia: University of Pennsylvania Press, 1943), 17.

27. Ammon Monroe Aurand Jr., *Little Known Facts About the Amish and the Mennonites* (Lancaster, Pa.: Aurand, n.d.), 12.

28. Aurand, 7.

29. Aurand, 28.

30. Bernard McGrane, *Beyond Anthropology: Society and the Other* (New York: Columbia University Press, 1989), 93.

31. Thomas Spicher, conversation with author, June 10, 1995.

32. Elizabeth Horsch Bender, editor and master translator, had a hand in nearly all of H.S. Bender's published works from the 1920s to 1962; translated the *Mennonitishes Lexikon*, which became the core of the *Mennonite Encyclopedia*; performed editorial work on *The Mennonite Quarterly Review* from 1927-85; and for fifteen years translated German language materials for the Historical Committee of the Mennonite Church. Leonard Gross in Cornelius J. Dyck and Dennis D. Martin, "Bender, Elizabeth Horsch," *The Mennonite Encyclopedia* 5 (Scottdale, Pa.: Herald Press, 1990), 66.

33. Helen R. Martin, "The Pennsylvania Dutch," *Bookman* 38 (November 1913), quoted in Lillian L. Thompson, "A Critical Biography of Mrs. Helen R. Martin," Master's thesis (Pennsylvania State University, 1935), 46.

34. Letter to *The Middlebury Independent*, November 26, 1940, YF.

35. Rosanna McGonegal Yoder Hostetler forward to Joseph W. Yoder, *Rosanna of the Amish* (Scottdale, Pa.: Herald Press, 1995), 10.

36. Mary Louise Pratt, "Arts of the Contact Zone," *Profession* (1991): 33-40.

37. *Rosanna*, 84.

38. *Rosanna*, 177.

39. Quoted in John Ruth, *Mennonite Identity and Literary Art* (Scottdale, Pa.: Herald Press, 1978), 40.

40. *Rosanna*, 227.

41. *Rosanna*, 179.

42. *Rosanna*, 118.

43. Letter to Annenberg, October 2, 1950, YF.

44. Letter to Haas, October 2, 1950, YF.

45. *Rosanna*, 143.

46. *Rosanna*, vii-viii. Emphases mine.

47. Robacker, 283.

48. Andrea Fishman, *Amish Literacy* (Portsmouth, Nh.: Heinemann, 1988), 46.

49. Interview with Helen R. Martin, Lillian L. Thompson, "A Critical Biography of Mrs. Helen R. Martin," Master's thesis (Pennsylvania State University, 1935), 12.

50. John Umble. Rev. of *Rosanna of the Amish* by Joseph W. Yoder, *Mennonite Quarterly Review* 15 (April 1941): 144.

51. *The Sentinal*, December 18, 1940, 6.

52. All letters can be found with Yoder's 1940 correspondence, YF.

53. Umble, 147.

54. Letter to the Editor, *Budget* (February 8, 1951), YF.

55. *Boys*, 293-94.

56. Plato, trans. by Walter Hamilton, *Phaedrus and the Seventh and Eighth Letters* (New York: Penguin, 1972), 275.

57. *Boys*, 294.

58. Copies of *Amische Lieder* may now sell for $100 or more at auction or through book dealers in central Pennsylvania. Yoder's version of the "*Lobgesang*" from *Amische Lieder* was the basis of an arrangement of "*O Gott Vater*," which can be found in *Hymnal*, the 1992 worship book currently used by Mennonites, Brethren, and other believers church congregations in the United States and Canada. Elgin, Ill.: Brethren Press, Newton, Kan.: Faith and Life Press, Scottdale, Pa.: Mennonite Publishing House, 1992, 33.

59. *Boys*, 293.

60. *Lieder*, v.

61. YF, 1947 letter.

62. *Traditions*, 92-93.

63. *Traditions*, 93-94.

64. *Traditions*, 91.

65. Plato, 97.

66. John Umble, "The Old Order Amish, Their Hymns and Hymn Tunes," *Journal of American Folklore* 52 (April 1929): 93-131.

67. George Pullen Jackson, "The American Amish Sing Medieval Folk Tunes Today," *Southern Folklore Quarterly* 10 (June 1946): 151-57.

68. Christian Hege, *Mennonitisches Lexikon*, quoted in John A. Hostetler, *Amish Society*, 230.

69. *Boys*, 301-302.

CHAPTER 5

1. RG 13, Individual Collections: Yoder, Joseph W., Box 6a, YF.

2. *Traditions*, vii.

3. Many of these letters are preserved in the Juniata College Archive, L. A. Beeghly Library, Huntingdon, Pa.

3. YF, copy of the January 9, 1947 letter sent to members of the Renno church.

5. *Rosanna*, 84-85.

6. *Boys*, 92-93.

7. YF, July 5, 1948.

8. YF, March 28, 1950.

9. John R. Renno, *A Brief History of the Amish Church in Belleville* (Danville, Pa.: n.p., n.d.), 71.

10. *Traditions*, 3.

11. YF, January 5, 1948.

12. There were several brief accounts of church schisms written before this time. Shem Zook (1798-1880), a highly literate layman Amish farmer and publisher wrote a thirty-one-page account of the King division (1849) and the Peachey schism (1863), *Eine Wahre Darstellung u.s.w.* (A True Exposition), which John A. Hostetler has translated and published. In a February 3, 1949 letter to L. A. Miller, editor of *Der Herald der Warheit*, Yoder mentioned owning a copy of Shem Zook's history. Also in 1930, Samuel W. Peachey published *Amish of the Kishacoquillas Valley*, a local Amish history spanning 1793-1930, listing names of leaders but avoiding reasons for congregational schism. Unpublished chronicles of community life and diary-like records were also kept in the community, and some have been handed down in the families of their authors. S. Duane Kauffman's *Mifflin County Amish and Mennonite Story, 1791-1991* now offers a more complete description of Mennonite and Amish congregational history.

13. *Traditions*, 11.

14. This summary is based on the fuller account in John A. Hostetler, *Amish Society*, fourth ed. (Baltimore: Johns Hopkins University Press, 1993), 27-48.

15. Kauffman, 305, 307.

16. Among his papers are "essential parts" of an English translation that Yoder made of this document and his own commentary pertaining to it. In brief, the document, "passed in 1809 and 1909 by Lancaster County Old Order Amish" was written in response to a request for "a ruling pertaining to the Meidung as taught by the old Bishops." As reported in Yoder's translation, the document's four elderly authors offered these points on the Meidung practice:

> 1.) We desire nothing except to continue in the doctrine which we were taught, built on the foundations as taught by the Prophets, and the apostles where Jesus Christ is the cornerstone." 2.) Of the Ban and withdraw he wrote that the sinful, the vexatious, the disobedient and the carnal members shall be expelled and shunned, but after an honest repentance to be taken into the church again. 3.) In the year 1809 . . . there was a ministers meeting of which the report and resolution is at hand. Namely that all those who join other churches shall be considered

apostate (faithless) people according to the word of God and Ordnung, and they shall be excommunicated and be subject to the Ban, and the Meidung shall be kept according to the teaching of Christ and the apostles unto they are again taken into the church." 4.) Jesus teaches in Matthew XVIII:17 about those who will not obey the Church, that they shall be regarded as heathen and Publicans. . . . By this teaching we intend to stay, by God's help and we implore and admonish all brethren and sisters to join in willingly and piously so we may all hold our communion together in harmony and to the honor of God.

17, *Traditions*, 11-12.

18. YF, 1944.

19. Interview with John A. Hostetler, Willow Grove, Pennsylvania, August 8, 1995.

20. John A. Hostetler, *Amish Society*, 287.

21. John A. Hostetler, "An Amish Beginning," *American Scholar* 16 (1992), 562.

22. John A. Hostetler. "An Amish Beginning," 562.

23. YF, January 5, 1948.

24. YF, n.d. (late 1940s).

25. YF, February 2, 1951.

26. YF, July 6, 1944.

27. YF, January 9, 1947.

28. YF, January 9, 1947.

29. YF, Letter to John D. Yoder, November 28, 1947.

30. When I met John D. Yoder at the home of John R. Renno during summer 1995, he could not believe that letters he had written could be part of a college library collection and therefore would not give me permission to print them. Because he was blind, I made a tape recording of the letters he had sent to J. W. Yoder in the late 1940s and mailed the tape to him. He never responded to my request for a tape-recorded response to those letters nor for permission to print them, and he passed away during summer 1996.

31. YF, Letter to John D. Yoder, Novem,ber 28, 1947.

32. YF, January 9, 1947.

33. Copies of these letters and Yoder's responses can be found in YF, 1947.

34. *Traditions*, 53.

35. Interview with John R. and Salina Renno, Danville, Pennsylvania, July 2, 1995.

36. Renno interview.

37. Renno interview.

38. Renno interview.

39. John R. Renno, *Growing Up Amish* (Petersburg, Oh.: Pilgrim Brethren Press, 1993), 77.

40. Renno interview.

41. Renno interview.

42. YF, February 28, 1953.

43. Renno interview.

44. Renno, *Growing*, 86.

45. Renno interview.

46 This link between contemplative religious practice and literacy is central to the work of Walter Ong, *Orality and Literacy* (London: Methuen, 1982).

47. In any edition of the popular 1917 Scofield Reference Bible, the fifth "Dispensation: Law" extends from Exodus 19:8 to Matthew 27:35 as noted on p. 94, and the dispensation of "Grace" begins with the death and resurrection of Christ and extends until the dispensation of "Fullness of Times" or the Millennium, as noted on pages 1115 and 1250. I thank J. Denny Weaver for his assistance with the *Scofield Reference Bible.*

48. *Traditions*, 24.

49. George Marsden, *Fundamentalism and American Culture: The Shaping of Twentieth Century Evangelicalism 1870-1925* (New York: Oxford University Press, 1980), 87.

50. YF, January 25, 1948.

51. YF, January 28, 1948.

52. For a detailed analyses of the case, see Mami Hiraike Okawara, "The Samuel D. Hochstetler Case (1948)," *The Japanese Journal of American Studies* 8 (1997): 119-141; and Julia Kasdorf, "The Gothic Tale of Lucy Hochstetler and the Temptation of Literary Authority," in *The Body and the Book: Writing from a Mennonite Life* (Baltimore: Johns Hopkins University Press, 2001), 143-163.

53. *Traditions*, 72.

54. *Traditions*, 78.

55. *Traditions*, 37.

56. *Traditions*, 34.

57. *Traditions*, 71.

58. *Traditions*, 72.

59. *Traditions*, 148.

60. *Traditions*, 173.

61. *Traditions*, 199.

62. *Traditions*, 203.

63. YF, March 2, 1947.

CHAPTER 6

1. YF, March 1, 1948.

2. YF, July 30, 1954.

3. *Belleville Times*, February 26, 1942, quoted in Kauffman, 247.

4. *Traditions*, 205-213.

5. YF, November 11, 1952.

6. YF, April 9, 1948.

7. YF, 1947 (Harrisburg speech dated February 6, 1947, all others, n.d.).

8. YF, January 17, 1951.

9. YF, January 18, 1951.

10. Donald B. Kraybill, "Mennonite Woman's Veiling: The Rise and Fall of a Sa-

cred Symbol," *Mennonite Quarterly Review* 61, no. 3 (July 1987): 309.

11. In 1891 J. S. Coffman relegated the prayer veil to a "secondary" ordinance and "custom" his Fundamental Bible References but saw the covering and long hair as signs of a woman's relationship to her husband, who is her head, Theron F. Schlabach, *Peace, Faith, Nation: Mennonites and Amish in Nineteenth-Century America*, The Mennonite Experience in America, vol. 2 (Scottdale, Pa: Herald Press, 1988), 315

Quoted in Beulah Stauffer Hostetler's unpublished mss, *The Journey Home* (September 1996), 72.

12. Beulah Stauffer Hostetler, *Journey,* 70; Juhnke, 115.

14. Daniel Kauffman, *Manual of Bible Doctrines* (Elkhart, Ind.: Mennonite Publishing Company, 1898); Kauffman, ed., *Bible Doctrines* (Scottdale, Pa.: Mennonite Publishing House, 1914); Kauffman, ed., *Doctrines of the Bible* (Scottdale, Pa.: Mennonite Publishing House, 1928). For a survey of Kauffman's influence, see Leonard Gross, "Kauffman, Daniel," *The Mennonite Encuclopedia*, v.5, Cornelius J. Dyck and Dennis D. Martin, eds. (Scottdale, Pa.: Herald Press, 1990), 483.

15. Leonard Gross, "The Doctrinal Era of the Mennonite Church," *Mennonite Quarterly Review* 60, no. 1 (January 1986): 113-138.

16. James C. Juhnke, *Vision, Doctrine, War: Mennonite Identity and Organization in America 1900-1930*, The Mennonite Experience in America, v. 3 (Scottdale, Pa.: Herald Press, 1989), 130-31.

17. Kraybill, "Veiling," 303.

18. Juhnke, 131-32.

19. S. Duane Kauffman, *Mifflin County Amish and Mennonite Story, 1791-1991* (Belleville, Pa.: Mifflin County Mennonite Historical Society, 1991), 317.

20. Telephone interview with an elderly member of Maple Grove Mennonite Church who wishes to remain unnamed, June 30, 1995.

21. John Christian Wenger, *Separated Unto God: A Plea for Christian Simplicity of Life and for a Scriptural Nonconformity to the World* (Scottdale, Pa.: Mennonite Publishing House, 1951).

22. Kauffman, 337.

23. Paul Erb, rev. of *Amish Traditions* by J. W. Yoder, *Gospel Herald* 44, no.24 (June 12, 1951), 575.

24. YF, June 22, 1951.

25. YF, June 26, 1251.

26. YF, June 26, 1951.

27. YF, August 12, 1951.

28. J. W. Yoder, Letter, *Gospel Herald* 44, no. 39 (September 25, 1951), 922.

29. Yoder letter to *Gospel Herald.*

30. YF, June 22, 1951.

31. J. W. Yoder, Letter, *Belleville Times*, August 16, 1951.

32. Interview with James and Marian Payne, Belleville, Pennsylvania, June 18, 1995.

33. Payne interview.

34. James Payne, Letter, *Belleville Times*, August 25, 1951.

35. Payne interview.

36. Levi K. Yoder, YF, September 14, 1951.

37. J. W. Yoder, Letter, *Belleville Times*, September 20, 1951.

38. Paul Bennett, Letter, *Belleville Times*, October 4, 1951.

39. J. W. Yoder, Letter, *Belleville Times*, October 18, 1951.

40. Paul Bennett, Letter, *Belleville Times*, October 25, 1951.

41. Payne interview.

42. Payne interview.

43. Payne interview.

44. YF, July 1, 1951.

45. YF, July 10, 1951. The General Conference Mennonite Church (GC) was formed in 1860, by three congregations of recent Mennonite immigrants in Iowa and the "new" or reform-minded Eastern Pennsylania Conference of Mennonites that was the result of an 1847 schism from Franconia Conference and became the Eastern District of the General Conference. In addition to the founders, the General Conference included many more recent Mennonite immigrants from Germany, Switzerland, and the Russian Empire, who settled in the Midwest and Plains states. In 2001, the General Conference integrated with the Mennonite Church (which for many years was called the "old" Mennonite Church) to form the Mennonite Church USA. From its inception in 1914, the GC school in Ohio, Bluffton College, attracted scholars such as Noah Byers and C. Henry Smith, who had grown weary of battling conservatives in the "old" Mennonite denomination. If J. W. Yoder had joined the General Conference, he would have followed those progressives of his generation, like Smith and J. E. Hartzler, who traveled the path from Amish to Amish-Mennonite to GC without ever entirely leaving the broader Mennonite family. For a history and discussion of the General Conference as a progressive movement, see Schlabach, chapter five.

46. YF, December 18, 1950.

47. YF, January 28, 1950.

48. YF, August 13, 1951.

49. Susan Fisher Miller, *Culture for Service: A History of Goshen College, 1894-1994* (Goshen, Ind.: Goshen College, 1994), 60-66.

50. YF, August 13, 1951.

51. Juhnke, 265.

52. Hartzler was among the athlete-scholars trained by Yoder in the Elkhart Athletic Association during 1900-01; he received a BA from Goshen College, BD from Union Theological Seminary in New York City, MA from the University of Chicago, law degree from Hamilton College and PhD from Hartford Thelogical seminary. In additional to teaching at the Mennonite Witmarsum Thelogical Seminary at Bluffton Ohio, he taught at the American University in Beirut and the Near East School of Religion before joining the faculty at Hartford Theological Seminary. J. Denny Weaver, "Hartzler, John Ellsworth," *Mennonite Encyclopedia* v. 5, p. 363.

53. YF, January 17, 1951.

54. YF, August 13, 1951.

55. YF, August 21, 1951

56. YF, August 13, 1951
57. YF, January 17, 1951.
58. *Prayer Veil*, 8.
59. *Prayer Veil*, 22.
60. *Prayer Veil*, 51.
61. *Prayer Veil*, 35.
62. *Prayer Veil*, 38.
63. *Prayer Veil*, 39.
64. *Prayer Veil*, 43.
65. *Prayer Veil*, 15.
66. *Prayer Veil*, 15.
67. *Prayer Veil*, 35-36.
68. *Prayer Veil*, 32.
69. Levi Bontrager, YF, July 18, 1955.

CHAPTER 7

1. Thrin T. Minh-Ha, *Woman Native Other* (Bloomington: Indiana University Press, 1989), 11.
2. *Rosanna*, 85-86.
3. YF, January 5, 1948.
4. Michel Foucault, *The Order of Things* (New York: Random House, 1970), 17-30.

CREDITS AND IDENTIFICATION

1.1   Photographer, Willis Peachey
1.2   Juniata College Archives
1.3   Personal collection of Polly Scully
1.4   Kline Studio, Huntingdon, Pa. Juniata College Archives
1.6   Kline Studio, Huntingdon, Pa. Juniata College Archives
1.7   Juniata College Archives
1.8   Photographer, Willis Peachey

2.1   Archives of the Mennonite Church
2.2   Archives of the Mennonite Church
2.3   E. M. Mudge Fine Art Studio, Mennonite Historical Library.
Front Row: (l-r) Mrs. McCracken, pianist; Abram B. Kolb, Director and Tenor Soloist;
       Lillian Smailey, soprano soloist; Emma Clouse; Addie Brunk, alto soloist; Joe
       Brubacker, bass soloist; Rev. Breightenbach, organist.
Row 2: (l-r) unknown, Henry Reist, Ella Kulp, Grace Lehman, Clara Mumaw, Lizzie Ja-
       cobs, Alice Miller, Barbara Coffman, Anna Brunk, unknown, unknow, J.W.
       Yoder, Will Coffman, Jacob Coffman, Aarthur Lehman.
Row 3 (l-r) A. R. Miller, Irvin Detweiler, Dan Weldy, unknown, unknown, Lavona
       Berkey, Anna Ranck, unknown, unknown, Verda Brunk, Mrs. Byers, un-
       known, Ira Johns, unknown, Sam Miller, Vernon Hartzler.
Row 4 (l-r) C. K. Hostetler, Levi Hostetler, Frank Ebersole, unknown, unknown,
       Martha Funk, Lena Williams, unknown, unknown, unknown, unknown,
       Elsie Kolb, Dan Coffman, unknown, Fred Blessing.
Row 5 (l-r) Aaron Kolb, unknown, unknown, unknown, unknown, unknown, Fannie
       Coffman, unknown, unknown, unknown.
Back Row (l-r) unknown, unknown, Celesta Hartzler, Anna Kulp, Madge Work, un-
       known, unknown, unknown, Phoebe Funk
2.4   From the 1900 Northwestern University *Syllabus*, Courtesy Northwestern Uni-
       versity Archives.
2.5   Frank S. Ebersole Photograph Album, Archives of the Mennonite Church.
2.6   E. M. Mudge Fine Art Studio, Mennonite Historical Library, gift of John S.

Row 1 (l-r)John S. Umble, unknown.

Row 2 (l-r) Sam T. Witmer, Glenn G. Unzicker, William S. Gehman, Purl R. Zook, Anthony C. Moyer, Harvey L Stump, Albert Stump.

Row 3 (l-r) Harold Buzzard, John I Byler, David B. Zook, Jonathan M. Kurtz, Joseph W. Yoder, Ellsworth Troyer, Paul Wesley Dierberger, Orvain C. Kurtz, C. Edward Bender.

Row 4 (l-r) John S. Musselman, Frank E. Dreisbach, unknown, Reuben R. Ebersole, Henry Frank Reist, Louis C. Schertz, John Ellsworth Hartzler, Walter B. Christophel, Frank S. Ebersole, Ira Musselman, Orie C. Yoder.

2.7   Juniata College Archive

2.8   Frank S. Ebersole Photograph Album, Archives of the Mennonite Church

2.9   Juniata College Archive

2.10 Juniata College Archive

2.11 *Women's Physical Development*

2.12 Juniata College Archive

2.13 Juniata College Archive

3.1   Richard Mellanger Collection, Box 4, album. Lancaster Mennonite Historical Society

3.2   *Catalogue of the Central State Normal School*, Lock Haven, Pennsylvania, 1907-08

3.3   Personal collection of Mary Yoder

3.4   Lock Haven Hospital Charity Minstrels, GPC 1-209, Annie Halenbake Ross Library.

3.5   Frank S. Ebersole Phorograph Album, Archives of the Mennonite Church

3.6   Photographer, S. Duane Kauffman

3.7   Frank S. Ebersole Photograph Album, Archives of the Mennonite Church

3.8   Yoder Papers, Juniata College Archive

3.9   Juniata College Archive

3.10 Newtown Enterprise, Feb. 6, 1915

3.11 Personal collection of Polly Scully

3.12 Mennonite Heritage Center, Harleysville, Pennsylvania

3.13 —

3.14 Personal collection of Kermit Yoder

3.15 Personal collection of Polly Scully

3.16 Original source of photo unknown, Joseph W. Yoder Photograph Collection, Archives of the Mennonite Church.

4.1   —

4.2   —

4.3   Yoder papers, Juniata College Archive

4.4   Das Lobsang as printed in *Amische Lieder*

4.5   —

5.1   Photograph by David L. Hunsberger for Mennonite Community (Aug. 1948), John E. Harshbarger Photograph Collection, Archives of the Mennonite Church

5.2   Photographer W. W. Cooke, Jr.; photograph taken from original newspaper clipping as found in the Samuel d. Hochstetler Collection, Archives of the Mennonite Church.

5.3   Photographer W. W. Cooke, Jr.; photograph taken from original newspaper clipping as found in the Samuel D. Hochstetler Collection, Archives of the Mennonite Church

6.1   Photograph by David L. Hunsberger, John E. Harshbarger Photograph Collection, Archives of the Mennonite Church

6.2   Photographer, E. M. Mudge, Phoebe Mumaw Kolb Photograph Collection, Archives of the Mennonite Church. Women (l-r) Lavona Berkey, Barbara Blosser, Minnie Stauffer, Addie Brunk, Anna Holdeman, and Elsie Kolb.

6.3   Graduation Class, Elkhart Institute, 1901. Frank S. and Lavona (Berkey) Ebersole Photograph Album, Archives of the Mennonite Church. First Row: (l-r) I.R. Detweiler, Olivia Good, John Umble. Second Row: (l-r) Lavona Berkey, Alice M. Landis. John L Steiner. F. S. Ebersole, J. M. Kurtz, Anna Holdeman, Adeline V. Brunk. Third Row: (l-r) Amelia Bergey, William S. Gehman, John S. Musselman, Carrie Ecker, Noah E. Byers, I.W. Royer, Lina Zook, C. Edward Bender, Anthony C. Moyer, Blanche Dickinson.

6.4   Photographer, Charles F. Kauffman

6.5   From personal collection of Mary Yoder

6.6   Photographer, Willis Peachey

7.1   Photographer, Willis Peachey

INTERVIEWS AND SPECIAL ARCHIVES

Preliminary Interviews

Kauffman, S. Duane. Harleysville, Pa.. 24 Feb. 1995.
Luthy David. Alymer, Ontario. 18 March 1995.
Peachey, Twila. Belleville, Pa. 1 Aug. 1994.
Ruth, John. Harleysville, Pa. 25 Feb. 1995.
Sharp, John. Telephone interview. 14 Oct. 1992.

Interviews

Brenneman, Maude. Belleville Pa. 20 June 1995.
Beiler, Abner. Intercourse, Pa. 11 Jan. 1997.
Byler, Sadie. Belleville, Pa. 21 June 1995.
Crosby (Eby) Jane. Huntingdon, Pa. 14-18 June 1995.
Durnbaugh, Don. Huntingdon, Pa. 2 Feb. 2001.
Glick, Elam. Belleville, Pa. 20 June 1995.
Hostetler, John A. and Beulah Stauffer Hostetler. Willow Grove, Pa. 8 Aug. 1995.
Hostetler, John A. Willow Grove, Pa. 26 Oct. 1995.
King, Daniel. Barrville, Pa. 20 June 1995.
Payne, James and Marian. Belleville, Pa. 18 June 1995.
Peachey, Elsie and Miriam. White Hall, Pa. 19 June 1995.
Peachey, Corrie N. Danville, Pa, 2 July 1995.
Peachey, Twila, Belleville, Pa, 20 June 1995, 15 Sept. 2001.
Renno, John R. and Salina. Danville, Pa. 2 July 1995.
Spicher, Jesse and Annie. Union Mills, Pa. 20 June, 1995.
Spicher, Thomas. Huntingdon, Pa. 2 July 1995.
Yoder, Dorothy. telephone interview. 20 June 1995.
Yoder, John D. Danville, Pa. 21 June 1995.
Yoder, Katie. Belleville, Pa. 21 June 1995.

Yoder, Mary. telephone interview 19 June 1995, 15 Spet. 2001.
Yoder, Naomi. Belleville, Pa. 21 June 1995.
Yoder, Percy. Belleville, Pa. 20 June, 1995.
Zook, Martha. Belleville, Pa. 20 June, 1995.
Zook, Yost and Amelia. Belleville, Pa, 19 June 1995.

SPECIAL ARCHIVES

Archives of the Mennonite Church, Goshen, Indiana. 28 June 1995, Jan. 3-5 2001.
Heritage Historical Society (Old Order Archive), Aylmer, Ontario. 18 March 1995.
Juniata College Archive, Huntingdon, Pa. 13-16 June 1995; 26 October 1995; 2 Feb. 2001.
Lock Haven University Archives, Lock Haven, Pa, 10 May, 2001.
Mennonite Heritage Center, Harleysville, Pa, 27 October, 2000.
Mennonite Historical Library, Goshen, Indiana. 28 June 1995, Jan. 4-5, 2001.
Mennonite Historical Society, Belleville, Pa. 19 June 1995
Mennonite Historical Society Library, Lancaster, Pa. 27 September, 1995, 14 June, 2001.
Mifflin County Historical Society, Lewistown, Pa. 27 Nov. 2001.
Annie Halenbake Ross Library, Lock Haven, Pa. 10 May, 2001.

TIMELINE

1872 - 1956
æ 84

1860s   American Civil War, Amish church divides in Big Valley, separating Rosanna and Crist from their parent's congregation.

Church House Amish meetinghouse built at Belleville (Maple Grove).

1872   Joseph Warren Yoder is born on September 22.

1877   Crazy Horse is captured, marking a decisive turn in the U.S.-Indian wars. Little Crist is ordained a minister in the Peachey Amish Church.

First transcontinental rail road spans the United States.

1890s   First singing schools in Big Valley; Yoder attends one taught by his brother-in-law, John M. Hooley.

1892-94   J. W. Yoder teaches school at Milltown, two miles from his parents' home.

Jan. 1894   Yoder enrolls in the English Normal Program at Brethren Normal School, Huntingdon, Pa., and boards with John M. Hooley.

1895   Yoder graduates with Normal Diploma; Yoder's mother Rosanna dies.

1895-96   Yoder is principal at Milroy, applies and is accepted into medical school.

1897-98   Yoder teaches English and music, Elkhart Institute; boards with J. S. Coffman.

U.S. at war with Spain and in four months prevails as world power, gaining possessions in the Far East.

1898-00   Yoder studies at Northwestern Academy and University, Evanston, Ill.

Church House Amish division in Belleville; part singing one issue (Locust Grove formed)

J . S. Coffman dies; Theodore Roosevelt makes his "Strenuous Life" speech.

1900-01   Yoder teaches English, Greek, and light gymnastics, Elkhart Institute. Institute faculty and students break with Prairie Street and Bishop John Funk.

1900   L. Frank Baum publishes *The Wizard of Oz*, sometimes read as a social allegory. In it a female protagonist travels with three male companions seeking the attributes symbolized by the YMCA triangle: head, heart, and brawn.

1901   Theodore Roosevelt becomes president.

1901-04   Yoder serves as Athletics Director at Juniata College while completing his bachelor's degree. A campus leader in the glee club, debate team, health club, he publishes bilingual poems, begins to annotate Amish hymns, and writes Amish history as a protegé of M. G. Brumbaugh.

1904   Yoder leads singing at his first Teacher's Institute.

1905   Yoder decides against studying journalism at Harvard University and goes instead to Lancaster to teach singing schools for the Mennonites.

1905-09   Yoder teaches logic and math, coaches basketball, baseball and debate teams at Lock Haven.

1910   Yoder lives and works with evangelist John H. Cassady.

1911   Yoder buys farm with John M. Hooley near Richboro, Pa., continues itinerant singing school and Teacher's Institute work.

1915   Father, Little Crist dies; Yoder and Hooley unsuccessfully attempt to dissolve their household and farm. Yoder begins formal recruiting work for Juniata College.

1915-19   M. G. Brumbaugh is Governor of Pennyvania.

1917-18   U.S. involved in World War I.

1920   National prohibition and women's suffrage achieved through the passage of the Eighteenth and Nineteenth Amendments, respectively.

1923   Yoder buys Hooley's share of the farm at Richboro.

1929   Yoder sells the Richboro farm to Hooley for $1.

1932   Yoder marries Emily Lane on February 18 and buys a house in Huntingdon, Pa. The U.S. economy hits a low point with 12 million people—one quarter of the work force—unemployed.

1933   Yoder begins twenty-year tenure as president of the annual Yoder Reunion.

1940   Yoder publishes *Rosanna of the Amish*.

1941   Yoder retires from his college recruiter job at Juniata College, and with the bomging of Pearl Harbor in December, the U. S enters World War II.

1942   Yoder publishes *Amische Lieder*.

1945   World War II ends.

1947   Yoder sends the *meidung* letter regarding the excommunication of John D. Yoder to sixty members of the Renno (formerly Peachey) Amish Church.

1948   Yoder publishes *Rosanna's Boys*; Lucy Hochstetler is discovered chained to her bed by her father near Goshen, Indiana.

1950   Yoder publishes *Amish Traditions*, anticipates church trouble; Korean War

1950s   Elam Glick leads last singing school in Big Valley, uses Yoder's *Cardinal Songster.*

1951   Paul Erb denounces *Amish Traditions* in *Gospel Herald* and *The Budget*; Yoder argues with Preacher Aaron Mast; J. C. Wenger publishes *Separated unto God.*

1952   John A. Hostetler publishes *Amish Life* in response to negative stereotypes of the Amish in tourist literature.

1953   John R. Renno excommunicated from the Renno Church.

1954   Yoder publishes *The Prayer Veil Analyzed.*

1956   Yoder dies of stomach cancer in Huntingdon, Pa.; Aaron Mast officiates at funeral in the meetinghouse at Maple Grove; Mennonite publisher and bishop A. J. Metzler preaches; Belleville Mennonite School chorus sings.

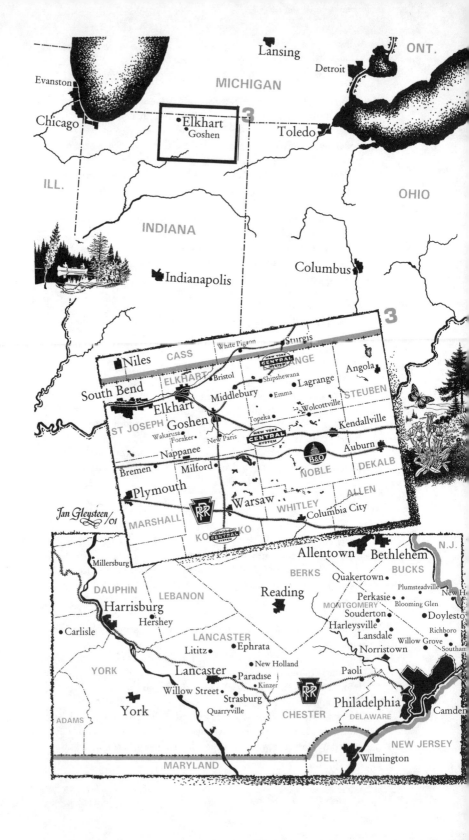

Lansing

ONT.

MICHIGAN

Detroit

3

Evanston

Elkhart
Goshen

Chicago

Toledo

ILL.

OHIO

INDIANA

Indianapolis

Columbus

3

Niles CASS

White Pigeon

Sturgis

NGE

Angola

NEW YORK CENTRAL SYSTEM

South Bend

ELKHART

Bristol

Shipshewana

Lagrange

STEUBEN

Elkhart

Middlebury

Emma

Wolcottville

Kendallville

ST JOSEPH

Goshen

Topeka

Wakarusa
Foraker

New Paris

NEW YORK CENTRAL SYSTEM

Auburn

Nappanee

B&O

Bremen

Milford

NOBLE

DEKALB

Plymouth

Warsaw

ALLEN

WHITLEY

Columbia City

Jan Gleysteen /01

PRR

MARSHALL

KO

CENTRAL SYSTEM

CO

Millersburg

Allentown

Bethlehem

N.J.

BERKS

Quakertown

BUCKS

DAUPHIN

LEBANON

Reading

Perkasie

Plumsteadville

New H

Blooming Glen

Harrisburg

MONTGOMERY

Souderton

Doylesto

Carlisle

Hershey

Harleysville

Richboro

Lansdale

Willow Grove

LANCASTER

Lititz

Ephrata

Norristown

Southam

YORK

New Holland

Paoli

Lancaster

Paradise

PRR

Kinzer

Willow Street

Strasburg

Philadelphia

DELAWARE

Camden

York

Quarryville

CHESTER

ADAMS

NEW JERSEY

DEL.

Wilmington

MARYLAND

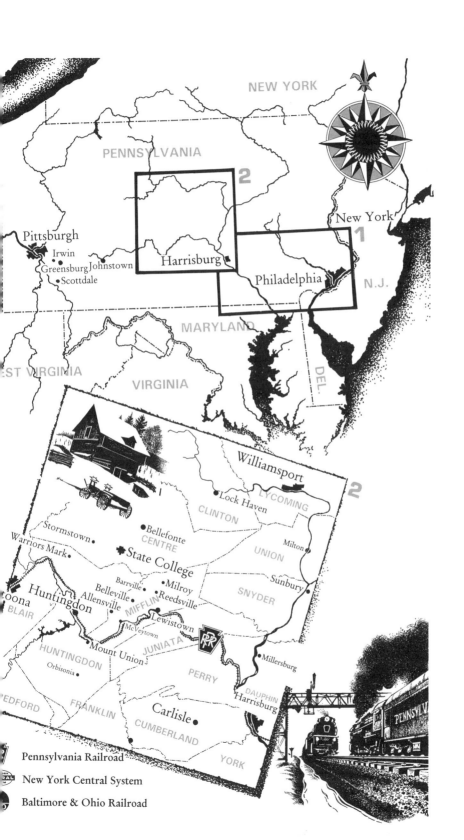

NEW YORK

PENNSYLVANIA

2

Pittsburgh
Irwin
Greensburg Johnstown
Scottdale

Harrisburg

New York

1

Philadelphia

N.J.

MARYLAND

WEST VIRGINIA

VIRGINIA

DEL.

Williamsport

LYCOMING

Lock Haven

CLINTON

2

Stormstown

Bellefonte
CENTRE

Milton

Warriors Mark

State College

UNION

Barrville
Belleville Milroy
Allensville Reedsville

MIFFLIN

Sunbury

SNYDER

Altoona
Huntingdon

BLAIR

Lewistown
McVeytown

Mount Union JUNIATA

PRR

HUNTINGDON

Orbisonia

Millersburg

PERRY

BEDFORD

FRANKLIN

DAUPHIN
Harrisburg

Carlisle

CUMBERLAND

YORK

PENNSYLVANIA

Pennsylvania Railroad

New York Central System

Baltimore & Ohio Railroad

THE INDEX

X

Y

Yoder, Christian "Little Crist" Z.,
23, 112, 124, 149, 161
Yoder, Don, 135
Yoder, Elizabeth, 23
Yoder, John D., 178-180
Yoder, Joseph Warren.
    and Addisville Reformed
        Church, 119
    Amish identity, 30, 103-104
    Amish history and culture, first
        studies of, 90-91
    on Amish religious practices,
        167. See also *Rosanna's Boys*
    and attire, 50
        and plain suit, 213
        track suits at Juniata College,
            78-79
    as bachelor, 98-99
    birth of, 24
    and Blooming Glen, 128
    and bodybuilding and physical
        culture, 47-49, 64, 70-72, 84,
        199
        football at Juniata College, 80
        Ralston Health Club, 48-49
        track (gymnasium exhibition),
            80
    at Brethren Normal School. See
        Yoder, Joseph Warren, at Juni-
        ata College
    and Central State Normal
        School. See Yoder, Joseph
        Warren, at Lock Haven State
        University
    and Church of the Brethren, 47
    and circus, 72, 231
    and "closed" communion, 219
    death of, 227-228
    and Deep Run, 126-128

    at Elkhart Institute of Science,
        Industry and the Arts
        (Goshen College), 70, 104-
        105
    Athletic Association, presiding
        over, 71
    Tennis Association, helped or-
        ganize, 75
    and family and filial devotion,
        54, 95-96
    as gentleman farmer, 120
    and German translation and in-
        terpretation, 196
    at Goshen College. See Yoder,
        Joseph Warren, at Elkhart In-
        stitute of Science, Industry
        and the Arts
    and Harvard University, 103-
        104
    and health, 81-82, 84, 200-202
        scientific medicine and alter-
            native healing, interest in, 54
    and higher education, promo-
        tion of, 65-66
    and Hochstetler case, 192-194
    and homes, 116-119
    Hostetler, John Andrew, rela-
        tionship with, 177
    Irish identity, 30-31, 103-104
    at Juniata College, 42-47, 50,
        170
        Athletic Director at, 36
        Health Club, 81
        Lyceum Literary Society, in-
            tercollegiate debate team
            under auspices of, 87
        as student recruiter, 125-126,
            132
        Varsity Quartet, and forma-
            tion of, 92-94
    at Lock Haven State University,
        106-107, 110, 116

THE AUTHOR

Julia Kasdorf was born in Lewistown, Pennsylvania, and grew up in Irwin, Pennsylvania. She attended Goshen (Ind.) College and New York University and lived in Brooklyn for more than a decade before returning to central Pennsylvania in 1996.

Her first book of poetry, *Sleeping Preacher*, published in 1992 by University of Pittsburgh Press, was awarded the 1991 Agnes Lynch Starrett Prize and the 1993 Great Lakes Colleges Award for New Writing. A second collection of poems, *Eve's Striptease*, was published in 1998, also by the University of Pittsburgh Press. In 2001, Johns Hopkins University published her book of essays, *The Body and the Book: Writing from a Mennonite Life*.

Kasdorf is an Associate Professor of English and directs the graduate creative writing program at the Pennsylvania State University. She lives in Bellefonte, Pennsylvania.